Raves for

YOUR DOG
THE OWNER'S MANUAL

"Not only do we learn a lot about the marvelous dogs Dr. Becker has known and loved, we feel like we're sitting with him as he tells us stories of his life and family...His writing is filled with humor, intelligence, and, most importantly, the wisdom that comes from a life well led."
—Homer Hickam, author of *Rocket Boys* and *October Sky*

"An easy and fun read...We all want a happy dog that is easy to live with. Dr. Marty Becker does a great job shedding light on the foundation necessary to enjoy life with a dog as a part of the family."
—Tamar Geller, author of *The Loved Dog*,
founder of Operation Heroes & Hounds

A must-have book for any dog-lover. It provides current facts with helpful recommendations for loving and living with our dogs through their lifespan."
—Rebecca Johnson, PhD, RN, FAAN, director,
Research Center for Human Animal Interaction,
College of Veterinary Medicine, University of Missouri

"An insightful and positive guide to making the most of life shared with a canine friend...encouraging and thorough: Fewer dogs would end up in a shelter if their owners read this book!"
—Wilma Melville, founder, National Disaster Search Dog Foundation

"At last! One commonsense book leading the new pet parent through the sometimes-daunting maze of raising the perfect dog."
—Susan Sims, publisher, *FIDO Friendly* magazine

"This is a must-have, one-stop-shop for anyone who has a dog or wants a dog. Rooted in science and written with love, this book will help us all become better people to our dogs."
—W. Bruce Cameron,
author of the *New York Times* bestseller *A Dog's Purpose*

"Dogs make us human, and with this much at stake you want your dog at your side and this book backing you up."

—Michael Capuzzo, bestselling author of *The Murder Room* and co-author of *Mutts: America's Dogs*

"Excellent educational value and practical guidance."

—Karen Pryor, author, biologist, CEO KPCT/clickertraining.com

YOUR DOG
THE OWNER'S MANUAL

Hundreds of Secrets,

Surprises, and Solutions

for Raising a Happy,

Healthy Dog

DR. MARTY BECKER
with Gina Spadafori

Foreword by Dr. Nicholas Dodman,

Cummings School of Veterinary Medicine,

Tufts University

GRAND CENTRAL
Life & Style

NEW YORK · BOSTON

Grand Central Life & Style
Hachette Book Group
237 Park Avenue
New York, NY 10017

www.HachetteBookGroup.com

Grand Central Life & Style is an imprint of Grand Central Publishing.
The Grand Central Life & Style name and logo are trademarks of Hachette Book Group, Inc.

The publisher is not responsible for websites (or their content) that are not owned by the publisher.

Printed in the United States of America

First Edition: April 2011
10 9 8 7 6 5 4 3 2

Library of Congress Cataloging-in-Publication Data
Becker, Marty, 1954—
Your dog: the owner's manual : hundreds of secrets, surprises, and solutions for raising a happy, healthy dog / Marty Becker with Gina Spadafori ; photographs by Quicksilver Studios.—1st ed.
p. cm.
ISBN 978-0-446-57132-6
1. Dogs—Training. I. Spadafori, Gina. II. Title.
SF431.B4136 2011
636.7'0887—dc22
2010044058

For Reagan Avelle

CONTENTS

FOREWORD

Times change, needs change, but what seems to never change is our desire to share our lives with dogs.

That sharing was once based on partnerships. Dogs worked with us to protect our families and property, to help us hunt for and herd our food animals, and to help get us and our goods from one place to another by pulling wagons or sleighs. The dogs bred selectively for these jobs were used to hard physical work, as were our own ancestors. *Dog-tired* had a real meaning then, for both a working dog and the person who owned the animal.

The change in our relationship with the dog has been astonishingly fast. In less than a single person's lifetime—as my friend Dr. Marty Becker likes to point out, because the lifetime is his own, and my own, too—dogs have gone from the farmyard to the backyard to our kitchen to eat and the bedroom to sleep. Ever resourceful and adaptive, dogs have adjusted to the change, in many ways better than we have.

Our own new and mostly sedentary lifestyles, though, have been a challenge to us and to our dogs.

Many of us now think of our dogs as "fur children," while even the fluffiest little purse dog has a truer sense that he is, in fact, still a dog. He needs exercise—both physical and mental. He needs work to do and he needs structure to be happy with his place in the world. When he doesn't get those things, his owner will likely need some help to cope with illnesses and unwanted behaviors.

That's where veterinarians like me step in, to sort out the problems and offer some solutions to save that relationship, and often, that dog. I do not lack for work, I assure you.

In this book, my friend Dr. Marty Becker offers just what this doctor ordered, with surprises and solutions on every page to address the challenges of keeping a dog with less time and less space than our forebears could ever have imagined. Backed by more than thirty years of hands-on experience along with unquenchable desire to know the latest and the best veterinary medicine has to offer, Dr. Becker puts it all down on paper in his own lively and entertaining style.

The result is truly as advertised: an "owner's manual" that covers it all, from nose to tail and inside and out. A modern guide to the modern dog-lover's life, stressing an educated, science-based, and cooperative approach to keeping everything going smoothly in your life with your dog.

Whether you're still thinking about a dog, have one that's not quite what you'd hoped for, or want to make a great relationship even better, you'll find the information you need inside these covers. Dr. Becker and I have been friends and respected colleagues for going on two decades now, and I simply cannot put you in hands any better than his.

Enjoy!

Dr. Nicholas Dodman
Cummings School of Veterinary Medicine at Tufts University

(Dr. Dodman, a board-certified veterinary behaviorist and anesthesiologist, is the author of *The Dog Who Loved Too Much: Tales, Treatments and the Psychology of Dogs*, *The Well-Adjusted Dog: Dr. Dodman's 7 Steps to Lifelong Health and Happiness for Your Best Friend*, and other best-selling books, along with respected research in peer-reviewed academic journals. He is also a sought-after and popular speaker to veterinarians, trainers, and those interested in a better relationship with their companion animals. A professor of veterinary medicine, he directs the animal behavior program at the Cummings School of Veterinary Medicine at Tufts University. His website is ThePetDocs.com.)

YOUR DOG
THE OWNER'S MANUAL

INTRODUCTION

You'd think after so many thousands of years together, we humans would have dogs all figured out by now. How to choose one. How to raise and train one. How to get (or better yet, prevent) one from humping a visitor's leg. Feeding, getting a veterinarian's help on the health front, training, choosing cool gear and toys, how to manage basic home care, and how to recognize a veterinary emergency. And so important in these get-thrifty times, how to spend well and wisely, but not unnecessarily.

Yeah, we ought to all know all that by now. Really, we should. But we don't.

As a practicing veterinarian, I can tell you this from my side of the exam-room table: many dog lovers really don't know everything they need to about their dogs, except for the one thing we all know—we love our dogs, and our dogs love us.

In my book—which this is, of course—that's a great place to start.

After thirty years as a veterinarian, and half of that as an "I play a veterinarian on TV—and I *am* one, too!" for *Good Morning America* and, recently, *The Dr. Oz Show*, I still get many of the same questions I did my first day of practice. I'm still answering those questions every day, not only from people who see me in practice (yes, I still practice, because I love it), but also from people who recognize me in an airport (I travel about half my life) and even from my own mother, eighty-six-plus years young with a newly adopted shelter dog she has taken to obedience class to train as a therapy dog.

Part of the problem is that while dogs haven't changed that much, our relationship with them has changed a great deal in a short amount of time. I grew up on a dairy farm in Idaho, one of those storybook places where we had a little bit of everything growing and needing care. Even as a young boy, I was involved in caring for animals—and my dad meant it when he said to treat them right. One of my first farm jobs was collecting eggs from our chickens, and I figured out I could get all those hens out of the nest if I just walked into the coop and yelled, "Boo!" They'd run and collecting those eggs would be easy—or so I thought until my dad caught me at this and let me know what I was doing would not fly.

That was an early lesson. Next up: my youthful amazement at watching a veterinarian come out to our farm and bring back a downed cow from what seemed near death with a simple infusion of what he called sugar water. A miracle!

Is it any wonder I do what I do and love it? Animals, the people who love them, and the profession that cares for and about them both: these are the reasons I was put on this earth, I know.

But back to dogs: In my farm-boy days, our dogs lived outside. A lot of dogs in town did, too. This was just how it was then. Oh sure, our farm dogs had warm places to sleep on cold nights and cool places to relax on hot ones. The food was good, the water was clean, and there were kids to hang out with and nasty things to roll in. It was a dog's life, and it was a good one. The town dogs didn't have barns, but they each had a doghouse knocked together by the family's dad as a Sunday project, with the dog's name painted over the entrance.

Maybe in the Big City (for me, that would have been Spokane, or Boise, back in the those days before TV studios in Manhattan and Southern California became my "other" homes), rich ladies had little dogs they doted on—remember Tricky Woo, you Dr. Herriot fans?—but the rest of the dogs? They spent their lives in the doghouse. Often on a chain attached to an eyebolt.

Flash-forward to now, and let me tell you I'm more likely to end up in the doghouse than any of the dogs at our Almost Heaven Ranch are. My wife of thirty-plus years, "Glam-ma" Teresa (yes, I'm a grandfarter—I mean, grandfather), wouldn't hear of our little dogs Quixote or Quora out in the elements. Heck, we make room for them on the bed! (Or is it the other way around?)

Think about it: we humans have had dogs in our lives for thousands of years, and in a single generation (mine) they've gone from the dog-house (comfy enough) to the kitchen (but only on really cold nights) to the house (but never on the furniture) to the bedroom (with a dog bed) to the bed. (Yes, we bought the biggest bed we could. We needed room for the dogs.)

In the same time veterinary medicine has changed, in many ways for the better. We can prevent diseases that once killed dogs the way polio ruined lives for people before Drs. Salk and Sabin changed that. We have even changed the ways we give vaccines so their risk is less (fewer vaccines less often, and tailored to an individual dog's lifestyle). We have available almost all the offerings of human medicine, from chemotherapy to hip replacements and more, and we also have pet health insurance to help with the costs of such lifesaving treatments.

Every year I attend and speak at veterinary conferences, and I'm also a regular at the massive trade show put on for buyers in the pet-supply industry. I see everything new, and I share the best with my readers and viewers. You wouldn't think there'd be that much new, but there always is, even when you're looking at something as basic as a leash. And while everyone with a pet may know how much veteri-nary medicine has changed, advances in dog training and dog gear have tracked right along even if you haven't noticed.

I see it every day. That's why I wrote this book; my life is helping pets and the people who love them, and some people could really use a hand.

We have leashes that help train dogs to walk nicely and dogs who help people to walk, period. Pet bowls that fill themselves, and so many different kinds of food to fill them that listing every brand would fill this book. (And even that isn't good enough for everyone. A lot of people prepare homemade meals for the dogs—and do a pretty good job of it, for the most part.) When you get beyond the basics, things can really amaze some old-timers. Did you know that there are hotels that have a room-service menu for dogs? Before you make tracks for such a sweet spot, be sure you buckle up—your dog, that is.

What you need to get the most out of a relationship with your dog is a manual.

Yes, I know a lot of people pride themselves on never reading the manual. But life is so complicated these days that if you don't read the manual, you're missing out. With a new smartphone, you may be missing that tip that's going to save you lots of time. With a new dog, you may be missing out on a great way to spend that time you saved: with your dog. You're going to have me, "America's Veterinarian," with you on every page, answering every question old and new with the latest information drawn from the best veterinarians in the world.

You and your dog are worth it, and I'm happy to help.

Dr. Marty Becker, "America's Veterinarian"

PART ONE
FRESH STARTS AND NEW BEGINNINGS

Everyone has a unique idea of the perfect dog, and how they arrive at that vision seems to have a lot to do with logic and a lot to do with love. Think about it: the world knows about five hundred kinds of dogs loosely or definitely defined as breeds, and that doesn't begin to count the "canine cocktails," the one-of-a kind dogs that are a complete mix-up, or a recent addition of "designer dogs" bred on purpose, such as the Labradoodle or the Puggle.

When you ask a dog lover what kind of dog is his or her favorite, you never get an answer such as "Well, I evaluated my family's available free time, the size of my house and yard, my tolerance for shedding, and my need for increased security since that break-in at the neighbors'."

What they tell you is this: "The first time I saw that dog, I fell in love."

I'm going to tell you love will get you a long way, sometimes. After all, I've been married for more than three decades to a woman I adored from the day I met her. And she and I have both been known to take home pets on impulse, although that last thing is pretty typical among us veterinarians. We tend to collect hard-luck cases. (My very funny friend, Dr. Tony Johnson, an emergency and critical care specialist at the Purdue University College of Veterinary Medicine, has an entire family of pets, all named for what they were suffering with when he met them in the ER. There's Arrow, the cat who'd been shot by one, and Crispy, the burn victim cat, and I'm sure I don't have to explain about his dog, Tripod.)

That tugging of heartstrings is another of those motivations. While some wonderful pets never seem to catch a break in their shelters, a littermate who's "lucky" enough to be found a victim of abuse or be plucked out of a raging canal by a firefighter on national TV will have more homes lined up for him than you can count. In human matchmaking, "hard-luck cases" don't get the time of day, but a pet with "baggage" will get the attention of people who want to help.

This is the generous side of human nature, and it is all good. But as much as I love a good "how we met" story and celebrate when a hard-luck dog finds a forever home, I'm also aware that adoption decisions made on impulse and emotion can turn out to be disasters. And that's why it's important that even as you listen to your heart, you use your brain as well.

Now, let's get choosing. Look at you: you need a dog. And just as importantly: there's a dog out there who needs you.

Start your search for the perfect dog by putting aside the cuteness factor as much as you can. While no dog will be cuter than this West Highland White Terrier puppy I had the pleasure of meeting, such an active, noisy breed, with more than its share of genetic disease, is not the right dog for everyone. The dog who's perfect for you may be one like this purebred pup—or it may be a different breed or mix, or an older dog instead of a puppy.

Chapter 1

WHAT ARE YOU LOOKING FOR IN A RELATIONSHIP?

All dogs started pretty much the same, as wolves who hung out around humans for scraps. Eventually, the relationship grew closer; the animals best suited to hanging around were the ones who bred, and they started to change to suit the environment they were in. In time the dogs evolved into something like what's called a pariah dog—a medium-sized, brown, agile, short-haired dog with a long snout and erect ears. You can still find dogs like these all over the world, hanging out on the edges of human society. If dogs are left to breed as randomly as possible, the pariah dog is what they look like.

But we like a lot of different things in dogs, don't we? We like dogs in all sizes, shapes, and colors, with all kinds of ears and tails, long-haired, curly-haired, short-haired...the list goes on. It wasn't just for reasons of appearance, of course. For many years we counted on dogs to help us by herding our livestock, protecting our homes, pulling wagons or sleds, or helping us to hunt our dinners.

While a few kinds of dogs, mostly small, were developed solely as companions—and even they had some purpose as heating pads in the days long before central heating was invented—all the rest had jobs. Our ancestors no doubt liked their dogs, told them they were good dogs, and were even proud of the work they did and how well they did it. But few could afford to keep a dog who didn't earn his own way.

Today, it's the reverse, and very few dogs earn their own way. Our dogs, as I always say, are "born retired." Despite all that work ethic and all those differences we've bred into them, they're all doing pretty much the same "work," these days—hanging around with us when we're home, and sleeping on the couch when we're not.

But the dogs they once were are still in there, and that means you have to figure out if you can live with who they are and find things for them to do if they aren't the couch-potato type. If you don't, neither you nor your dog will be happy—and speaking as a veterinarian, I can tell you that what happens when a dog is bored and unhappy is going to be a bad thing for the dog. He'll either be fat and sick before his time (if he's the kind of dog who can stand just being on the couch) or, if he can't stand snoozing while you're at work and does an Unwanted Extreme Home Makeover, he'll soon be looking for a new home.

Yes, love can and does conquer all, but it doesn't do so easily. I'm suggesting some introspection before you get a dog so you have fewer problems and more love.

DEFINE ME, DEFINE MY DOG

Who are you now, and who will you be in ten years? You might be surprised at how different those answers can be. While nothing in life's a sure thing, if you're going to spend the next ten years building a business empire, raising kids or retiring to a life of active leisure, you need to think about how this is going to affect your choice of a dog. Because in fact, there really is a dog for almost everyone who wants one, but dogs can be so different—even siblings—that you really need to put some effort into getting a dog to have any hope of keeping a dog.

Take me, for example. I'm farm kid, born and raised on an Idaho dairy. I grew up with big dogs, farm dogs and hunting dogs who worked as hard as we did with all the hard physical labor of country life. I'm still a country boy, and home is our ranch in northern Idaho. My wife and I have been around large animals—cattle and horses—all our lives, and we still get up at dawn every day and do ranch chores. We love the outdoors, and I don't even mind putting on my overalls and barn coat on bitter, cold days to go out and care for the horses.

Bet you have me pegged as a guy who'd have a big, strong dog, right?

For much of my life, you'd have been right, and our family still has a beloved Golden Retriever, Shakira, otherwise known as She-Crazy for her boundless enthusiasm and her ability to play fetch until long after my arm wants to call it quits. But chances are she may be the last of the big dogs at our Almost Heaven Ranch. We've gone crazy for little dogs, starting with Quixote, the little canine cocktail you see on the cover of this book. Sure, I tell my poker buddies that he's my wife's dog, but that's as big a bluff as the aces I want them to think I'm holding. Quixote and the more recent addition, Quora, another little pooch pastiche—along with my dog-trainer daughter's little dogs, Willy and Bruce—I call them the GrandPugs—are where we are now. We're older, we love to travel, and we like having smaller, more portable dogs. Ones that fit in the seat between us or under the seat on the airplane.

That's not to say I don't love all dogs—I'm a veterinarian, after all— but my own perfect match in a family dog has been downsized, and I was smart enough to know it. Or my wife was, really.

Just don't anyone tell my poker buddies that my little dogs not only wear coats in the winter, but that I'll actually put the coats on them. Repeat that, and I'll deny it to the end of my farm-boy days.

But enough about me. Who are you? Are you a runner looking for a trail companion? A busy parent looking for a little help with babysitting and teaching kids responsibility? A young city hipster looking to impress others at the dog-friendly café? A person looking for a new hobby to go with a new dog? Are you slowing down—or do you want to? Are you living in an apartment, on an acre in suburbia, or on a hobby farm?

If you want a dog who needs more than you can give him in terms of time or exercise, do you have or can you afford to pay for a support system? Do you hate dog hair or are you good with picking the occasional strand off the butter or business suit without a flinch? Are you, personally, ready to take on the care of another living being, or is getting your own self fed and dressed about as much as you can handle? (I throw that one in for those Paris Hilton wannabes who forget that dogs aren't fashion statements or canine accoutrements, and they do need to get out of those designer handbags to do their business.)

In other words, figure out who you are, and you'll be better able to make a good match. Owning a dog is a lot like finding a mate, after all—except that odds are for many people that their dogs will live longer than their marriages last. Take your time and know yourself. (Not bad advice for that marriage thing, too.)

Think Twice about That New "Hot" Dog

How do dogs go from "What on earth is that?" to "I gotta have one, too"? Publicity, of course. A breed or mix turns up in a popular movie (like Disney's Dalmatian movies), on a hot advertisement (think the Taco Bell Chihuahua), or a long-running TV series (*Frasier*, whose cast included a Jack Russell Terrier) and suddenly you have a new "it" dog.

There are two problems with choosing the popular dog of the year. First, the breed may not be right for you. Canine actors are well-trained and never reveal the true characteristics of a breed, such as high-energy (Dalmatian), barkiness and pushiness (Chihuahua), and high-energy barkiness, pushiness, and an unstoppable desire to dig (Jack Russell). While every breed is right for someone, no breed is right for everyone. If you're thinking of a breed that's suddenly popular because of a turn in the spotlight, make sure you're not being swayed by a passing trend.

The second problem: When a breed becomes hot, it tends to encourage people who should not be breeding dogs at all to jump into the market. The resulting puppies are more likely to have health problems or be poorly socialized because of the corners cut getting puppies produced and sold before the next star dog starts rising.

THE COST OF HAVING A DOG

Once you've figured out the kind of person you are and will be in the lifetime of your prospective dog, it's time to look at the life you lead.

After all, the fact that you love to run, and would love running even more if you had a dog with you, doesn't mean a thing if you can't fit running into your schedule. And while there are lots of ways to save money on caring for your dog while not scrimping on the necessities, if you're really struggling to make ends meet you might need to put off owning a pet until things are going better for you.

Money is an issue with all dogs—small dogs aren't all that much less expensive to care for than large ones, except in the category of food. They still need regular veterinary care, and many have health issues that are related to their size, especially the tiniest of dogs. And lots of smaller dogs need professional grooming that big dogs don't.

Doggie Details

How much does it cost to keep a dog? Trade groups that track these things put the start-up cost after adopting a dog (which doesn't account for the cost of purchase or adoption) at an average of about $1,000, with annual upkeep of about $700 a year. Bear in mind two things: first, that costs are often higher in urban areas and on both coasts, and less expensive in rural areas and in the Midwest and South; and second, that "average" includes people who frankly are barely spending enough on their dogs to keep from being hauled in by humane officers and charged with neglect.

If you opt for a high-quality diet (recommended), a solid preventive-care regimen from your veterinarian (also recommended) including parasite control (protecting your dog and your human family, too), along with some fun purchases that can also make your life easier and keep your home cleaner (fun? easy? you bet!), you can easily double those guesstimates—and still be hit with some big expenses that can be financially and emotionally devastating.

Is a dog worth it? That's a question only you can answer, but if you think you want to have a dog in your life, do be prepared to spend some money on your pet. A high-quality diet and good preventive care may seem like one area where you can scrimp, but it's really not. Tak-

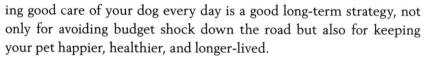

ing good care of your dog every day is a good long-term strategy, not only for avoiding budget shock down the road but also for keeping your pet happier, healthier, and longer-lived.

Taking good care of your dog is a good investment, and it's a responsibility you owe to your dog. Cut the budget in other places if you must—your pet doesn't need a biker jacket or an expensive collar, and no dog was ever hurt by an owner who buys in bulk—but make sure you can cover the basics.

Calamity Coverage: The Time Is Now, For You, Your Pet—and Your Vet

As a veterinarian, I've seen too many pet owners faced with the worst choice of all: choosing euthanasia over treatment for no reason other than expense. There's even a term for it—*economic euthanasia*.

I don't want this to happen to you or any other pet lover, which is why I'm a firm advocate for pet health insurance. With so many good companies and such variety of choices available now, I've simply never been a bigger believer.

Truth to tell, I don't think there's a veterinarian alive who hasn't given away care, reduced the cost or offered payment options, but you can go only so far with that. After all, a veterinary hospital costs money to run, and as with all businesses those expenses go up all the time. Trust me when I say: if you were in it for the money rather than the emotional rewards, veterinary medicine would be a very poor choice of profession.

I'm not complaining. I'm just explaining why you need to think about what you'd do if you were facing a really big veterinary bill. Because you might need to, and your veterinarian can help only so much and no more. And even if you can come up with the money—

on credit, for many people—is paying off that charge or loan a good plan for you down the road?

Pet health insurance is really more like car insurance than an HMO: Although companies such as Veterinary Pet Insurance (VPI) do offer wellness plans that may be helpful, especially if you're not good at saving or budgeting, the real benefit of the plans is that they cover a large part of the cost if something really bad happens—if your dog gets loose and is hit by a car, for example, or eats your underwear and needs surgery to clear the obstruction, or starts limping and it turns out to be cancer (which has never been more treatable, but treatment can be very expensive).

You'll still want to put some money aside—a pet health savings account set up like the old Christmas club savings plans (putting a set amount aside every month into an account with a dedicated purpose, whether it's buying gifts or paying for a possible pet emergency) is a great idea. Pet health insurance reimburses you for part of the expenses, not all, and you still have to pay your veterinarian up front, even if you're using a credit line as a temporary measure.

Pet health insurance isn't supposed to pay off more than you put in every year. It's not supposed to save you money on veterinary care and won't if your pet stays healthy. That's what insurance is all about: it's there when you need it, and it could save your pet's life.

Check it out. You'll want to look at all the companies, talk to your veterinarian, read the reviews, and fiddle with the formulas online to see what company and choices best fit your pet. Preexisting conditions are never covered, but a great many other things are.

It's worth it to never have to say, "I can't afford that, Doc, you'll have to put him down," or what most people say in order to live with themselves—"We decided we didn't want him to suffer anymore," which could be interpreted as "I can't afford to do what's best."

TIME: NO ONE EVER HAS ENOUGH OF IT

You have enough money—or at least you're pretty sure you do. Do you have enough time for a dog? Some dogs, like some people, are high maintenance—they need lots and lots of attention. Sometimes that attention is in caring for a complicated coat, but usually the big time suck is in the category most Americans say they don't have time for already—exercise.

All dogs need exercise. Even little ones. Even old ones. Even ones who really don't seem to mind a sedentary lifestyle. They need exercise, just as you do, and for the same reasons. Exercise helps keep their heart healthy, helps keep their joints strong, helps keep their weight down. (Did you know that veterinarians say the majority—yes, more than half—of all dogs they see are overweight or obese? The statistics are even worse for some breeds that just seem to be born to blimp—Flabadors, er, I mean Labradors, Beagles, and Pugs, to name just three.)

Exercise—or more specifically, the lack of it—is also one of the main reasons why dogs misbehave. They need to burn energy. If you don't find something for them to do, they'll find something to do on their own, and chances are you won't like their choices in activities.

Now, while it's true you can get a doggy treadmill (some look like human treadmills; the ones for small dogs look more like hamster wheels), or get someone else to exercise your pet, the fact is that getting out with your dog is good for you both. That's not just me talking, by the way: studies have shown that people who walk their dogs benefit from the activity as much as their dogs do. So much so that I wrote a book on the subject, *Fitness Unleashed: A Dog and Owner's Guide to Losing Weight and Gaining Health Together*, with Robert Kushner, MD, an internist and nutritionist who's an expert on human weight loss.

The least amount of time you can get away with is probably an hour a day, all total, for feeding, cleaning up after, and a little play and exercise. For larger dogs—or high-energy small ones, such as most of the terriers—there simply isn't a high end on the amount of time you could spend with them. They'll happily jump up and be ready to go every time you pick up the leash or the car keys.

There are always imaginative ways to get your dog exercised without you exhausting yourself, of course. Fetch is always great for this, and swimming is another energy burner, especially when combined with fetch. Toys that require dogs to work for small food rewards also count, and are really well suited to those times when you simply can't keep your dog busy, such as when you're out earning the kibble.

If you can't carve some time out of your schedule for a dog of your own, you might consider volunteering at a shelter, fostering now and then for a rescue group, or walking a neighbor's dog. If you can make time for your own dog, though, you'll be healthier for the time you spend.

Day Care, Dog-Running, and Poop Scoopers

Gina Spadafori, who coauthored this book, has a friend who's an ultramarathoner. The regular twenty-six-mile endurance run is nothing for him—his hobby is running in races of fifty to a hundred miles or even more. He has been a runner all his life but just started ultramarathoning in his fifties.

That sort of athletic endeavor requires a lot of training, so he figured he might as well start a business to take other people's dogs with him on training runs. Gina's three retrievers go out with him two or three times a week and are far happier for it (as is Gina).

While you'll surely find more dog walkers than dog runners, the trend toward a wider array of pet services has been growing in recent years, in ways people never could have imagined.

People may roll their eyes at the idea of doggy day care, for example, but if you dream of having a large, active dog but you work long hours, a place for your dog to play and run all day may be just the ticket. No "dog guilt" for you, and at the end of the day your pet will be dog-tired and just as happy to crash on the couch as you are.

(Continued)

What about paying someone to clean up your yard? If you can afford it and have better ways to spend your time, why not? After all, it wasn't that long ago that paying a service to keep your lawn mowed or your house clean was unusual, and now it doesn't even raise eyebrows.

All of which is why dog walkers/runners, doggy day-care centers, and professional poop scoopers are joining groomers, boarding kennels, pet sitters, and dog trainers—not to mention the most important "service" job of all, the veterinarian—as canine companions that are here to stay, offering help to those who need it.

Of course, check references and the Better Business Bureau, and look for membership in trade associations while considering whom to trust with your dog—or to come onto your property.

WHEN I SAY, "IN THE DOGHOUSE," IT'S A COMPLIMENT

Buying or building a doghouse used to be one of those things you did when you got a dog. These days, although some dog owners keep their dogs outside some or all the time, their numbers are dwarfed by people for whom keeping dogs off the furniture doesn't even happen.

In my life, being in the doghouse has gone from being banished to the barn—and even that eventually changed as the years passed—to enjoying the same environmental amenities human family members enjoy, including comfy beds and climate control.

What this means is that the rules for what kind of housing is appropriate for what kind of dog really don't work anymore. Great Danes live in big cities and meet their friends at the dog parks for playtime, and tiny toy breeds ruff—I mean rough—it inside cozy ranch houses, whether they're houses on real ranches (like mine) or the tract home kind scattered throughout every community, the classic three-bedroom/two-bath with a yard the dog uses for a bathroom but not much more. If you're willing to make it work, you can. In fact, one of the writer/editors who works with me all the time has two giant-breed dogs—a Scottish Deerhound and a Borzoi—in a San Francisco home that's not much bigger than our kitchen. She makes it work because she wants to, and so can you.

Dog Parks: Fun, But Not Always Friendly

One of the reasons having a large living space isn't so critical in keeping a dog anymore is that many communities have become much more dog-friendly. Cities large and small have responded to dog owners' desire for off-leash play areas, and have even allowed businesses to let dogs dine on patios in the style long enjoyed in many parts of Europe.

Dog parks, though, tend to be only as good as the people using them, and as a dog owner you need to look out for the safety of your dog as well as making sure he's not causing problems for other dogs. Yes, there are dog-park bullies!

The best way to check out a dog park is to go during off-peak hours. You want to see clean grounds and clear rules for pickup and good behavior. A double-gated entry, so dogs don't walk in on a leash (a known fight trigger), and, in the best parks, a separate area for small dogs so they're not trampled or looked at as prey by large ones.

Whether or not children are allowed is a matter of controversy, but dog experts generally agree that it's safer for all involved if they are not. And of course, all dogs should be current on their vaccines (that means no puppies), well socialized, and nonaggressive. People should be paying attention to keeping their own dogs out of trouble, not answering their e-mail.

When they work, dog parks are great for getting pets the exercise they need. When they don't work, they put people and pets at risk of injury, perhaps even deadly ones. So go forth and unleash, but do so with common sense and caution.

My daughter, Mikkel, is a dog trainer and author, and she sees a lot of dogs in her work. She loves Pugs, especially her dogs Willy and Bruce. They came from a breeder, and her other dog, Teddy, a Pomeranian, came from a shelter when he was ten years old. She knew to make sure before saying yes to either dog to understand their activity level, their appropriateness for life with children, and the health issues she'll be dealing with in their lives.

Chapter 2

WHICH DOG FITS AT THE OTHER END OF THE COUCH?

You want a dog. You're ready for a dog. You know what it takes to keep a dog, and to keep a dog happy. When you see people walking their dogs, you want to run out and scratch those dogs behind the ears. You look at those "pet of the week" pictures and think, *I ought to run to the shelter now!* Or you look at Petfinder and scan the ads like it's a dating site. This one? Nah, too big. This one? Hmmm, "no kids." That one? Cute face, but what about the other one here? *Click. Click. Click.*

Or maybe you've got your mind set on a particular breed. The one you grew up with, maybe? The one so great with your sister's kids? The one your coworker's always saying is the best dog he ever owned?

Choice, choices, choices. They're endless, and you can make a lot of good ones. But you can't know what will work for you, your family, and your lifestyle until you narrow the choices.

Now, as a veterinarian, I've treated just about every kind of dog you can imagine, from the tiniest Chihuahuas to the tallest Great Danes to Mastiffs and mixes of every variety. While there have been a few individual dogs I could have lived without knowing—and like every veterinarian, I have the scars to prove it—I can't say there's any type of dog I don't love.

But I do see a lot of mismatches, and I feel just awful when a relationship's not working out. My daughter's a professional dog trainer, so I am well aware that many problems can be fixed, or at least managed with some—and sometimes a lot of—effort. Life is full of compromises, true, but you're better off starting out with some commonsense foundations when you're looking for a dog.

AS HYPER AS YOU WANNA BE

First, let's get this out there: All dogs need exercise. All of them. The amount of exercise varies by the type of dog, the shape, the size, and the original purpose of the breed or breeds that lurk in the genetic code of a particular dog, but all dogs need something to do.

Bored dogs can be destructive, and you wouldn't believe all the things we veterinarians have surgically removed from the insides of dogs who didn't have anything better to do than eat a doll, a remote control, rocks, or a hamper full of dirty underwear.

And it's not just boredom that's the problem. Sedentary dogs can become overweight, which leads to all kinds of health problems. If you want to be a good dog owner, you'll have your dog's heart pumping at an aerobic rate on a regular basis.

But…some dogs need more exercise than most people are willing to give them. These guys are often tagged as "hyper," and you can find a lot of them in the shelters. Now, the truth is that you can settle a hyper dog by making sure those exercise needs are met. It takes time (yours) to set aside a daily workout for your dog, such as a long walk, a trip to the dog park for a meet-up with play buddies, a good game of fetch, or a few miles of biking. If you can't do that, money (also yours) can fill the gap, especially if you live in an urban or a suburban area. Most cities have doggy day care, and large cities usually have dog walkers. If these businesses don't exist in your area, you might ask around to see if you can get another dog lover to dog-sit while you're at work, or a neighbor kid to walk or run your dog.

If none of those options are possible, you'll need a dog who needs less exercise. Here's what you'll be looking for:

Older. Even dogs who will one day grow up to be the most mellow of companions are born as…puppies! Everyone loves a puppy, but not everyone is well suited to raising one. Puppies have two speeds: dead battery and fully charged. Growing takes a lot of rest, and the truth is puppies sleep a great deal. When you're raising one, though, you'll swear they never sleep. So if you're hoping for a quiet, calm, low-energy dog—and especially if you have to have one from the get-go—adopt an older dog.

Most people think of *older* as about a year old. Bad call. Dogs are still in their adolescence at that age, and that means you can add "testing limits" and even "hormones" (if they're not altered, which they should be) to the mix. Most dogs settle down at about two years of age, and are really in their prime at three to five years of age. And don't dismiss even older dogs: shelters and rescue groups say people often draw the line at five, and that's leaving a lot of wonderful dogs out of consideration, including many who have a lot of years of love left to give. Just as this book was being finished, my dog-trainer daughter adopted Teddy, a ten-year-old Pomeranian. She knew he was meant for her from the minute they met.

Puppies fly out of the shelter, but many times they come back just about the time they would be settling down if their owners knew to get them some training and have some patience. Their loss can be your gain.

Smaller. It's not that small dogs are inactive—a lot of them are active nonstop—but because they are small, their exercise needs are pretty easy to meet. You might need to run with a young Border Collie for five miles or play fetch for forty minutes in an open field to get the exercise you would get taking a small dog for a spin around the block, or playing fetch with it in a long hallway. This goes not only for small dogs but for a lot of the dogs who wouldn't be as small as they seem were it not for short legs—Dachshunds, Corgis, and Bassets, for example. They can be busy dogs, but you can meet their exercise needs without too much trouble.

Remember, though, that some small dogs are high-maintenance in other ways, which I'll get to soon enough. But exercise? Piece of cake with these guys. You can tire them out without working up a sweat yourself, and that's not often true of the big dogs.

Short-nosed. Some of the most popular kinds of dogs around these days are what we veterinarians call brachycephalic: they have a pushed-in face with short breathing passages. Pugs, the beagle-pug crosses known as Puggles, English Bulldogs, French Bulldogs, Pekingese, Shih Tzus, and others like them. Some of these dogs were originally bred with the idea that the short faces gave them the ability to latch on to other animals (such as cattle) and hang on while being able to keep breathing. But their popularity these days, without much need today for holding on to cattle, is that their broad, flat faces remind us of our own. They look like us, and we love them for it.

These dogs are really cute, but they're notoriously intolerant of exercise, especially when it's hot and humid. In fact, you have to be really careful not to stress them. That means they're generally on the low end of the exercise-demand scale; but again, other problems with these dogs—Bulldogs and Pugs in particular have a lot of life-threatening congenital health problems—mean you need to look at the big picture.

Breed types. While a dog's size and shape can be a good indicator of exercise needs, so, too, can be the breed or breeds in a dog's makeup. Learning what a breed was developed to do—often listed in the first paragraph of a breed description—can tell you how much exercise that animal is likely to need, with young dogs on the high end of the scale and old dogs on the low end. What about mixed breeds? Not that many dogs are really, truly mixed: most are a combination of a couple of breeds, or a couple of related breeds, at best. Shelter and rescue groups are often pretty good at guessing what breeds went into these canine cocktails, and even if they're a little off, they can often tell you from a dog's behavior in the shelter or a foster home how active that dog will be. But in general, you can expect some apples to fall not very far from the genetic tree.

What's in That Canine Cocktail?

One of the most interesting developments I've seen is the DNA tests—the Canine Heritage Breed Test and Mars Wisdom Panel are two in a growing market—that tell you from which breeds a particular dog is descended. From a medical standpoint, the information can be important when you're trying to avoid or deal with certain breed-specific health problems (such as known drug sensitivities in some breeds).

From the standpoint of a dog owner, the point of these tests can just be plain fun—and often very surprising. I decided to use the Mars Wisdom Panel to check out the DNA of my own two canine cocktails, Quixote and Quora. Want to take a guess? We let the readers of our PetConnection.com blog take their guesses, and folks came up with a lot of different ideas.

A small blood sample gave us an answer. When we adopted Quixote as a little fuzzy brown puppy, we were told he was a mix of Papillion, Poodle, and Yorkshire Terrier. The DNA testing told a slightly different story: Quixote is a mix of Chihuahua, Yorkshire, and Pomeranian. Our girl, Quora, adopted as an adult because we thought she looked enough like Quixote to be related, turned out to be a Pomeranian and Cairn Terrier mix, with a dash of a breed absolutely no one could have guessed, Shar Pei. (Guess her wrinkles came out in the wash.)

Did you guess right on cover dog Quixote? Only a couple of our blog readers nailed it, so don't feel bad if you didn't. While these tests have their skeptics, there's certainly no harm in checking out your own dog—and a fair amount of benefit to be gained. Ask your veterinarian about them.

With more than five hundred breeds recognized by various registries and countless crossbreeds—the so-called designer dogs that have become stupendously popular in the last few years—it's impossible to fit a comprehensive list in a book. So let me give you some guidelines.

Breeds and mixes with high exercise needs are generally dogs bred for jobs that required working for long periods of time at high levels of energy. That would certainly include dogs developed to herd livestock (Border Collies, Shelties, Kelpies, German Shepherds, and the Belgian herding breeds, the Malinois being the most common) and dogs expected to find and retrieve game for hunters (setters, pointers, spaniels, retrievers, and "scent" hounds—such as Beagles and Foxhounds—so called because they hunt by picking up and following a scent trail). You can also figure in the sled dogs, because any dog who can keep moving for hours on end through almost any wintry landscape (think Iditarod) is not going to be happy sitting on your couch for days at a time.

On the smaller side but no less energetic are many terrier breeds, which were developed to keep vermin out of houses and barns. While some terriers are more easygoing than others, dogs such as the Jack Russell Terrier (also known as the Parson Russell) are about as high energy as a dog can get. And while some of these breeds—Labradors are famous for this—often mellow significantly over the age of five or so, some of these canine go-getters simply never slow down. Their motto: I'll sleep when I'm dead. If that's not your motto, you might think twice before jumping into this end of the gene pool.

Breeds and mixes with lower exercise needs are dogs whose ancestors were developed for short periods of activity. They are often pretty easygoing companions, regardless of size. And that surprises a lot of people, who assume that a breed such as a Greyhound will always be on the run. Not so! Greyhounds and other sight hounds—so called because they spot their targets by movement and run down their prey with astonishing bursts of speed—are actually pretty hedonistic layabouts most of the time. They're up for a good, long walk, and they'd love to be let off the leash to really stretch out in a safe, fenced area (coming when called is a foreign concept to many of these dogs—once they're in hot pursuit, it's hard to stop them). But the other twenty-three and a half hours of the day? Soft beds and couches are their preferred environment, especially warm ones, since their low levels of body fat leave these lean running machines almost perpetually cold. Groups that place retired racing Greyhounds market them as "40 mph couch potatoes," and it's truth in advertising. Greyhounds, Scottish Deerhounds, Irish Wolfhounds, Borzoi (also known as Russian Wolfhounds), Saluki, and the glamorous Afghan Hounds (among others) are happy in almost all environments, as long as they can stretch those long legs on a regular basis.

Guarding breeds—including dogs meant to protect livestock rather than herd them—can also be pretty laid-back most of the time. Mastiffs, Great Pyrenees, and even all the dogs commonly lumped under the general heading of *pit bull* are happy to chill until they're needed to do something.

"Designer dogs"—purpose-bred crossbreeds—can be less intense than their purebred forebears, as can out-and-out "Heinz 57s," the all-

American mutt. Tossing a few breeds together can take the edge off the most intense traits of dogs bred to do a job. It's not always true—each dog is an individual—but it's true often enough to take into consideration.

Now, of course, I've tried to point out the dogs who are too much for most families—herding breeds, sporting breeds, and terriers—because the truth is most people aren't all that active, and even those who do find time for exercise often do it in a gym or on exercise machines. If you are a fit and athletic person who wants to spend your exercise time with your dog, you're probably just fine with all but the most exercise-intolerant dogs, because with proper training and conditioning most dogs can keep up with the busy bodies among us.

The important thing is whether or not you have the time and energy to meet a dog's exercise needs. Find a dog who will match your lifestyle. When dogs are brought to trainers or behaviorists for problems that put them at risk of being given up, the number one thing that these experts suggest is almost always more exercise. They even have a saying, "A tired dog is a happy dog," and I would add "a healthy dog." If you're meeting your dog's needs from the start because you're well matched, you've got an advantage.

Pitch Like a Major Leaguer

We have a full range of canine activity levels in the Becker family, from the easygoing pugs who belong to my dog-trainer daughter, to our little canine cocktails, to our gorgeous and energetic Golden Retriever. Now, I usually don't like it when people dis their dogs as "hyper," especially when it comes naturally to them. But Shakira? If I were to use that description, she'd be a likely candidate.

Mind you, we live on a ranch, so it's not exactly hard for a dog to stretch her legs up here in northern Idaho. But Shakira wants to share the fun, and she doesn't understand that you might occasionally have something else you want or need to do besides keep her busy.

(Continued)

Enter one of the best inventions ever, as far as owners of dogs like Shakira are concerned: the Chuckit. Made of a long, flexible piece of durable plastic with a tennis-ball-sized cup at the tip, the Chuckit gives you the rocket arm of a major-league outfielder, if not the accuracy. With one of these babies—and the Chuckit and products like it do come in smaller sizes and even collapsible models—you never have to touch a slobber-slick tennis ball. Press the cup over the ball, rear back and fling. And fling. And fling.

Shakira and dogs like her would probably keep retrieving until they dropped from exhaustion, so stop long before that happens. But if you have or can get to some open space, and you have a dog who loves or can learn to love retrieving—which is most of them, if you train them—you can get some serious exercise into your dog without a lot of time or effort. Or toss a floating ball into the water for an even more amped-up exercise. Bow-wow-wow-flex, you can call it, an all-in-one workout that you can find at any pet store.

THE FUR FACTOR

Doggie Details

The number one complaint pet owners have about their pets? Shedding. And while it's true that you can cut down on the fur you find on your floors, furniture, and clothing with some basic strategies, if you find shedding really annoying you need to choose a dog who doesn't shed as much.

First, some more myth-busting. All dogs shed. Some more than others, but even so-called hairless breeds shed (the hairs are just sparse and fine). And, in case you were wondering, the related misconception is that some dogs won't trigger allergies—also not true. If you read somewhere on some Internet site or someone you once knew told you that some breeds, most usually cited is the Chihuahua, actually cure allergies and asthma, put that one out of your head as well.

Dogs shed. And what comes off them—from the fur and skin cells that come off naturally to all the sneeze-inducing stuff they pick up in their travels as furry Swiffers or dust mops, such as pollen, dust, mites, and more—will trigger allergies if you're the allergic type. Most people can live with a certain amount of hair and other allergens, with the help of an allergist (the human kind) and a few basic strategies. The same is true of shedding.

The first strategy, if you need or want a low-shed, less-allergenic dog, is to get a small one. The logic here is easy to follow: less dog, less hair.

The second criteria is to get a long-haired dog and keep the fur clipped short. That's because long-haired dogs drop hair less frequently than short-haired dogs, and keeping the hair clipped means less hair less often, and the hair that does come out is short and easy to pick up.

The third tip is to bathe and brush your dog frequently. Bathing weekly is fine, and even more often is fine, too, if you use a good shampoo (your veterinarian can suggest one). As veterinarians we also recommend more frequent bathing if a dog has so-called "environmental allergies" to pollen, dust, mites, and so on, and needs the coat kept exceptionally clean to prevent explosive skin problems. If you're highly allergic, have the brushing done outside by a family member, and have that person wipe down the coat with a damp towel or a disposable wipe to reduce dander. Ask your veterinarian for recommendations for shampoos, conditioners, wipes, and more.

The final tip is to dress your dog. Yes, that's right, I said put clothes on your dog. It works better—or at least, it's more socially acceptable—if you have a purse-sized dog, but if you're really troubled by fur you can look into body suits for any size of dog, and these will contain the shedding nicely. And since your dog is wearing the body suit at home, no one knows—just like no one knows that when I'm working at home I'm not wearing my "signature TV outfit" of khakis, a denim shirt, a red tie, and a stethoscope—I'm in pajama bottoms and a pocketed Carhartt T-shirt.

Many people swear the Poodle—and breeds similar to it, such as the Bichon Frise or the Portuguese Water Dog (adopted by the family of President Barack Obama)—don't shed and don't trigger allergies. It's true that they shed less, and many allergic people find them easier to live with, but it's not guaranteed. Some people suggest that adding a Poodle to any other breed, from Labradoodle to Schnoodles to Cockapoos and so on, somehow transfers the low-allergy status to the resulting mix. Maybe yes, maybe no. Again, there are no guarantees.

I can guarantee you that there are a few breeds (and mixes of those breeds) you most certainly will not like if you cannot stand living in dog fur. Top among them is likely the German Shepherd, with a year-round shedding of world-class standing. Northern breeds such as Alaskan Malamutes and Samoyeds can also leave you up to your ankles in fur, but at least with them the shedding is seasonal, typically a major coat blow in spring and fall. As for our beloved Quora and Willy the grandpug, well, we call them hairy hand grenades or the furry jack-in-the-boxes.

What about short-haired dogs? They're easy to keep brushed, but they shed those short bits of fur constantly. Unless you want to coordinate your wardrobe to match, you'll need a sticky tape roller like the ones you see in every veterinary hospital, or a newer product like the Pledge Fabric Sweeper for Pet Hair, to cope.

IS THAT A SQUIRREL...OR ARE YOU GONNA PUT A SADDLE ON THAT?

No animal has been more dramatically altered by selective breeding than the dog, and these amazingly adaptable animals range in adult size from a couple of pounds to a couple hundred, and from dogs not as tall as your average cat to those bigger than some small horse breeds. They've been called the most plastic of all species.

Activity levels are probably a bigger problem for most people than size, with the exception of the truly giant breeds, which can be hard to fit into a studio apartment even if they are generally pretty easygoing. From a health standpoint, you're going to have fewer problems if you avoid dogs at either extreme. Teeny-tiny dogs—less than ten pounds and certainly less than five—are very fragile and prone to an array of congenital health problems. Giant breeds have the shortest average life span of all dogs, and that means early heartbreak. At either extreme you're generally not looking at animals who are likely to live long lives of robust good health. Small- and medium-sized dogs generally fare better, so unless you're willing to put the extra effort, money, and some difficult decisions into caring for a dog at either extreme, stay on the small to medium size.

You'll also find small- and medium-sized dogs less expensive to feed and easier to transport (it's hard to fit a Great Dane in a Mini Cooper). Smaller dogs also offer more housing options, since many homeowners' associations and apartments allow pets under a certain weight (typically twenty-five pounds). Even hotels are more likely to allow these smaller dogs.

Netting the Best Information

Put the name of any recognized breed or designer dog into an Internet search engine and you'll come back with plenty of information—a lot of it incorrect, especially if it's from people who are trying to sell you a puppy.

Do I need to tell you that a lot of these folks are puppy millers? They've got oodles of different breeds stacked in cages or jammed in filthy runs, but they'll put a couple cute puppy pictures on their websites and they'll take your credit card. You may call it love at first sight, but ask a veterinary health-care professional to view the same site and he or she will probably be thinking *fright at first sight*, as many of these pets are doomed to a lifetime of increased medical and behavioral problems.

I encourage looking on the Internet for information on the breed or breed type you are researching, but take what you see with a few grains of salt. You should make a list of the potential problems with a breed or crossbreed so you can ask individual breeders about those problems (if you're buying a puppy) and judge their answers. Go to a dog show and see, touch, hear, smell, and experience the various breeds up close and personal. Or so you can ask a veterinarian, shelter, or rescue group for more information on the animal whose picture you've fallen for on the web.

I've had all kinds of dogs in my life, and the truth is I love them all. The current canine residents of the Almost Heaven Ranch, though, Quora, left, and Quixote, are mostly canine cocktails. We also have a Golden Retriever, Shakira. We've done a DNA test on the little dogs, and if you forgot what their tests showed, turn to page 25.

Chapter 3

LOOKING FOR LOVE IN ALL THE RIGHT PLACES

Time to get your dog at last! You now have a realistic idea of how much effort you will want to—or be able to—put into caring for your dog. You've looked at the various kinds of dogs and done your best to match them against your needs, dreams, and future.

Now it's time to find the right source—a shelter, rescue group, or reputable, ethical breeder. You really want to avoid the puppy mills and other disreputable puppy sellers out there. And that's important, because you can toss out all that research you've done if you get a puppy or dog from an operation that breeds sick dogs and raises the puppies in conditions more likely to produce emotionally damaged pets (that will be nearly impossible to house-train). Not to mention that every time someone buys from a filthy, high-volume facility, a careless and clueless small breeder, or a shady roadside seller, the cruel business of bad breeding continues. You may save one dog, but you've condemned others to miserable lives.

Finally, I'm not going to lecture you if you decide to buy from a breeder. While there are plenty out there who say the only responsible choice is to adopt, I'm not going to dissuade you from making your own choices that fit you and your family. That may be a purebred puppy or an intentionally produced crossbred one (the so-called designer dogs). There's a world of difference between a reputable, ethical breeder and the rest, and there's nothing wrong with supporting the labor of love that is the work of a good breeder. You are not denying a home to a shelter pet in doing so. If everyone chose either shelters/rescue groups or good breeders, there would be more than enough homes for all—and puppy mills would be history.

I've had many dogs in my life, and known many, many more in my thirty-plus years as a veterinarian. Loved every single one of mine, and all but a few of the ones I've seen in practice (but no, I won't dish on the ones I didn't like so much). I wholeheartedly support shelters and rescue groups, and also good, responsible breeders. I want you to get the dog who fits with you for life, and that's the bottom line.

DIRTY YARDS AND DIRTY SECRETS: NOT RECOMMENDED

There's nothing harder than walking away from a puppy, especially when you think you can make that puppy's life better by taking that animal home. But the fact is that sleazy sellers of sick, unsocialized puppies are everywhere, from roadside stands, flea markets, and the seediest parking lot to the swankiest pet store. When you buy a puppy from someone whose primary motivation is a sale, you're doing something you probably never thought you'd do, and it isn't good.

When you buy a puppy from a less-than-reputable source, you

may be saving that one puppy. In fact, you are indeed saving that one puppy. But when you support a less-than-ethical source of a puppy, you are guaranteeing that there will be more puppies who need saving. And those puppies need someone to look after them. And so do the parents of those puppies, even more, because they aren't ever going to be saved as long as people keep making it profitable for them to spend their lives in misery.

When you don't adopt from a shelter or buy from a reputable breeder (more on both later in this chapter), here's what you are likely supporting:

- Trashy, backyard breeding operations where the mothers are chained to barrels or put in cages their whole lives, never given good veterinary care (if they get any at all), rarely have their water changed, and starve themselves to nurse their puppies. When those puppies sell, those mother dogs are bred again, and again, and again. When they can no longer turn a profit they are dumped, often turned out on the street, or even shot—and some of their daughters take their place in confinement.
- Overseas breeding operations in Mexico or the former Soviet Republics that mass-produce hot breeds such as Chihuahuas or Bulldogs. The Mexican puppies are smuggled into the United States stuffed into the side panels of cars, their mouths and legs taped to immobilize and quiet them, and sold at flea markets, in parking lots, or on the roadside. The Eastern European pet trade is little better, especially when you consider that their breeds of choice usually require Cesarean sections, something they can't be bothered to pay a veterinarian to do—so they cut open the mothers themselves.
- High-volume commercial breeders in the United States, typically in the Midwest and in Pennsylvania and Ohio (where, sadly, the Amish have discovered how lucrative the trade can be). The worst of these operations are called puppy mills, and their abject cruelty has been well documented for decades. Even the "best" of these operations—with clean kennels and decent care—don't concern themselves with the importance of screening for genetic defects, or socializing puppies to prepare them for lives as pets. Commercial breeding is overseen—to the extent it's overseen at all—by the U.S.

Department of Agriculture, and to this industry, what we see as pets and family members are nothing more than livestock. USDA requirements for the "breeding stock" require barely enough room to take a few steps and stand up straight. It's no way to treat man's best friend—and it's no way to start life as a family companion.

Don't "save" a puppy from sellers such as these. To date, it has been impossible in any practical sense to come up with a fair way to legislate against poor-quality breeders without hurting ethical, caring breeders who are working to preserve breeds and raise healthy, well-socialized family pets from health-certified, well-loved family pets.

That's why the only real way to change the situation is for buyers to walk away from breeders or sellers who see dog selling as a profit center, with corners to cut and merchandise to move. Or better yet, never put yourself in a position to consider a puppy from such a source. Because it's really hard to say no, but say no you must.

The Right Source for a Healthy Dog

Aside from the importance of voting with your feet when it comes to puppy mills and other less-than-ideal dog sellers and breeders for the sake of the dogs, you're also helping to keep your dog-care costs low by going with either a shelter/rescue dog or a reputable breeder.

While the evidence isn't certain—and includes purebred dogs from bad breeders as well as good ones—veterinarians have long felt that canine cocktails are healthier than purebreds. And when I say *canine cocktails*, I mean a really mixed-up All-American mutt— or Heinz 57, as my parents used to call them—not a so-called designer dog. The puppy product of two unhealthy dogs of different breeds with poor temperaments isn't going to be instantly rendered perfect because of the "hybrid vigor" bad breeders hype to justify their jaw-droppingly high prices.

Shelter/rescue dogs can save you money because of their mixed-up backgrounds, and even more so because they're often adult dogs, so you know what you're getting into in terms of health and temperament and can make your decision accordingly. (Hey, who am I to suggest you not get a dog who really needs you—as long as you're rescuing with your eyes wide open?)

As for purebred puppies, reputable, ethical breeders screen the parents for every health issue they can, have them certified healthy by an organization with a database you can check for yourself, such as the Orthopedic Foundation for America. They then raise the puppies in the house and underfoot using well-proven methods of socializing and early training. Some of the designer-dog breeders are now doing the same, although with both purebreds and crossbreds, you have to look for a good breeder—and know what you're looking for.

Shelter/rescue puppies and dogs and, surprisingly enough, puppies from ethical breeders usually cost less than a pet-store puppy born in a mill. And they'll more than likely cost you less at the veterinarian's in the long run. Trust me on this one. Too many people make the wrong choice, buy an expensive pet-store puppy, and end up proving a veterinary saying: "Pay a lot to buy and spend a lot to keep"—versus a shelter rescue or puppy from a good breeder that a loving owner will spend little to acquire, spend less to maintain, and be rewarded emotionally for a good deed.

RESCUE DOGS: GOOD DEAL, GOOD DEED, BUT SOMETIMES SOME BAGGAGE

You'll find an amazing number of really wonderful dogs out there, and there's no doubt you can find the perfect pet through a shelter or a rescue group, especially if you're patient—and even more so if you're willing to be flexible in your choices. Small dogs, young dogs (especially puppies), and dogs who don't look scary—in other words, dogs who aren't dark-colored large dogs or pit bulls or pit bull mixes—are in high demand at many shelters, and if you will not budge from look-ing for a puppy who'll be a small dog, you may be on a waiting list for a long time, even though with sites like Petfinder.com your search can range from the local shelter to one in the next community or county, or clear across the country.

But if you're willing to make some concessions, you may end up with a dog who's actually a better choice for you anyway. Older dogs (five or above) or senior dogs (seven to ten or above) are often healthy, well mannered, well trained, and, well, just plain wonderful. But they tend to be passed over because people figure that they'll be saying good-bye too soon or that they'll have a lot of health problems.

My daughter, Mikkel, wanted another dog for her Pugs, especially since she knew dogs in multiple-pet households are sick less often and live longer. She chose a ten-year-old Pomeranian, Mr. Teddy, who ended up in a shelter after his original owner had died. He may have almost no teeth, but he still has at least half a tank of gas, and he has proven to be a wonderful companion for Willy and Bruce, a wonderful companion to my granddaughter, Reagan, and a best friend and demo dog for Mikkel, who's a dog trainer.

I say life is full of uncertainties when it comes to life span, and a puppy may not live as long as the healthy middle-aged dog you can adopt. You just never know, and you really shouldn't rule anything out.

If you're thinking you have to have a small dog because you're look-ing for a pet who's less active, you may be surprised: many small dogs never stop moving and are quite noisy besides. The bigger dogs you passed up? Many are happy with not as much activity, and they're not likely to be as reactive from a barking standpoint than many of those little dogs. So if you're looking for peace and quiet first and foremost, you may actually be happier with a larger, older, and more mellow dog. The shelter or rescue group will be able to tell you the energy level of any dog you're considering.

And while some of these dogs get tagged as rejects—they were, after all, given up by their owners—many rescue and shelter dogs have no problems at all; they were often abandoned because of their own-ers' circumstances (lost job, moving across the county, new housing doesn't allow pets, etc.). And many of the ones that do have problems can be fixed pretty easily with a minimal expenditure of time or money. That's true of both health and behavior problems, by the way. Many shelter dogs are diamonds in the ruff, and it doesn't take much for them to gleam.

Do think twice before taking on a dog the shelter or rescue group says has a serious behavior or health problem (such as aggression, incessant barking, separation anxiety, or any expensive-to-maintain health issue) unless you're an experienced dog owner with time and money to spend. Too often, well-meaning people fall for a sad story or a sadder face. If you can handle it—with the help of trainers, behaviorists, and veterinarians—then go for it. But if you're just looking for an easy family pet, leave the hard cases for others. That's especially true when you're dealing with a dog with a known history of aggressive behavior. Many of these dogs can be rehabbed, but not by most pet owners.

The Particular Problem of the Pit Bull

If you look in a lot of shelters, especially those in urban areas, what you'll be looking at is a lot of pit bulls—dogs who are from a number of related breeds and all their mixes. There are those who argue the number one breed in the country is not the Labrador Retriever—which leads American Kennel Club registrations—but is in fact the pit bull, which isn't registered and still seems to be the most popular—or unpopular—kind of dog in the country.

Because of fear, many adopters have the attitude: "anything but a pit bull." Frankly, that's a shame. Because a good pit bull was the quintessential American dog—a calm, good-natured, outgoing dog who was an excellent family pet. These were also dogs that personified another American trait: a good pit bull never goes looking for a fight but won't run from one, either.

(Continued)

So what happened? A couple of things, really. One, the dogs became the darling of criminals, who bred them to be aggressive to everyone. (Old-time dogfighters, while not by any means saints, would not breed a dog who was aggressive to people, if for no other reason than that a dog who bites the hand that feeds him isn't much use.) The other thing is that the pit bull became the dog the media most loved to hate, the latest in a long line of breeds that has included German Shepherds, Dobermans, and Rottweilers.

But a funny thing happened on the way to the complete vilification of these dogs: Michael Vick was arrested in connection with dogfighting, and public sentiment switched in large part to seeing the dogs not as criminals but as victims. That became even more true when these dogs became among the first fighting dogs to be given a second chance—and proved that they were not stone-cold killers. Many of them are now normal pets in loving homes.

Still, because the problems of bad breeders are even worse when you're talking about pit bulls and pit mixes, you need to be careful. A good pit bull is still a great family pet, but make sure you adopt from a shelter or rescue group that knows the breed and is adept at evaluating temperament. While life provides no guarantees—and every kind of dog can and will bite (you just hear less often about ten-pound dogs that bite than you do about hundred-pound ones, or about a Pekingese that bites than about a pit bull that does)—a pit bull from a good shelter or rescue group is more than worth taking a chance on.

PICK A PUPPY, ALL BY YOURSELF

One of the signs you're dealing with a good breeder—and more on the other signs in the next section—is that the breeder will not let you pick out your own puppy. That's because, left to their own devices, most people will pick the most active and bossy—"She chose us!"—or the cutest, or the shyest. None of these may be the best match with a given family.

A buyer also sees a litter once, typically, while a good breeder has been living with, watching, and making notes on the entire litter for two or even three months. A good breeder has a better idea of what each puppy is really like, not what those same puppies might be like in the presence of strangers on a given day. A good breeder will respect and honor your wishes—male or female, or certain colors or markings—if at all possible, but the most important factor is whether or not that puppy is a good match in terms of personality. You may be surprised to find out that some of the most experienced dog owners and dog handlers—people who compete with their dogs in sports events, or train them for jobs in search-and-rescue or drug detection—completely trust their breeders to choose for them, and never see their puppy until they open the crate at the airport.

But what if you aren't dealing with an experienced breeder, but rather a shelter or rescue group that lets you choose (although they may make suggestions) or a less experienced home-based breeder who otherwise seems to be doing a good job with the litter?

Can you make a good decision? You bet you can! Just put your heart aside for a little while and really put your brain into play, keeping in mind what it is you want in a companion.

Puppy-testing methods vary widely, but in general the purpose of testing is the same. You're trying to figure out:

- How bossy or shy is the puppy? While a lot of people are inclined to pick the boldest pup of a litter—because he seems to pick them—he's probably not the best choice for most homes. He *may* be just the ticket for someone with a great deal of dog-training experience who intends to work with her dog constantly, and maybe even compete in a sport such as canine agility, but for an average home a less dominant dog's a better choice. Avoiding the shyest, least dominant puppy, which some people pick "because he needs us!" is best, too.
- How much do the puppies like people? Some puppies are more dog oriented or really don't care much about anything at all. A puppy who's not curious and interested in people—perhaps because of little or no socialization—isn't a very good prospect as a pet. You want a pup who wants to be with you, because that's the pup who'll be loving—and trainable.

☙ How happy are the puppies to learn? The goal here is a puppy with the ability to concentrate—as much as any baby can—and absorb information. A puppy who is so busy bouncing off the walls that he can't give you even a moment's attention is going to be one you want to avoid.

Take each of the puppies to a safe, secure area away from littermates. Observe how the puppy reacts to the change—tentative exploration is okay, but beware the puppy who's so terrified she won't move, even after having a couple minutes to settle in. Look, too, for how busy a puppy is: playfulness is fine, but full-out go-go-go is maybe a little too much.

Remember, ideally your observations should be compared and discussed with the observations of others who have looked at these puppies, such as the volunteers and staff at the shelters, the seller or foster family, or a dog-savvy friend.

The puppy who's probably going to be the best for most people is going to be medium in personality. She may not be the smartest in the litter, but she may be more interested in your point of view than the one who is the smartest. She has an attitude, but not so much that she'll drive you crazy. She's willing to try new things, but she'll like them better if you are with her.

> You can size up a puppy's personality in several ways, but here are a few exercises anyone can do well:
>
> **I want to be with you!** Walk a few steps away, bend over, and call to him. (Bending over makes you less intimidating.) If the puppy seems a little tentative, crouch and open your arms. You're not ordering the pup—he doesn't know what you want, after all. You're trying to see how attracted he is to a nice person. So be nice. Call gently, click your tongue, squeak a toy. The medium puppy you want will probably trot over happily, perhaps after a slight hesitation. The bossy puppy may come over and nip at you, and the shy one may not move except to shiver in terror. The one who doesn't care a bit about people may go investigate a bug in the corner of the room.

I don't want to be bossy with you! Gently roll the puppy onto his back and hold him there with your hand. The medium pup you're looking for will fuss a little, settle down, and maybe even lick your hand. Bossy pups usually keep struggling, and the shyest ones generally freeze in terror.

I want you to love me! Praise and petting are integral parts of training and communicating with your dogs, and so finding a puppy who wants affection enough to earn it is important. Talk to the puppy lovingly and stroke him, but let him decide whether he stays with you or not—don't hold him. The medium puppy will probably lick your hands and be glad to stay with you. Rolling over is okay, and don't be surprised if he urinates a little, since it's a kind of a canine compliment, especially in puppies. A puppy who bites hard may have missed the lesson that teeth hurt and should never be used on skin. The one who wants nothing to do with you probably isn't people oriented enough. Stay away, too, from the one who's terrified of being touched.

Almost any puppy can overcome a bad start or a personality that's too bold or too shy. But training the puppies on the extremes of ideal personality is not a job most people can handle. If you choose a puppy at the extremes—too bold and bossy, or too shy and scared—you may become so frustrated and unhappy with the adult dog he becomes that you'll not have the dog you need. And that means you may even give up on that dog. Better you pick the right puppy for you from the start rather than break both your hearts later, don't you think?

BUYING FROM A BREEDER:
HOW TO FIND A GOOD ONE

A reputable breeder can be very hard to find and may not have a puppy available when you want one, like now. Those facts alone send many puppy buyers to other, less-than-ideal sources. If you want a particular breed or crossbreed, there's nothing more important than finding the right breeder. Nothing.

If everything goes well, you'll have your dog for more than a decade. Doesn't taking a little time to find the right breeder seem reasonable? To make a few phone calls, take a few field trips? Trust me, it is, and I tell you that as a veterinarian who sees problems well-meaning people could have avoided had they just taken their research one step further and put as much emphasis on finding the right breeder as on finding the right breed (or crossbreed, such as the popular designer dogs). When you're dealing with a reputable breeder, their commitment to the puppy you buy doesn't end when the sale is final. You get a healthy, well-socialized puppy and technical support that would be the envy of any electronics company. You get help and advice for life, and you get a safety net for your puppy if you ever can't keep your dog.

Very few breeders are downright evil and fail to provide for even the basics of their animals' needs. A few more are mentally ill, living in filthy homes packed to the rafters with freely mating dogs. These people are fairly easy to spot and avoid—unless their pups are cleaned up and sold elsewhere.

Here are the things that should give you pause when dealing with a puppy seller:

Lack of knowledge about the breed. Someone who doesn't know about the history of the breed or how suitable it is for different homes probably isn't someone who's too concerned about breeding dogs that are healthy, outgoing representatives of the breed.

Ignorance or denial of genetic defects. Every breed has some problems, and some of the most common ones—such as hip dysplasia—can cause great pain and cost big bucks. A person who isn't aware of congenital defects almost certainly isn't screening breeding stock to avoid these problems. Sellers who aren't spending money to certify that their breeding dogs are free of congenital defects—and can't prove they have done so—are taking a big risk, and so are you if you buy from them.

No involvement with other reputable breeders. Most good breeders are active with their dogs, and well-connected with others who share their love of their breed or crossbreed. Some compete in dog shows, some in other sports (agility, fly ball, hunt tests). Some are active in working their dogs, such as in search-and-rescue or herding. A person completely isolated from the community of people who also love the same kind of dogs isn't usually that interested in doing things right.

Not letting you observe the litter, meet the mother or other dogs, or see where the puppies were raised. Healthy, well-mannered adults and a clean home are a breeder's best testimonial. If a person doesn't want you to see anything except the puppy she's trying to sell, you ought to be wondering why. (It's often common for the father of a litter not to be there, since the best choice for breeding is often a dog owned by someone else, often many states away.)

No documentation. If the purebred puppy's represented as registered, then registration papers should be available when the puppy is. So, too, should any certifications backing up health claims. A sales contract spelling out the rights and responsibilities of both parties is another must. Such a document provides you with recourse should the puppy not turn out as promised—if he has congenital health problems, for example.

Doesn't seem to understand the importance of socialization. Puppies need to be nurtured, loved, and handled to make good pets. Someone who can't explain what they've done in this area, or who tries to sell a puppy less than seven weeks old (and many good breeders hold on to puppies far longer, up to twelve weeks), probably doesn't understand enough about puppy raising to be breeding dogs.

While you'll likely find a reputable breeder in your area, or within a few hours' drive, that's not always going to be the case, especially if you've set your heart on a puppy of a less popular breed. In such cases you'll have to decide if you want to buy a puppy you've never met and have him shipped, probably by air.

Buying a puppy unseen may seem a risky business, but perhaps not so much as you may think. Before you consider this option, you'll have checked out the breeder thoroughly and talked to references and none of the red flags will have been raised. If everything seems in order, go for it. It's likely better to deal with a reputable breeder a time zone or two away than a clueless one in your hometown—or a puppy-mill dog in the nearby mall pet store.

Think Twice about Less Healthy Breeds

Let me say this up front: I love my "GrandPugs." But Pugs are one of the breeds that really give veterinarians like me pause when it comes to recommending them as pets. Not because they're not adorable and lovable, but because they've been bred to fit a fashion that isn't really conducive to a healthy, normal canine life.

Some of these defects are obvious. Dogs with short faces (Pugs, Bulldogs, Pekingese) are incredibly intolerant of warm weather and all but moderate exercise, and should never be sent as cargo in an airplane because they're at higher risk of death in transit. Dogs with long backs (Dachshunds, Corgis) are prone to back problems and rear-end paralysis. Other problems aren't so obvious: breeds with severe heart problems (Cavalier King Charles Spaniels), cancer (Golden Retrievers), or both (Boxers).

Reputable, ethical breeders test their dogs for congenital defects and do not use dogs with problems that can be detected. But design defects such as long backs and short noses will have to be fixed by a change in fashion, and endemic levels of disease may have to be dealt with by deepening the shallow gene pool of many breeds with some outcrossing to healthy dogs in other breeds.

The future will be interesting for many breeds, as pressure builds to change the fashionable looks of many and adapt the breeding practices to break genetic bottlenecks that produce disease. The science and veterinary communities will be a large part of the solution, as will those same ethical, reputable breeders who are doing what they can now to avoid problems within the system they have.

But for now, some breeds are difficult to recommend because of the health liabilities they bring with them. Consider the worst-case scenario when looking at a breed and see if you can live with that; if not, choose a healthier breed or mix. If you go forward, find a good breeder who's doing the best she can within the constraints of tradition and dog-world rules to breed healthy dogs.

Does your dog need a crate? It's really not optional equipment anymore for the modern dog. A crate makes house-training easier, helps your dog relax at the veterinarian's, and provides a safe way to transport your pet, especially in an emergency.

Chapter 4

BASIC GEAR AND COOL PUP STUFF

No matter where you get your puppy or dog, you need to acquire all the pup paraphernalia your pet needs to be safe, comfortable, and entertained. That's right: it's time to go shopping!

The items you purchase will affect your dog's well-being in many ways, from ensuring that he doesn't munch on your Manolos (I don't wear them, but you might!), or gnaw his way through your new kitchen cabinets, to providing him with appropriate bedding, dishes, and, yes, toys, toys, toys. Having everything on hand before you bring him home will help make the transition easier for both of you.

If you haven't visited a pet supply store since Scooby-Doo was a pup, you're probably in for a shock. There is a never-ending supply of items made for dogs and their people. High-end to mass-market,

Pick of the Litter for Your Pup

It's easy to get lost in the miles of aisles as you seek out what your pup needs versus what's cute but not crucial. The important

(Continued)

thing is to look past the marketing tools of packaging, color, and "pet guru recommended" blurbs to assess quality: the features that come together to make a product that is well designed, sturdy, attractive, and easy to use. Here's a look at some other factors to take into account:

Breed or Mix. Your dog's breed or mix of breeds affects his choice of toys and the type of play he enjoys. Retrievers and spaniels like to chase, carry, and chew things while dogs such as Greyhounds would rather pounce on and "kill" a stuffed toy, shaking it by the neck until the fur flies. Herding-type breeds enjoy going after airborne objects such as flying discs and bringing them under control. Choose toys that are likely to suit your dog's favorite forms of fun.

Size. Yes, it matters. Whenever possible, choose items that can grow with your puppy. Collars and crates are examples of items that can be adjusted along with a puppy's growth spurt.

designer chic to bare-bones functionality—everything a dog could possibly need or that you could want can be found at your local big-box pet-supply store or Bark Avenue boutique.

THE NONOPTIONALS

Some things a dog owner just can't do without. Before you bring your new dog home, be sure you purchase the following supplies: crate, food and water dishes, a collar, a leash (or harness and leash), some basic grooming tools, a jug of enzymatic stain and odor remover, and a couple of toys. These essentials will help your pup settle happily into his new digs. How do you know which ones to get? Here are a few tips on which ones to get, depending on your dog and your lifestyle.

A Room of Their Own

The first thing to know is that a crate isn't a cage or a jail. Think of it as a nice, cozy bedroom where your dog will sleep at night and rest comfortably during times when you are busy and can't supervise his every move. A crate is a restful retreat for a dog who needs a break from noisy kids, unfamiliar house guests, other pets, or simply too much activity. When you travel, your dog's crate is his home away from home. It keeps him safe while he's riding in a car and makes him feel secure in a hotel room or a new house. And it's a familiar enclosure on an airline flight, whether he's traveling first-class in the cabin or as cargo in the, well, cargo area.

A crate keeps your puppy out of trouble and out of harm's way. When he is safely tucked into his crate, he's not chewing on electrical cords, nibbling on tasty but toxic plants, destroying that antique wood sculpture that you brought back from your first trip to Thailand, or swallowing those AA batteries you were planning to recharge. The savings in veterinary bills alone makes a crate well worth the price.

With a crate as his own personal den, your dog can still enjoy time with the family without getting underfoot. It's easy to move a crate from room to room so your pup can be in the kitchen with you while you're preparing meals, in the family room while everyone watches television, and in the bedroom at night for some quality sleep time. A puppy in a crate with a chew toy is happy, and your home and belongings are safe from destruction. That's much kinder than banishing him to the backyard, away from the family, because he damaged something you valued or hurt himself because he got into something he shouldn't have.

Doggie Details

The best thing about a crate is that it is a fabulous house-training tool. Dogs are very clean, and they learn at an early age not to soil in their sleeping area—the crate. Your favorite rug, sure, but a properly crate-trained pup won't slip up and make a mess in what he views as a room of his own.

The first decision you need to make about a crate is which type to get. Crates come in three basic materials: wire (metal), plastic, or nylon or some other strong, soft material. You can find good arguments in favor of each, so your choice simply depends on your needs. Will you move the crate frequently? Do you have little room to spare in your home? Will greater air flow or increased privacy be more important to your dog? Will you need to ship your dog by air? Will you also use the carrier to transport a pet to the vet? The answers to these questions will help you decide which crate to purchase.

Wire crates. Wire crates offer good ventilation and allow your dog to see out on all sides. If you want to give him some privacy or a greater sense of security, it's easy to purchase or make a cover. Wire crates are easy to stack if you have more than one dog, and they fold up when you aren't using them. Some wire crates come with divider panels that allow you to purchase the size crate your puppy will need as an adult but limit the amount of space he has in it (see below for preferable size), gradually increasing it as he grows. One drawback is that wire crates are not appropriate for air travel. If you plan to ship your dog at some point in his life, he will need a hard plastic crate.

Plastic crates. Plastic crates are more private for dogs who like their space. Like wire crates, they can be stacked, but they don't break down easily for storage. They are well suited to safe air and automobile travel. Some come with wheels for easy transport through busy airports.

Soft-sided crates. These are lightweight and easy to move around. The front and sides have panels you can roll down if your dog needs to rest, or roll up to let him see what's going on. They collapse easily when not in use and are easy to clean. A soft crate can be a good choice for a mellow dog who uses it primarily as a retreat or nighttime sleep spot. This is not the crate to buy, however, if your dog is a chewer or an escape artist who knows how to operate zippers. Even a small dog can damage or destroy a soft crate if he is determined to get out of it.

Now, let's talk size. For house-training purposes, your dog's crate should be just big enough for him to comfortably lie down and turn around but not so spacious that he can use a corner as a potty area and still have room to get away from the mess. Remember, a crate should be cozy, not castlelike. If your pup will grow from the size of a Tonka truck to the size of a tanker truck, get a full-sized crate with a divider panel so it can grow right along with him.

Dish It Up

This should be pretty straightforward, right? I mean, how much is there to know? You just plop the food in a bowl or fill it with water, and you're good to go. If that's what you think, well, you probably haven't purchased dog dishes lately. Food and water dishes can be utilitarian stainless steel or good-looking ceramic, and they come in more styles than you can shake a stick at. Here's what to consider when making your choice:

Stainless steel. If your middle name is practical, there's no question: go for stainless steel. It's dishwasher safe, nonallergenic, and lasts forever. Some stainless steel dishes are lightweight, and exuberant dogs will use them as hockey pucks, but you can get around that problem by looking for one with a weighted or rubberized bottom. One drawback is that they can't be used to warm food in the microwave, which can help to intensify food's aroma if you have an old or a sick dog whose sniffer is on the fritz.

Ceramic. Looking for dishes that match your decor? Ceramic is the way to go. It's heavier than most metal dishes, so it's more difficult for a rambunctious dog to tip over, and you can find designs in just about any color or pattern. The good? Ceramic dishes are both dishwasher and microwave safe. The bad? They're likely to shatter if you drop them on the floor or your granite countertop.

Other types. What about plastic? It's inexpensive, colorful, and easy to clean, but it's not as durable as stainless steel or ceramic. Plastic bowls often bear tooth marks from dogs gnawing on them, and bacteria can enter through the chewed edges. Plastic also retains odors, and lots of dogs are allergic to it, developing acne on their chin or face.

Shape and diameter are other factors to consider. Choose a bowl with a narrow diameter or one that slants inward if your dog has droopy ears or you feed him canned food. This way, your dog's ears will hang outside the bowl, and he won't get them wet or messy. For a dog who slurps water out of his dish onto the floor, look for a water dish surrounded by a guard that will catch any overflow. You can also find dishes designed to slow down fast eaters.

Finally, check out the variety of travel dishes. From collapsible soft dishes to canteens with fold-down dishes to dispensers that fit in a minivan's cupholder, there's no end to the ingenious variety of on-the-go dishes these days.

Throw Out Your Dog Dish!

Yes, I just talked about dishes, because the fact is that most people will buy them anyway, and you'll need dishes for water, too. But here's what I'm really recommending these days: throw out your dog's food dish, or never get one at all.

Did you double-take? I bet you did, but here's the thing: My own dogs don't have food bowls. They have food...*puzzles.* These come from several companies and in a lot of different styles, but the basic premise is the same: you put kibble into the toy, and your dog has to work to get it out. Think of them like canine slot machines; sometimes they pay nothing, other times a little, on occasion a lot. Dogs love having to hearken back to their ancestors and work for their food.

The benefit is exercise to both body and mind, and our born-retired dogs need more of both. My dogs love food puzzles, and I recommend them to every dog owner I see. Check out the variety and buy a few of them, and rotate them to keep your pet interested. Your dog will really enjoy them, and you'll get a kick out of seeing how much fun it can be for your dog to work for his meals. (More on dog puzzles on page 98.)

Control and Contain

Your dog thinks what you offer the food in is most important, but collars, leashes, harnesses...they're all pretty high on the must-have list, too. And they're the most fun to shop for, with an endless array of choices.

Collars. A flat collar in nylon or leather with a buckle, plastic snap, or safety release is the go-to choice for everyday dog wear. Look for one that's sturdy and well made, with strong stitching. Nylon comes in many colors and designs, and it can be personalized with your dog's name and your phone number. Leather has a classic look and a natural appeal.

My favorite collars have one D ring at the buckle to which you can attach an identification tag and another D ring on the back for attaching the leash.

Nylon and leather are both long-lasting materials, but for a young puppy with a yen to chew, nylon has the edge. Leather smells good, so good that your pup may try to use his collar as a chew toy. Wait to purchase a leather collar for him until he is well past the destructive chewing stage.

If you are purchasing a collar for a puppy, check the fit regularly and adjust it as needed. It should lie snugly without being too tight. Make sure you can comfortably insert two fingers between the collar and your pup's neck.

Are there any types of collars you shouldn't get for everyday wear? You bet! Chain or nylon slip or choke collars and metal prong collars, which have inward-facing teeth, are training devices with specific uses and should never be left on a dog as a regular collar. Chain collars, especially, can get hung up on shrubbery, fences, or even other dogs' mouths and choke the dog wearing them.

Above all, make sure your dog's collar has some bling around it: an ID tag that will get him home if he gets out. And if the shelter or breeder didn't insert a microchip, ask your veterinarian to do it, pronto. ID tags and microchips are the best insurance against loss you'll ever buy. (For more on collars and tags, see pages 131–135.)

Wish I'd Thought of That!

The Tagnabbit (from Petmate) is an inexpensive, double-ended clip that holds ID tags and license on one end and clips to a collar at the other. For just a couple bucks you can move tags easily from one collar to another. Why is this...genius? Because it's actually not a bad idea to have a variety of collars—quick-release for in the home, nylon for swimming, higher-control for leash walks, blaze orange for wilderness hikes in hunting season, reflective for night-walking...and so on.

Not to mention some dogs are clothes horses—there are so many attractive collars available, so why limit your dog to just one? With the little Tagnabbit, you can have as many collars as you have days to play and things to do, and switch tags with just a snap.

Harnesses. People with small dogs or short-faced (brachycephalic) breeds often prefer a harness to a collar. These dogs can suffer neck injuries or have difficulty breathing if they pull hard against a collar. Some dogs learn to back out of collars, which is a safety concern. A harness helps to prevent these issues. It is also useful for safely securing dogs that ride in car seats or attached to canine seat belts.

In choosing a harness, consider the same features you would in choosing a collar. A good harness fits well and doesn't rub against your dog's skin or fur, causing raw or bare spots.

Leash. When it comes to leashes, leather and nylon have the same advantages and disadvantages as they do in collars. If you're a fashionista, nylon leashes and collars are usually available in matched sets. Whichever material you choose, the leash should be lightweight but sturdy. Avoid chain leashes, which can be heavy and noisy.

The best length for a leash is four to six feet (four feet may be too short for teeny-tiny dogs). This length gives your dog a little space

Power Steering for Power Dogs

For dogs who don't walk well on a leash—and owners who aren't that interested in or good at training—there's a kind of harness I just can't recommend enough: the front clip or snap that fits around the front legs and shoulders. More than half of the average dog's weight is on his front legs; control his forward momentum and you control his movement, like power steering. The front clip uses the dog's own strength to stop him from pulling on the leash (the harder he pulls away the more the harness turns him from going forward). They really work, even for big, strong dogs.

while still keeping him close to your side, and it's not so long that he or you will always be tripping over it.

Reel-type leashes are popular, but they're often misused. They're not suitable for using with a dog who isn't properly leash trained, or when they are used with an unruly or untrained dog. You have much more control with a dog at the end of a sturdy six-foot leash versus one at the end of a twenty-five-foot retractable leash. If you do choose to use one after your dog is trained, be sure to follow the directions, and use a wrist loop for safety so the handle doesn't pop out of your hand.

Looking Good: Choosing Grooming Tools

When we look good, we feel good. Dogs are no different. You can see the spring in their step after a good grooming. Some dogs even admire themselves in the mirror! Keeping your dog groomed is an important part of his physical and mental well-being. Grooming removes excess hair, distributes oils across the skin and coat, helps remove parasites and debris, and keeps air flowing to the skin.

Every dog's grooming needs are different, but all dogs need the same basic grooming: brushing or combing, nail trimming, tooth brushing, and ear cleaning. With the grooming tools listed below, you'll be equipped with the basics to keep your dog clean.

Brush. The brush you choose depends on your dog's coat type. A rubber curry brush, which has short, flexible rubber nubs, is a good choice for dogs with short coats. It removes dead hairs and distributes skin oils, making your dog's coat shine. Dogs with longer coats need a pin brush, which has long metal pins that help lift away dead hair without removing the protective undercoat. If your dog sheds heavily, you may want to purchase a wire slicker brush or shedding blade to easily remove excess coat.

Comb. Look for a steel comb, sometimes called a Greyhound comb, with half wide teeth and half narrow. It is useful for removing tangles from your dog's coat. You may also want to purchase a fine-tooth flea comb. It won't get rid of the tiny vampires, but it will alert you to their presence. A couple new twists on the traditional brush have become popular in recent years: brushes with rotating teeth to help work through the coat, and a shedding rake with the dynamite name of the FURminator. I especially love the latter: it gets all the loose hair off our dogs, and that means less shedding.

Dental care. Dental disease is the most commonly diagnosed problem in veterinary medicine. Dental problems are expensive to treat and take years off your dog's life. To keep your dog's fangs gleaming, his gums a healthy pink, and his breath pleasant, you need to practice daily oral care. Daily brushing is best, but every other day is great and weekly is better than nothing. You can buy a toothbrush made especially for dogs, with a triangular head that is useful for getting at the back cheek teeth and brushing all tooth surfaces with one pass, or you can simply use a soft toothbrush from your own dentist. Another option is a finger brush, sort of a little rubber cap with bristles that fits over your finger.

When it comes to toothpaste, buy the type made for dogs. Human toothpaste isn't made to be swallowed, and it can give a dog an upset stomach. Besides your dog will prefer poultry or beef flavor rather than a minty fresh taste.

If you can't or don't want to brush your pet's teeth, there a several good options for practicing daily oral care, including dental diets that provide abrasion to help keep teeth cleaner, dental vaccines for periodontal disease, enzyme-impregnated rawhide chews, dental treats, cloth tooth scrubbers, and even toys that help scrub plaque and tartar off teeth. Ask your veterinarian about these products, some of which are only available from a veterinary hospital or clinic.

Nail trimmers. Dogs have thick, tough toenails. To trim them, you need nail trimmers that are up to the task. Look for a nail clipper with a sharp blade that will slice through the nail rather than crushing it. Keep some styptic powder on hand in case you misjudge where to cut and nick the quick, a blood vessel inside the nail. A cotton swab dipped in styptic powder will apply pressure and a coagulant and stop the bleeding fast. After trimming, smooth the nails with a metal file.

BY YOUR ENERGY AND STRENGTH
SHALL YOU BE JUDGED

Don't think you are through shopping for your dog. The basics are just the beginning. If you have a dog with special needs or abilities—a high energy level, a strong desire to pull, a talent for making a mess—there are products that can help. Ingenious pet-product manufacturers have come up with numerous aids for people who need help to keep their dogs busy or under control. These items can help level the playing field when you're feeling overwhelmed by your dog's exuberance, strength, or just plain sloppy nature.

Keep 'Em Rolling

Are you exhausted at the end of your dog's walk while he's ready to go another few miles? Are you working overtime on a project that keeps you from walking your dog at all? There's an app for that. Well, actually, it's a treadmill. Don't laugh. Treadmills made for dogs are a great way to give your dog a workout if you don't come home until after dark, if it's raining or snowing outside, if you live in a high-rise, or if you're just too pooped to exercise your pooch. Canine treadmills are available for dogs of all sizes. And if you get a treadmill for yourself, the two of you can work out side by side.

Tidy Dog

We love our dogs, but we don't always love the mess they make. They sling slobber after they drink, they track dirty pawprints through the house, and they spill food on the floor. Teaching them to clean up after themselves is a lost cause, but the solution is underfoot. You can buy mats at home-supply stores made of high-performance fabrics that absorb liquids, block stains and odors, and remove dirt from paws. Place them at doorways or beneath your dog's food and water dishes. They wipe clean and are machine washable. Look for one with a nonskid backing.

MATTERS OF CONVENIENCE

Beyond the essentials and the special-use pet products are the things that just make life a little easier for both you and your dog. Without them, life would be a little hairier, in more ways than one. Here are some items you might appreciate.

Sofa covers and car seat covers help keep furniture and vehicle upholstery fur free. They come in every possible color and pattern to match any decor or car interior. Look for one that's machine washable, and buy at least two so you'll always have one available if the other is being laundered.

Puppies and older dogs can benefit from steps or ramps to help them get on and off furniture or, let's be honest, your bed, without injuring still-developing joints or aging and brittle bones. A ramp can also help an older or a smaller dog get in and out of the car easily.

Puppy gates and playpens are perfect for confining your dog to areas where he can't do any damage. A good puppy gate is adjustable so it can be placed in doorways of different widths. If you have a dog who can jump like Superman, you may want to invest in an extra-tall gate or a playpen with a cover. Make sure the gate or playpen you use offers no way for the pup to stick his head through and get caught, although there's even a solution for that—a product called Puppy Bumpers that fits around a dog's neck to prevent him from slipping through. (Yes, innovation is alive in the pet-products world.) Puppy gates used to be baby gates, really, and baby gates are designed to be used for a couple years. Several companies have noticed that people with dogs often use these barriers forever, and they don't want them to be ugly. In recent years these companies have come out with gates and barriers that not only don't take away from the look of a home but match and even enhance it.

The final thing every dog owner needs? Something to scoop the poop. That can be a designated tool for your backyard, but when you're on the go, make sure you have poop bags along. While you can reuse plastic grocery bags, you might find rolls of plastic bags designed for the purpose to be easier, especially since many come in dispensers that snap on your leash. Don't ignore cleanup when you're out: put the bag over your hand like a mitten, pick up the poop, invert, tie, and drop in the nearest appropriate receptacle. In your own yard, you might want to look at an appliance that fits on your sewer line or clean-out, so you can send the waste straight to the sewage plant instead of to the landfill.

THE DOG WHO LIVES WITH THE MOST TOYS WINS

Dogs just wanna have fun, and with all the different types of toys available to them, there's no reason for them ever to be bored. And toys are for more than playtime. A hard rubber chew toy helps soothe the aching mouth of a teething puppy and exercises and develops his jaws. A puzzle toy filled with kibble is a great way for your dog to exercise his mind and body while getting a meal. Stuff a hollow Kong with peanut butter and other goodies to entertain your dog for hours while you're working, or fill a Kong or Squirrel Dude with canned food, insert a pencil rawhide fuse, freeze, then deliver for an afternoon of nibbling away at the slowly defrosting delight.

Every dog has a different favorite toy. A tiny Japanese Chin pup may not be interested in a tennis ball, while a Golden Retriever will love it, love it, love it. Some Beagles enjoy cuddling up to a soft stuffed toy while others would take the same toy and shake it until the stuffing flies. Pugs are fond of fleeces, and terriers go for anything they can pounce on and "kill," especially if it makes a squeaky noise. Try different types of toys until you learn what your dog loves best.

Before you buy, check out toys for any features that might not be safe. Soft toys should be well made, with nontoxic stuffing and no bells, button eyes, or ribbons that could be chewed off and swallowed. Some plastics break easily, leaving sharp edges. Make sure your pup doesn't gulp down any squeakers if he is shredding a toy. With the exception of toys such as Kongs, which are about as tough as dog toys come, few toys should be left with an unsupervised pup. And don't forget that dogs like variety, so get lots of toys and retire some for reappearance later, when they're "new" again.

THE SILLY STUFF: HEY, WHY NOT? DOGS ARE SUPPOSED TO BE FUN

What would shopping for dogs be without the T-shirts, the sunglasses, the hats, the popsicle makers? Sure, none of those are requirements for your dog's well-being, but there's nothing wrong with indulging in something frivolous as long as it's not harmful. Besides, sometimes those silly products serve a purpose, too.

Take T-shirts and other clothing. Even the silliest clothes also help protect light-colored dogs from sunburn. They contribute to your dog's social skills by making him seem more approachable. An approachable dog meets more people and has more opportunities to learn how to interact with them. In wet and cold weather, raincoats and jackets keep thin-skinned dogs warm and dry. Boots keep pets from burning feet on hot pavement or damaging them on winter sidewalks covered in salt or other ice melters.

Hats and sunglasses serve the same dual purpose of protection and socialization. Doggles, strap-on eyewear that offers UV protection and impact-resistant lenses, put the *fun* in *functional* for dogs that enjoy beaches, boating, four-wheeling, and car rides. So ignore those people who say it's criminal to make a dog wear clothing and dress your dog with pride. If he likes it and you do, too, where's the harm?

What about items like the Kool Dogz Ice Treat Maker? That doesn't really have any redeeming value, does it? Sure it does. It helps dogs stay cool and hydrated on hot days. Freeze some favorite treats and water-proof toys inside the popsicle, and it keeps them entertained, too.

Don't be afraid to have fun with your dog! He is your best friend, after all.

Keeping Up with the Latest

Every year Team Becker heads to Global Pet Expo, the world's largest trade show for the pet-care industry. The show draws companies from all over the world, and is so big that the buyers would be well advised to bring a GPS to help them navigate the twelve football fields' worth of products.

With the help of my team of writers, editors, videographers, photographers, and producers, I pick Becker's Best: the products that I find the most innovative and useful, and that I most want pet lovers to know about. We shine the light on these great products through all my media platforms, including our PetConnection.com website, YouTube, Facebook, and Twitter. If you want to keep up with the latest, come find me!

For puppies nothing is more important than learning that the world isn't a scary place. When you're raising your puppy, be sure to take him safe places to socialize. Avoid parks, pet stores, or anyplace where you don't know the health of the other dogs until your veterinarian gives you the go-ahead. Instead, plan socializing with other healthy, vaccinated puppies and dogs (such as those belonging to friends and family), and go to places where your dog will see a wide variety of people, such as the outdoor patio of a coffeehouse. Let strangers give your puppy love and treats.

Chapter 5

TIME TO BRING HOME A NEW FAMILY MEMBER

You've taken your time in choosing a breed and a source, and in finding the perfect puppy or dog to join your family. You've been a responsible, thorough, and sensible person, hard as that may have been when all you really wanted was to sniff puppy breath or enjoy the wagging tail and dancing eyes of an adult dog who knew he was going *home*.

You deserve to enjoy the moment—take pictures, show off, enjoy—but you also need to be a solid, responsible person for a while longer, no matter how much you want to do the Snoopy dance when you bring your new companion home. That's because the first days and weeks (and, really, months when it comes to puppies) of effort you put into getting the relationship off right will set the tone for a lifetime of good health and behavior.

You'll both be better off for the effort you put in from the beginning. The major spoiling? There's plenty of time for that later.

GETTING A PUPPY OFF TO A GREAT START

Your puppy starts learning the moment he's born, and by the time you get him—seven to ten weeks of age—he's as absorbent as a bath towel, taking in the sights and sounds of his world and trying to figure out his place in it. The answer he arrives at on his own may be quite different from the one you want him to have, which is why you need to be involved in the process. Don't let your puppy grow up without you. Every minute you spend with your puppy is not only delightful but also an investment in the future.

A Rose by Any Other Name Is Sadie

One of the things I always do when I meet new pet owners is ask how they came up with the name of their pet. I love the stories! But I also love how the names we choose have a lot to say about how we consider our pets as family today. I'm no longer surprised to find out that people check out lists of baby names—as in human baby—to get a name for a pet.

And it's not just my impression. Every year Veterinary Pet Insurance (VPI), the pet-health insurance company, releases a list of the top names for dogs. While there are always some real head-scratchers—the company chose Pickle Von Corndog as the wackiest name of 2010—the top names for pets are now people names such Max, Molly, Charlie, and Sadie.

Do you need to keep anything in mind when naming a dog? A little, maybe. Avoid names that sound like common obedience commands. Sitka, as in Alaska, is a pretty name, but you can imagine you'll be confusing your dog when you try to teach her to sit. Otherwise, keep names short, one or two syllables, although your dog can have as many nicknames as you want, of course, and they can be as long as you want. I sure do know a lot of dogs who, like a lot of children, know they're in trouble when they're called by their full name—Charles Lexington Smith, aka Charlie, you are in the doghouse, buddy.

THE FIRST NIGHT: EVERYONE RELAX

Your puppy will probably be so overwhelmed by the new sights, sounds, smells, and all the attention that she won't much miss her littermates and her old home. Don't worry, that will come soon enough—and last most of the first few nights.

Keep things nice and easy at the start. Everyone will want to hold the puppy and play with her, and that's fine, but remember she's still a baby and gets worn out quickly. She needs to sleep, but she may not eat much on that first day. She has a lot to get used to; don't worry about it very much. Let her explore.

Puppies aren't stuffed toys, and you must help your children to realize that. Small children—especially those under five—can't really help being a little rough with puppies (and dogs), and they must be carefully supervised to ensure that neither hurts the other.

Where should your puppy sleep? That's for you to decide. Ours sleep on the bed, and studies show we're not alone in this. In most cases—the exceptions being allergies (human) or bad attitude (canine)—sleeping on the bed is fine. But not for your puppy, not at first. In the beginning, you'll want a crate in the bedroom for house-training purposes.

The first couple of nights are very tough on a puppy. The reassuring warmth of her littermates is gone and everything has changed. She's going to have a lot to say about this, so be prepared. She will fuss less if she's in your presence, if she can be reassured by your smell and the sound of your breathing.

Set up her crate next to your bed and prepare it with a soft blanket to sleep on and a chew toy or two. Tell her "crate" firmly, put her inside, and close the door. Ignore the cries and whines, but don't punish your puppy, and don't take her out when she's carrying on—you'll teach her that all she need do is fuss and she gets what she wants. She'll probably settle down and then wake once or twice in the middle of the night. Do take her out to relieve herself—and praise her for doing so—and then put her back in her crate.

In a day or two, the worst of the heartbreaking crying is over.

A POSITIVE APPROACH TO HOUSE-TRAINING

Crate-training is the fastest, neatest way to teach your puppy not to do his business in the house. Learning to be comfortable in a crate is also an essential part of being a modern dog, since confinement is a normal part of every dog's life, whether it's at the veterinarian's or in a car or on a plane. A dog who is comfortable in a crate is also easier to evacuate and house during a disaster. All dogs should be familiar with and comfortable in a crate.

And that starts with house-training your puppy. During training he's either:

* "on empty" and playing loose under your supervision;
* relieving himself, where you choose; or
* confined to his crate for quiet chewing or sleeping.

Crates work for house-training because your dog wants to keep his "den" clean. Puppy mothers keep the whelping box clean by eating what tiny babies produce, and good breeders pick up where Mom left off by offering puppies who are weaned but not yet ready to go home—from about three weeks of age to between seven and twelve weeks of age—a clean puppy area with a place perfect to step away and potty. (The work of a good mom and a good breeder is another reason to avoid pet-store puppies. Trainers have long known that many of these puppies are hard to house-train, because they grew up accustomed to living in their own filth.)

Doggie Details

A general rule of thumb is that a puppy can hold it for about as many hours as his age in months—two hours for a two-month-old puppy, four hours for a four-month-old puppy, and so on. Like human babies, though, every puppy is an individual, and many are quickly able to sleep through the night. Don't push your luck, though. Give your puppy plenty of chances to go out.

Take your puppy out of the crate first thing in the morning and coax him to follow you outside to the spot you have chosen for him to relieve himself. If he starts to relieve himself on the trip outside, give him a firm no and take him to the area you've chosen for him in your yard. (Make sure it's safe and that there isn't tall grass there—your puppy doesn't want to push through a scary jungle.) Give the command you've chosen—"hurry up," "get to it," or whatever—and praise him for going. Take him inside and give him food and water, and then go outside again immediately—a full tummy puts pressure on a puppy's bladder. Give the command and praise him when he goes. Remember a puppy has to go to the bathroom within fifteen minutes of eating or drinking, upon waking up, and after play or exercise.

Let him play in a small area under supervision, take him out again in an hour or so, and then put him in the crate for a nap. Repeat throughout the day.

What if you work? If you can, it's always a good idea to take a little vacation time to start a puppy out right. You may think you're wasting vacation time, but really . . . what could be a better vacation than hanging out with a puppy? If that's not possible, then get help. Find a friend or neighbor to handle the duties when you can't be home, or hire a pet-sitter. Whatever you do, never—and I mean never, ever—punish a puppy for going in the house. The fault is yours, not the puppy's.

If you're doing everything as you should be and your puppy isn't getting the concept, see your veterinarian—first, to rule out a health issue, and second, to refer you to a trainer or behaviorist for help.

Quicker Cleaner-Uppers

Puppies and dogs will return to the scene of an accident because it smells like a place to go. Even if you clean up all visible signs of the mess, enough smell may remain to keep the area attractive to

(Continued)

your dog. Keeping on top of messes isn't hard, but it is essential to house-training. What you need to know:

🐾 Don't use ammonia-based cleaners. They smell like urine to a puppy—ammonia being one of the by-products of decomposing urine. So instead of making the area smell clean, ammonia products make a mess site seem even more attractive.

🐾 Use products designed for pet mess cleanup. These liquid products contain enzymes that break down the waste and neutralize odor. Use lots: the wet spot on top of the carpet can be the size of a quarter, but the plume under the carpet pad can be the size of a salad plate—and your pet can smell it!

🐾 Clean up the area as soon as possible. Do this before the mess has a chance to soak through to carpet padding, where getting the smell out is very hard. Once the urine soaks through, you have to pull up the carpet to ensure that the area's truly clean.

🐾 Search for and destroy old stains. Even if you can't smell anything, old stains may still have a lingering odor that can attract your puppy. Remember dogs have been trained to sniff out explosives, termites, mold, accelerants in arson cases...their sensitive sniffers don't have any problem finding every spot that's ever been soiled on. Pet-supply outlets offer black lights that show old messes you may not be able to see. Veterinarians and trainers sometimes have these available for rent. Cleaners that have mess-eating enzymes—all pet stores have them—will do the best on old stains, but you may need to treat the area a couple of times.

When your puppy's completely house-trained, you'll most likely want to have the carpets cleaned; but if you are diligent during the training period, you'll probably end up with no permanent stains. Keep cleanup supplies on hand, though, because accidents and illnesses occur throughout your dog's life. You've been sick as a grown-up, right? Your pet's the same. Mess happens.

THE SOCIAL ANIMAL: GETTING YOUR PUPPY
INTO THE WORLD

There is no lesson you can teach your puppy that's more important than getting along. A good breeder or foster home would have started the process by safely introducing your puppy to a variety of experiences—carpet and tile, different substrates to soil on such as grass, gravel, and concrete, brief periods of warmth and cold, all manner of normal household sounds, all kinds of people of various ages, and so on. The staff at the veterinary hospital where your puppy went before you adopted your new baby was also likely savvy in making the world less scary—praising your puppy and his brothers and sisters, giving treats while shots and microchips were given, and taking time to kiss those irresistible puppy faces with those sweet plumes of puppy breath. Puppies are one of the best things about working in a veterinary hospital!

When you get your puppy home, you need to keep the good times rolling—and that means getting out and about with your puppy.

Oh, but wait: didn't your veterinarian warn you to keep your puppy safe from disease by keeping him away from other dogs or places where other dogs roam, such as parks?

Yes, we do say that. And it used to be that we veterinarians were at loggerheads with trainers and behaviorists—even our own colleagues, veterinary behaviorists—by insisting on isolation until that final puppy shot is in place. After all, preventing and curing disease is our thing.

But...we also know that an unsocialized puppy is at far greater risk of not staying in the family, so we have had to balance the risk a little in giving our advice. This is why you shouldn't go anywhere where dogs you do not know hang out—parks, dog events, or pet stores—until your veterinarian gives the go-ahead. You should take him to places that are probably safe—to see friends and play with their healthy, vaccinated dogs, for example, or to places humans frequent, such as the outdoor seating area of a sidewalk café.

So use common sense. Plan safe outings, and carry your puppy if you're not sure. And when that last puppy shot has been given—at fourteen to sixteen weeks—then really pull out all the stops when it comes to socialization.

Finally, remember that it's normal for puppies to be scared, but your response to their fear sets the stage for their future. Don't soothe a frightened puppy. Petting him and saying, "It's okay, baby" or something similar gives your puppy the idea that being scared is okay, that you're rewarding him for the behavior.

Be matter-of-fact and encouraging. Let him know that you think there's nothing to be afraid of. Let him work it out, and when he takes that step forward, praise him for his courage. And then move on.

SET THE RULES AND STICK WITH THEM

Puppies are adorable, even when they're naughty. Maybe *especially* when they're naughty. If you want your puppy to learn, you need to be consistent about what's acceptable behavior and what's not. The easiest time to teach a dog to walk on a leash, sit when asked to, learn to love a crate, accept and enjoy the attention of strangers, and stay off the furniture is when your dog is a puppy.

> ### Doggie Details
>
> Think about the dog you want to have, and never let your puppy get away with what you don't want a grown dog to do, no matter how cute he is. And if there is one major tip for minimizing the training time and maximizing the effectiveness, it would be to use positive, reward-based training as much as possible. Show your pet what to do and reward him for doing it right. It's that simple.

Sure, you might have to discipline a pet from time to time, but if you keep the training positive, you'll be mostly rewarding good behavior, and that means less bad behavior.

First, envision the kind of pet you'd like to live with. Some people are considerably looser with their dogs (and kids) than others. If you think that allowing dogs on the furniture is okay, fine, then let your puppy up on the furniture. But if you think it's only okay for puppies to be on the furniture because you want to snuggle yours, then not so fine. You're not being fair.

Second, follow through with the ground rules, every time. No letting things slide because you're tired. No letting him get away with things because he's cute. When he jumps on the couch for the first time—and he will try it at least once—tell him "off" and set him on the floor. Praise him for being a good puppy on the floor. When he jumps on you, or the kids, tell him "off," then take his collar and show him what you mean. Praise him for keeping all four paws on the ground.

Consistency also means that every human member of the family is clear on puppy rules and helps the puppy learn and live by them. If you've decided you don't want your dog to beg for food, you're going to have a hard time enforcing the rule if your son is slipping the puppy French fries while watching TV. It also helps if everyone in the household tries to use a similar tone of voice (better than if Dad uses a big, gruff voice, Mom speaks in hushed tones, and children bark commands in the soprano range).

Loosening the rules is easier than tightening them. A puppy who grows up thinking every obnoxious thing he wants to do is fine is going to grow into a dog you're not going to enjoy living with or be able to take places. Once your puppy is a well-mannered dog, you can invite him up on the couch or teach him to put his paws on your shoulder and give you a big, slurpy kiss. The distinction between him doing what he wants and him doing what he wants with your permission is a big one.

In reality, in the wild dogs can do just about whatever they want: everything can be a chew toy and the world is their toilet. But domesticated dogs that want to live a happy, full life must learn manners that allow them to live in a human household. There's appropriate chewing (a toy) and inappropriate chomping (the leg of the table). There's an acceptable place to go the bathroom (in the yard, or perhaps in a litter box if your home's an apartment) and a livable amount to bark (to alert you somebody is at the door but not incessantly enough to cause the neighbor to complain to the authorities). Because I know you want to know more about training, remember that's all in Part Three. Get your puppy off to a great start and you can look at training as a joy, not a chore.

GETTING AN ADOPTED DOG OFF TO A GREAT START

While adopting a grown dog often isn't nearly the work that introducing a puppy is, you should still follow some guidelines to ease the transition. Your new dog will be a little disoriented under any circumstances. But if spaying or neutering was done just before adoption, the postsurgical fog may add to the stress and confusion. Anesthesia mixes up the brain chemicals, and it takes a few days to a couple of weeks on occasion for all the brain cells to march in proper formation again.

Remember the saying "You never get a second chance to make a first impression"? The idea works with dogs, too. No matter how happy you are to bring him home, no matter how much you want to make up for the shabby way he was treated before you got him, start him off right from the beginning. Decide what the house rules are and stick to them, at least for the first couple of months. Let him know that even though you're the nicest person on earth and the best human he could ever hope to find, your house does have rules and he must follow them. If your Ten Commandments for dog training are more like the Ten Suggestions, or if you are consistent and persistent in your training but you don't embrace positive reinforcement, then at best you'll have a relationship with your dog that isn't all it can be. Or an indoor dog becomes an outdoor one or, worse yet, it's removed from the home for poor manners that could have and should have been avoided.

House-training is obviously priority number one for most people, and many adopted dogs already have a pretty good idea what to do. An adult dog may not be as comfortable in a crate as a puppy quickly becomes, so get in the habit of making that crate a destination for good things. Give your pet tasty treats for going in, and praise as well. Build up the time and ignore the fussing. Choose a very special toy—one stuffed with food and treats—to give your dog when he's in the crate. And then follow the guidelines for puppies to house-train.

Since dogs can get out of sight and into trouble more quickly than a little puppy can, close doors and use baby gates to keep your dog where you can observe him when he's not in a crate. Take him outside on a leash and praise him for going. Not only does putting the behavior on a cue make the training go more quickly, but a dog who goes on command is a wonderful thing to have when traveling or with inclement weather.

While every dog is an individual, most adult dogs start feeling comfortable in their new homes in about a month. You can do a few things to help him understand that yours is his new home and he is a loved member of his new family, but he also has to understand his place in the family. For the dog who's really shy or anxious, there are pheromones on the market—such as DAP (for Dog Appeasing Pheromone)—that can help him get through the rough spots.

Many if not most adult dogs know how to sit when asked to do so. If yours does, great. If not, teach him (it's in Part Three), and use this behavior both as a substitute for things you don't want a dog to do (a dog who's sitting can't also be jumping up) and to teach your dog without punishment that you set the rules, and if he follows them, everyone's happy.

Doggie Details

Dog trainers and behaviorists call this NLIF—Nothing in Life Is Free—or Learn to Earn. What a dog wants—his dinner, a walk, a car ride, a belly rub—simply doesn't happen until he does something you want. Most often, that's a sit. Get in the habit of asking your dog to sit before you give him his dinner. Before you put on his leash for a walk. Before you open the door for him to go out, before you invite him up on the couch. Ask him for a sit before you pet him, and you'll never get that dog who paws and nudges for constant attention—that is a dog who has trained the owner, not the other way around.

While this seems like dog training, it's really a lot deeper than that. By setting limits and insisting on rules to follow, you're building a relationship where your dog knows what's expected and that you're in charge. Not a dominant person, but a leader. And your dog loves a leader. It makes him feel like a member of the team. Set the ground rules early, and stick to them fairly and consistently. You can always loosen up, but tightening up is awfully hard after your dog's out of control.

And speaking of teams, you need a veterinarian on yours. Do you have one yet? Read on!

PART TWO
HOME CARE TO KEEP PETS HEALTHY AND SAFE

The fact is, I wouldn't be a practicing veterinarian with more than thirty years of experience if I didn't love pets and people both. Pets, because, well, how can I not? I grew up on a small family farm, the old-fashioned kind where we had a little bit of everything—cows, chickens, pigs, dogs, and cats, you name it! I grew up loving and respecting animals and the many ways they help people. Veterinary medicine? There was never really any other choice for me. I love both pets and people, and as a veterinarian I could work with both.

But much as I love seeing pets and people when I'm working at the two veterinary hospitals—when I'm not on the road for TV appearances and veterinary conferences—I do sometimes wish I didn't have to see some of the pets I see. I wish I could get to their owners before their owners got into my exam room, to make sure they know what they need to do to keep their pets healthier. To save unnecessary pain, expense, or worse.

A veterinarian like me is a pet owner's best friend in keeping a dog healthy with robust, preventive health-care measures such as wellness exams, vaccinations as needed, spaying and neutering, and parasite prevention. But a lot of the things that have owners bringing dogs to the veterinarian stem from problems that would never have happened if home-care preventive measures—the old-fashioned word for that is *husbandry*—were in place from the first day a dog or puppy comes home.

And I want you to know what these things are so you and your veterinarian can focus on the health problems you can't avoid.

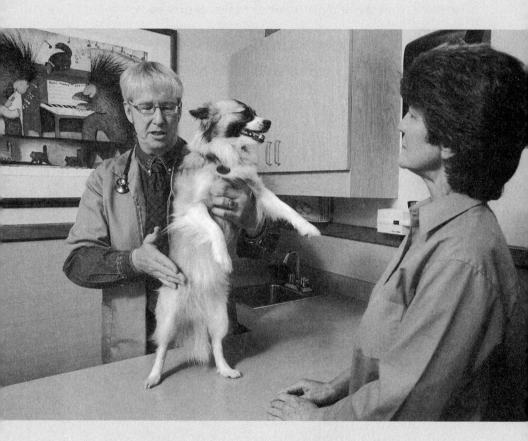

The most important thing you can do with regard to food is to not give your dog too much of it. Fat pets will live shorter lives, and the time they have will be less comfortable, with all the kinds of health problems that come with excess weight. Discuss your pet's weight at every veterinary visit, and if you need help slimming down your pet, ask.

Chapter 6

WHAT'S GREAT TO EAT AND WHERE TO FIND IT

magine your own personal food fairy—a benevolent guardian who chooses only high-quality, healthy meals and snacks, always in right-sized portions, always served with your satisfaction and well-being at heart. Like a spa chef and a mom in one. As chief shopper and food preparer for your dog, that's exactly the role you play in her diet. The foods you choose (and the portions you dish out) impact nearly every aspect of her life, including health, happiness, appearance, and longevity. In fact, how you feed your dog may be the single most important decision you ever make for her long-term health.

There's no end to the choices in dog food. Dry, canned, semimoist, freeze-dried, frozen, or homemade? Fifteen dollars a bag, or fifty? Generic, big-name, boutique brand, organic, or even kosher? You could spend all day trying to figure out the dog food options at a pet supply store and end up with little more than a confusion-induced headache. The labels are overwhelming, touting "fresh," "lean," "gourmet," "meaty," "holistic," "healthy," and "natural," and featuring ingredients that seem like those you'd be happy to serve your human family. And almost all say "Veterinarian Recommended"—something that's easy to put on packaging but can be very hard to get from your own veterinarian, who has his or her own ideas. Packaging on some foods makes it appear as if a gourmet chef just wrapped them up—heck, you can practically see the steam coming off the packaging. The direct and implied promises that your dog will be stronger, faster, thinner, wiser, or otherwise more agreeable if you feed her any given product are impossible to assess with any objectivity, no matter how many of the labels state their contents are "Veterinarian Recommended."

Turn Your Dog into a Hunter

Dogs and their wolf ancestors evolved to earn every bite they took. Hunting means hard and frequent exercise, but today's hounds rarely have to travel much farther than from sofa to food bowl. This doesn't just make them fat, it also makes them bored. You can help give your dog something to think about and do at dinnertime by getting rid of the food bowl and using a food puzzle instead.

These are toys designed to dole out small amounts of food when the dog makes the puzzle move or open in some way. They're made of everything from plastic to wood, cardboard, and even recycled water bottles, and are available in most pet supply stores. Some of my favorites are the Kong Wobbler and Genius, the Busy Buddy line, the Buster Cube, Twist 'n Treats, Nina Ottosson's Dog Pyramid, and the Kibble Nibble.

AN ENDLESS ARRAY OF FOOD CHOICES
FOR DOGS AND THEIR OWNERS

So how do you choose? You're smart enough not to be swayed by packaging, shelf position, and price alone, and the legally mandated labels leave lots to be desired, as any pet-food-industry critic is quick to point out.

As for "Veterinarian Recommended," well, which veterinarian? And what are her credentials? Many dog foods *are* veterinarian recommended—just not for your own particular dog. Your dog has a specific and unique set of dietary needs, and the single best way to decide which food to dish out at your house is to research, know your own preferences, and then discuss matters with your veterinarian. Together, you can weigh your dog's needs against all the products and sort through the complicated labels to come up with the one diet that works best, both for your dog and for your own sense of how your food purchases matter. Your veterinarian will help you consider the critical factors: your dog's age, lifestyle, breed, and health risks and conditions—as well as your budget and convenience. Don't be shy about sharing your limitations, whether that means you need to choose a food available at a grocery store, that you need to have a limit on your dog's food budget, or that you have an interest in preparing fresh meals at home from whole, locally obtained ingredients you can source.

Because my clients see that most veterinarians also sell pet foods I always recommend feeding a great food you don't have to buy it from me; I just always want you to get the recommendation of what to feed from me (nutrition is therapy, and that educated recommendation costs you nothing). Once you've found the right diet and decided on the right portion size for your dog, review your choice at each well-pet visit. Dogs' nutritional needs change with their life stage and lifestyle, so it's possible that the best food today may not still be the right choice a year or two down the road. In fact, I typically recommend at least four changes of diet in a dog's lifetime (puppy, adult, senior, therapeutic). Just as it would be interesting to ask a painter what brand of paint she uses to paint her own home or a mechanic what kind of motor oil he uses in his own car, I highly recommending asking a veterinarian what kind of food she feeds her own pets (also what kind of parasite control, dental treats, supplements, and so on).

Some experts want even more change than I do, saying that changing diets regularly—and mixing things up—is the best choice for a healthy dog. Variety is more than the spice of life: it's the one way to ensure that you're really covering all the bases when it comes to giving your dog what he needs. (That old saw about never switching food was created by pet-food marketing whizzes. Rotating high-quality foods regularly is never a bad idea.)

Here's a rundown of some of the other major factors to consider when choosing food.

Age and Activity Level

Puppies need more proteins and fats than adults, and they need foods that help them grow slowly and steadily. This is especially important for large dogs, as growing too quickly puts a major strain on bones and joints as well as major organs. Some companies have even made products that break things down further, with foods for small-breed puppies and large-breed ones.

Active adult dogs not only need more calories than their more sedentary peers, but they need a higher percentage of those calories to come from proteins and fats. For example, a dog who runs daily and competes in high-energy dog sports—or accompanies a human marathoner on training runs—may need as much as double the percentage of her calories from fat as her couch-potato canine counterpart. Just feeding more of the same food can't provide for that nutritional requirement.

Many senior dogs need foods with low calorie density and lots of fiber to work with their slowing metabolisms and digestive systems. For other older dogs, brain changes or sensory loss sometimes take away from appetite, and you need to find a food that recaptures their interest. Tip: Putting food in the microwave for a few seconds releases the aroma and amps up the taste.

The Breed's Needs

Your dog's breed or breed-mix makeup determines much more than appearance, favorite pastime, and energy level. Breed is also the biggest clue to the health complications any given dog might face in his lifetime. Choosing a food that anticipates health problems can help stave them off and keep your dog's body in the best possible shape to cope with trouble in the long run. For example:

🐾 Dalmatians, Boxers, Collies, Cocker Spaniels, and West Highland Terriers are prone to skin problems caused by food allergies. Unlike people, whose allergies are most commonly manifested through their respiratory systems, dogs suffer their allergies mostly through skin itchiness and irritation. The discomfort is a cross to bear for afflicted dogs—and it creates all kinds of extra work and expense for dog owners. In fact, skin problems (which include ear infections) are the number one reason pet owners take pets to the veterinarian. Anything you can do to head this problem off at the pass is a good turn for both you and your canine companion, which may mean a diet without common allergy triggers or therapeutic diets designed for sensitive pets.

* Labrador Retrievers, Golden Retrievers, German Shepherds, and many other large breeds have high incidents of joint disease. Choosing a diet with added neutraceuticals such as glucosamine, chondroitin sulfate to help foster cartilage growth, and that is high in fatty acids to deter inflammation may help a dog live years longer without symptoms of arthritis.

* Schnauzers are prone to genetic kidney disease and diabetes. A diet with high-quality protein and low carbohydrates can save years of wear and tear on their kidneys, before they ever have symptoms of illness.

* Small dogs are especially prone to painful, debilitating, and expensive dental problems. Foods designed with a more abrasive action help to scrape the teeth clean as the pet chews.

While there are foods designed to address all these potential health problems—and others—recipes developed by veterinary nutritionists can also help. Your veterinarian will work with you to decide what route is best to take for your dog.

Weight and Health Conditions

Overweight dogs and dogs with existing health conditions sometimes benefit from specially formulated diets or even therapeutic diets. Therapeutic diet options available only from your veterinarian range from foods targeted for dogs who are obese, arthritic, or suffering from diabetes, to diets that help control severe allergies or digestive distress. There are even special diets available from veterinarians for dogs who have cancer and those who are suffering from cognitive dysfunction.

I truly believe nutrition is therapy. Therapeutic diets should be given only when they are recommended by your dog's veterinarian.

Stop the Wolfing!

When you watch your dog consume his meals, does the expression "wolfing it down" come to mind? Dogs are scavengers, and because a scavenger never knows where his next meal will come from, the instinct to eat as much as possible, as fast as possible, is so strong in some breeds (and some individual dogs) they can make themselves ill with their rate of consumption. These are dogs who will kitchen-counter-surf and garbage-dive for any scrap of food they can scrounge. Heck they'll even raid the cat's litter box... yuck! Labrador Retrievers, Beagles, Bassets, Cocker Spaniels, Corgis, Dachshunds, and Pugs are among the breeds that come to mind—and, not coincidentally, the breeds that most often lumber into my veterinary office looking like they need to lose a pound or ten. Labs, in fact, are so well-known in the pet food industry for their willingness to happily eat anything at all that they have been banned as taste testers from some research trials. Eating too quickly is a bigger problem than just eating too much, also. It can lead to excessive gassiness and possibly contributes to a life-threatening emergency commonly known as bloat, where a dog's stomach enlarges and twists, requiring fast surgical response to hope for survival.

If your dog's a wolfer, here's a tip to slow him down: choose a couple of smooth stones (make sure they are too big for your dog to swallow), wash them, and put them in your dog's dish with his food. Arrange the food so the dog will have to move things around to get to his meal—thus making him take his time. You can also find bowls designed to make eating more time-consuming, such as the Brake-fast bowl that makes eating more difficult, or LeBistro food dispensers that slow the rate of food availability.

And you'll read this more than once in this book: get food puzzles or even scatter your dog's meal in the grass or on the vinyl flooring and let him graze. Anything that will make the wolfer slow down and work harder.

They contain supplements and treatments designed for specific health conditions, and just as you wouldn't randomly give your dog antibiotics or pain medications without cause, you should not give these diets to any dog for whom they are not prescribed. This is sometimes an issue in multidog households, but it's a necessary inconvenience to feed two different foods if you have one dog with special dietary needs and another without them.

HOW TO KNOW WHEN A DIET IS RIGHT—AND WRONG

How do you know the food you're feeding your dog is "the one"? Here are a few signs you've got it right:

- **A huggable coat and visible health.** An optimum diet gives your dog's coat shine, volume, and luster. It imparts to your dog shiny eyes, strong bones, and healthy skin. As a veterinarian I can tell from twenty paces if dogs are on a high level of nutrition; their coat announces it like a neon sign when they walk in the door or if I see them on a street. Pets with poorer nutrition have coats that are dull, brittle, and roughed up.
- **Vitality.** You might say that dogs on the best possible diet are blessed with an extra gear—they play a little harder, walk a little longer, and look healthy and strong. Does that mean your twelve-year-old Labrador Retriever can run with the four-year-olds? Probably not, but he ought to be able to outshine and outpace plenty of the other senior dogs on the block.
- **Green lawn.** If your lawn is dotted with yellow spots from dog urine—although a little spotting is normal—there's a good chance you're feeding your dog the wrong food. When a food has excessive amounts of nitrogenous waste products, they pass right through your dog—and end up ruining your yard. When I go through a neighborhood and see a yard that's spotted by Spot, I know the owners aren't making the best choices when it comes to their pet's diet.
- **Small, compact waste.** Nobody wants to talk about poop, but here's the little secret dog owners who are feeding the right food know: dogs eating their optimum diet produce less waste—sometimes *far*

less—than dogs who aren't. The fact is, if a high-quality food is suitable to your dog's nutritional needs, most of it is used during digestion—and little waste remains. If you put a high-quality food in your dog's mouth, what comes out the other end is small and firm. The food helps to express the dog's anal glands, and it's easy to pick up even if your dog has an accident. If the kibble is made largely of fillers, however, your dog will need to eat more to get adequate nutrition—and all that filler will end up working its way through the digestive system and ending up on your lawn or in your carpet, as poor-quality foods can cause dogs to have chronic diarrhea and accidents.

❧**Healthy weight.** If your dog is overweight or underweight, you may be feeding him the wrong diet—or you may just be giving too much or too little food. Talk with the veterinarian about both the food and the portion. As a general guideline, a small dog needs 40 calories per pound of body weight each day, a medium-sized dog needs 30 calories per pound, and a large dog needs 20 calories per pound. To figure out how much food your dog needs each day, multiply his weight by the correct number of calories per pound (for example, a 30-pound dog times 30 calories per pound per day equals 900 calories a day). Most dry dog foods contain about 350 calories per measuring cup—so your 30-pound dog would require slightly less than three measuring cups of food a day. (Canned foods are made up of at least 70 percent water, so your dog would need to eat more to consume the same number of calories.) Dogs who are spayed or neutered need fewer calories, by the way, about 10 percent less. You'll also need to adjust up or down if your dog is very active (up) or not (down).

Pay Attention to Prospective Problems

In 2007, thousands of pets were sickened and killed when adulterated ingredients from rogue overseas suppliers got into many different brands of dog food.

Because there is no central reporting system for pet deaths, many of the sick and dead animals were considered to be isolated incidents until routine product testing revealed the problem, and veterinarians and public-health officials started putting the pieces together to reveal how widespread the problem was. The unprecedented recalls of affected products went on for weeks as companies scrambled to find out the problem and pull affected food off the shelves.

Pet food comes from the same food-supply system as human food, and that means you must be aware of recalls for your entire family. Be sure to pay attention to any news about recalls. Sign up at FDA.gov to get recall information straight from the US Food and Drug Administration. If a product you've bought turns up in a recall, stop feeding it to your pet, and save the food to return and in case you need to make a claim. Call your veterinarian for more information.

If you routinely store pet food in containers, always save the part of the package with the manufacturer's contact information and lot number.

FORGET BRANDS FOR A MINUTE, AND JUST THINK ABOUT FOOD "FORMATS"

Confused yet? Hang in there, because I'm going to rock your world a little more and have you yearning for the days when there were only a few brands and two basic choices: wet food or dry. It's just not that simple anymore. And really, that's a good thing. So let's talk food "formats."

Kibble

Kibble is the food of choice for the vast majority of dogs. Dry dog food combines convenience, cost-effectiveness, and nutritional balance. It's easily portable and storable. There are formulations available to meet most dogs' nutritional needs, and dry food is easily supplemented when a dog needs or enjoys something extra in his diet.

The biggest challenge in using dry food is simply in the choosing. The differences in quality and content of dry foods are vast, ranging from foods that are concocted with precision from quality ingredients to foods that are, quite literally, made from the worst of the leftover junk from the food chain. Here are a few tips to keep in mind as you choose:

❧ Look for meats that have a name among the top ingredients. You don't want to read a vague reference to "meat" or "meat by-products." Honestly, that kindasorta meat listing could refer to anything from filet mignon to shoe leather. Instead, look for "chicken," "beef," and so on.

❧ Any acceptable dry dog food should be labeled as complete and balanced by the Association of American Feed Control Officials (AAFCO).

❧ When it comes to dry dog food, it pays to be a brand-name shopper. Choose foods from well-established pet food companies, not off-brands or unknowns. These corporations invest tens of millions of dollars a year in nutrition research and food testing, and they employ countless veterinarians and veterinary nutritionists to help them ensure a good product. As such, they are the safest bet as a source of your dog's nutrition.

❧ Buy the best you can afford. *Premium* and *super-premium* are largely marketing terms, but they do usually indicate a level of commitment to quality products and a commensurately higher-priced food. The most expensive dry dog food is not necessarily the best, but there is definitely a general correlation between quality and price. Bargain basement–priced foods tend to be made with lots of cheap fillers and inferior-quality ingredients. Ask your veterinarian to recommend a dog food brand and product that fit both your budget and your dog's nutritional needs.

Canned and Pouched

Canned or pouched food is a great option for some dogs. Finicky eaters and seniors who have decreased appetite often find strong-

The Benefits of Bacteria

In recent years many people have started taking probiotics—doses of beneficial bacteria to help the body break down food and fight off disease.

It's no surprise that the popularity of these products in humans has led to a corresponding increase in giving them to dogs.

Probiotics come in many forms, but one of the easiest to use is a simple powder packet or capsule that can be added to your dog's food. Some people give them regularly, especially if their dog is gassy—better digestion means fewer by-products, including gas.

Talk to your veterinarian about these products. Some of the products available from your veterinarian are specially formulated to survive the passage through the stomach so that more bacteria can be active in the intestines. For the dog whose idea of a well-varied diet includes anything he can find anywhere, a boost of beneficial bacteria may help keep him healthier.

smelling, moist, canned food more appealing than kibble. Dogs with serious dental problems can chew canned food more easily than dry nuggets. In some cases, dogs with voracious appetites find satisfaction in canned food over kibble because all the water in it means they get more per serving. The added moisture helps give them a sense of fullness.

If you are trying to find good-quality food without giving up the convenience of buying off (and storing on) the shelf, canned foods have the edge over dry products. The same companies that make the best dry food often have a line of canned products as well—and your veterinarian can advise you on choosing what's best for your dog. Creating canned food doesn't require the level of processing that making dry kibble does, so some canned foods contain portions of minimally processed, quality proteins and carbs.

Dehydrated, Freeze-Dried, and Frozen

The past decade has brought a huge surge in interest and availability of organic or local foods for people, and that enthusiasm and knowledge carries over into food for pets, too. Owners are more interested than ever in the quality and sources of ingredients, and they're concerned about the use of preservatives and fillers in dog food. Large dog food manufacturers address these concerns with super-premium, "all natural" food formulations, but there is another segment of the pet food market that is growing and expanding by offering top-quality pet foods in dehydrated, freeze-dried, and frozen forms.

The companies specialize in making pet foods with the same standards—and often, the same ingredients—as those used in human food, with an emphasis on a few select ingredients and the absence on their labels of ingredients you've never heard of or cannot pronounce. With content lists that begin with items like "USDA free-range chicken, organic flaxseed, potatoes," and so on, these products have a big appeal to pet owners who often eschew highly processed foods in their own diets as well.

Most of these products are found in the freezer case, as they are meant to be thawed and served raw. While there is no evidence that these products are worth their higher cost—a fact that their advocates attribute to the money no big pet food manufacturer will spend to prove the benefits of uncooked food—these small companies fill a growing niche and resonate with those whose personal values have created a similar trend in human food production. While many veterinarians consider these diets—especially raw ones that include bones—to be at least of no greater benefit and at most dangerous, their advocates believe their dogs thrive on these simple, less processed diets, and that these products help with many chronic conditions. My thoughts? I don't see enough advantage to these frozen or dehydrated diets to choose them myself or recommend them, especially considering that they are usually more expensive than kibble or canned food. But I don't see anything wrong with them, either.

Foods Your Pet Should Never Get

There are a number of foods that are safe for humans that can injure or even kill your dog. One of the most deadly of these is xylitol, a sweetener that is being ever more commonly used in foods for diabetics and dieters, as well as products designed to prevent tooth decay, such as sugar-free gum.

Xylitol in small amounts can cause fatal and irreversible damage to your dog's kidneys, so my advice to dog owners is to keep it out of the house entirely.

If you need to use it, make sure it's where your dog can't get it. While you might think to not leave bulk xylitol on the kitchen counter, you might not think to leave a purse containing gum within reach of a hungry or an inquisitive pet. Other foods that are toxic to dogs include raisins, grapes, onions, macadamia nuts, and chocolate. (Rule of thumb for chocolate: Milk chocolate and a big dog isn't a major concern. But the darker the chocolate and the smaller the dog, the more dangerous the combination.) Don't let your dogs eat bread dough, either; it can start to rise in their stomachs and cause an obstruction that can be fatal. Also avoid giving any amount of alcohol to your dog; their tolerance for it is much less than ours, and it can make them very sick.

Homemade Diets—Raw or Cooked

For most of recorded history and long before it, dogs were eating some kind of homemade diet. After all, the pet food industry has been around only for about a century, give or take. Dogs were fed leftovers from the table, slaughterhouse trimmings, and whatever else was on hand. These days, an emphasis on local, fresh ingredients is increasingly important to many people, so much so that it's revolutionizing agricultural policy and giving hope for the salvation of the true family farm and the revitalization of rural America. With people wondering if a processed diet is good for people, it's no surprise that they are likewise asking the same questions when it comes to feeding their pets.

At this stage, the scientific answers are not clear. But that has not stopped those who are making changes to their diets and to their pets' diets to facilitate what they believe is better health and better care not only for their animals but also for livestock, and also to show support for local farmers and ranchers who have returned to traditional ways of food production.

You cannot just throw a raw chicken breast (or raw chicken wing) in a bowl and call it a day, however. While preparing your dogs' meals at home does not require a PhD in nutrition—you manage to feed yourself without a team of advisors, don't you?—you do need to learn and understand some basics that can be found in any number of books on home-prepared diets (my favorite is by a veterinarian: Dr. Donald Strombeck's *Home-Prepared Dog & Cat Diets: The Healthful Alternative*), pay very keen attention to cleanliness, and realize that this route is generally more expensive and more time-consuming than pouring kibble in a bowl.

The Skinny on Home-Prepared Diets

I have be honest with you. Even a few years ago I would have strongly objected to any client who came in with a dog on a home-made diet, and I would have been even stronger in my objection to a raw one.

Now I'm not. While I do continue to have concerns about food-borne contamination involved in feeding a raw diet, and I'm just never going to feel comfortable watching dogs consume things like raw turkey necks, I do now believe that for the educated, careful, committed dog owner a well-considered home-prepared diet is an option I can support as a veterinarian. Truth is, even veterinary nutritionists working at the nation's veterinary colleges see about as many cases of nutritional deficiencies as I treat jackalopes. But veterinarians do see cases of nutritional imbalance from people who prepare a homemade diet incorrectly because they haven't done their research.

A few members of Team Becker, including my writing partner, Gina Spadafori, feed their pets a homemade diet, and I'm fine with that because it's an educated decision. If you want to go that route, get as educated as my colleagues are…or stick to a good commercial kibble.

So what do I feed my own dogs? Kibble, in food puzzles. Kibble, because I have been a veterinarian a long time, and I have seen many generations of healthy pets live long, healthy lives on commercial diets. Food puzzles because in recent years I have seen the bigger problem is not what you feed but how much and how, because few dogs get enough exercise of their minds and bodies. They are born retired, and when you make them figure out how to get their food out of safe toys, they are happier, more active, and eat less. And because dogs are still scavengers deep in their genome, they'll happily join the 50 percent of America's pets that are overweight or obese and will unknowingly be digging their own graves with their food bowls. Whatever you choose, keep your dog lean!

Treats

What a drag life would be without treats! For dogs, as well as people, treats are the wonderful little extras that add excitement and pleasure to a day. A dog that seems deaf suddenly hears your footsteps heading to the kitchen or the imperceptible creak of the treat drawer. Even if your dog is overweight, there's a place for treats in his diet. Everybody gives pets treats, yes, even veterinarians. The trick is in figuring out what his total food allotment should be, and then not going over that total—even *after* you count the extras.

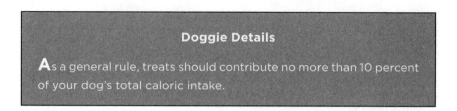

Doggie Details

As a general rule, treats should contribute no more than 10 percent of your dog's total caloric intake.

There are plenty of healthy choices in dog treats, and many of those aren't technically for dogs at all. In addition to biscuits and cookies marketed for dogs, try giving your pup cut-up carrots, snap peas, green beans, or apple slices. Most dogs love them. Mini or cut-up rice cakes (without salt or flavoring) make great dog goodies, too. Small amounts of cooked and cubed chicken, an occasional dab of peanut butter, poker chip–thin slices of a turkey hot dog or a little liver treat are all happy surprises for your dog.

While most foods are okay for once-in-a-while treats, keep in mind that your dog should not have much salt, sugar, or artificial colors and flavors. In addition, anything with nuts, raisins, chocolate, or onions should be strictly off-limits. A common veterinarian complaint is that owners overfeed their dogs unhealthy snack foods for people—in fact, one veterinary dentist reports that the one food he most wishes people wouldn't share with their dogs is—drumroll, please—gummy bears!

Fat Pets Are Not Funny!

If your dog is among the couch-potato majority that is overweight, you might need to learn some new tricks of the treats. While pudgy pooches might be funny in cartoons, in real life they're like tubby time bombs ticking away their health and vitality.

First, give smaller portions; a crumb of cheese or biscuit tastes just as good as a larger piece, and it's not likely your dog will even know the difference. I tell my clients to give half the portion with twice the enthusiasm (you know that nauseatingly whiny voice we use when giving our pets tasty tidbits). Second, dole the treats out like slot machines pay out; sometimes a little, rarely a lot. Research into gambling shows that the expectation of winning keeps people playing longer than a payoff every time, and the same is true in dog training. So don't give a treat whenever the dog sits on command. Instead, give a treat every third or fourth time (petting and praise should be a constant, though).

Last, the vegetable drawer of your refrigerator may hold the number one veterinarian recommended treat: carrots! They snap and crunch, are sweet, have no empty calories, and are good for your dog's teeth.

Food puzzles are a great way to make dogs work for their dinner. One toy that has stood the test of time is the Kong. Dog trainers such as my daughter, Mikkel, advise stuffing Kongs with kibble, pieces of biscuit, and filler, either ready-made or peanut butter. Add a rawhide twist as a "fuse" and freeze to make the chewing even more interesting. You dog will stay busy and happy for a long time.

Chapter 7

HEALTHY DOGS ARE BUSY DOGS

Pretend your house is an exhibit at the zoo. You wouldn't want visitors to come by, look at your dog, and think, *Oh, that poor thing.* He has the basics—food, water, shelter, and veterinary care—but never does anything but sit around. A dog's body is made for motion—as a hunter and a scavenger and, thanks to centuries of selective breeding, also for countless physical tasks in the service of a human owner. If you want to see it for yourself, just watch for your dog's prey drive. They all have it, though it's buried deeper in some dogs than others. Everything about a dog is designed to see and go after potential prey—the way his eyes focus, the way his nerves are routed, the way he's on his feet and after that squirrel, tennis ball, or the opening of the treat drawer, or the way he moves toward the door for a walk before even he himself seems to fully process what's going on.

Doggie Details

Get your dog back to his roots. He needs to move, to work, to play, and to prey to be healthy and happy. Movement helps dogs shed excess pounds as well as behavior problems. And keeping him active is good for you: studies show you'll be more likely to become more fit as well, and you and your dog will be more tightly bonded.

An animal with an instinct that strong to take off running wants and needs exercise to be happy and healthy—no matter how cushy his spot is on the couch.

EXERCISING THE BODY AND THE MIND—GAMES THAT WORK BOTH

Long before the canine family tree was split by human intervention into such diverse branches as the Irish Setter, the Bulldog, the Alaskan Malamute, and the Yorkshire Terrier (and all combinations thereof), feral dogs spent their waking hours using their wits and their bodies to search for food. Sometimes they hunted and sometimes they scavenged, but they were on the move, working for the next meal to keep them alive. When humans came into the picture, many kinds of dog became even more active (predators sleep when they're not hunting). The majority of breeds worldwide, developed through selective breeding, help hunters and farmers get and protect their own food supply. All the retrievers, hounds, terriers, setters, shepherds, and collies of the world are a testament to this work—dogs who are born with a drive to earn their keep by working alongside their owners.

Exercising your dog is a responsibility right up there with providing him with food, water, shelter, and veterinary care. Without an adequate outlet for their energy, even sweet, easygoing dogs can quickly develop a trifecta of serious issues: bad behavior brought on by boredom, excess weight, and potentially significant health problems.

The best exercise for any dog is something that engages both body and mind. These activities can help your dog prove to you the tenet all veterinarians hold dear: a tired dog is a happy dog. You can start with something simple, or dedicate your life to training and competing with your dog—it doesn't matter, as long as you start. As the saying goes, every journey starts with a single step, which is why there's a natural place to begin: walking.

Walking

A short walk may seem too easy a way to satisfy your dog's exercise needs, but it just might, especially if your dog is small, short-legged, or older. Walking gets your dog's blood pumping (and yours, too) while offering the mental stimulation of a change of scenery, a breath of fresh air, sun on the face, and new sights, sounds, and smells. Regular walks give dogs something to look forward to each day, and you'll quickly find that if you walk your dog at the about the same time daily, he'll help keep you to the schedule with reminders as subtle as a big sigh and pleading eyes, or as in-your-face as dancing around your heels with his leash in his mouth. Unlike human exercise partners, dogs never have a better offer, other deadlines to meet, or call in sick. As certain as death and taxes, dogs will get your feet on the floor and out the door by what I call "nagging you to life."

Even if you have a dog who is old, frail, arthritic, or disabled, try to find a way to work in a walk. Your dog doesn't have to walk long or far. If he needs extra support, you can use a special leash with a sling that helps you bear his weight. If he can't go far, bring along a wagon or stroller and give him a lift partway. Even if your dog can't achieve aerobic exercise, the benefits of getting him moving and taking in a good dose of the stimulation of the outdoors are priceless.

As for those big, healthy, active dogs, walking can work for them as well. You'll just have to go farther and faster. In other words: take a hike! And keep reading for more great exercise ideas.

Fetch

If your dog is a retriever, or any dog who's willing to learn to fetch, you've got a built-in exercise machine right there at the end of your arm. Just add a tennis ball and you're in business.

For some dogs, you could walk to the end of the world and not wear them out. Fetch is a terrific and flexible game you can adjust to your dog's needs. For the truly and deeply energetic, invest in a Chuckit (see page 27), a device designed to get the kind of distance on your throw that only a professional ballplayer could reach. Try tossing the ball up or down a hill or in the water for an extra-fulfilling workout. For small dogs who love the game, choose a favorite, right-sized stuffed animal or rubber toy and play fetch anywhere, including your living room or hallway.

After Fetch, Put Those Tennis Balls Away

I often suspect more tennis balls are used to keep dogs active than are used to play tennis. If you have friends who are tennis players, ask them to save their old balls for you. A tennis ball that hasn't the oomph for a good game of tennis is still perfect for playing fetch with your dog.

One important thing to know, though: tennis balls are not chew toys. Put them away when you're done with your game of fetch. Dogs have been known to compress tennis balls in their throat, and then die when the ball springs back to full size in the back of their mouth, cutting off air supply. And even if that never happens, the materials in a tennis ball are designed for…tennis! They're not made to be chewed on or swallowed by dogs.

Biking

Letting your dog run alongside a bike is a great way to help him burn off a day's pent-up energy without wearing yourself completely out in the process. Running with bikes is *not* for every dog. But for those with serious exercise requirements, it can be a perfect fit. If you choose to bike with your dog, start slowly (both in terms of speed and distance) to make sure this activity suits him. Don't even try it if he's a puller or doesn't respond to basic commands, including "sit," "leave it," and "heel." Stay on trails if you can and off busy streets, if that's your only choice.

Keep your dog at a trot, not a run, and watch for signs of over-heating—seeking shade, lagging behind, wanting to lie down, excessive panting. Never go out in the hottest part of the day, always carry water to offer frequently, and walk your bike and your dog for a cool-down before calling it a day.

Finally, invest in a bicycle attachment that holds your dog's leash and has a spring to take the abruptness out of sudden motions—

carrying the leash in your hand while biking is a recipe for a wreck, even if you have a well-behaved pup. After all, a teasing bird or furry animal is more temptation than even most good dogs can take.

Dog Park Play

You gotta love a dog park, a place where your dog can run to his heart's content, make friends, chase butterflies, drink and drool, even roll in the mud if he feels the urge. For a social dog, a good dog park offers all the benefits of Facebook, Twitter, and YouTube; all you have to do is sniff both ends of other dogs and be sniffed, check your pee-mail, then politely leave a message of your own. (I suspect check-in social media like FourSquare was invented by a dog!) All the activity, the excitement, and the freedom a dog park provides can give your dog a satisfying workout—even while you sit around and chat with the other dog owners.

As with all forms of exercise, dog parks raise their own special safety concerns. First and foremost, take a long look at who's hanging out in the 'hood before you enter with your dog. Though most dog parks attract a regular and well-socialized clientele, it takes only one aggressive or bullying dog to turn a fun outing into a disaster. Second, make sure your dog is up-to-date on all his immunizations and other preventive health-care measures such as parasite control. Socializing with strange dogs significantly raises his chances of being exposed to communicable diseases and parasites.

Watch your dog. If he's bullying or being bullied, take him out and go home. Some dogs are just not party animals and don't do well dealing with strange dogs. And do your part for the public good: pick up after your pet, and don't tolerate bad behavior from your dog or others. Finally, leave your young children outside the fence. Squealing, fast-moving children and loose dogs are a recipe for an accident, and you don't want your child to be knocked down or bitten.

Swimming

Water dogs love nothing more than to get good and wet (unless, of course, we're talking about the dreaded bath water, which has

S-O-A-P in it!). A dip in the pool, a romp in the lake, even the chance to splash around in a puddle or wallow in a kiddie pool are all it takes to make these dogs happy. Take advantage of this natural bent to help your dog get his exercise. Water workouts are wonderful, even if they're messy. They're great non-weight-bearing exercises that will get more work done in less time, since moving in water is harder than moving in air. Add a tennis ball, retriever bumper, or floatable Kong to up the fun factor.

Swimming dogs need to have extra attention paid to their ears, which tend to develop infections. Ask your veterinarian about products that clean and dry the ears after swimming, and don't delay a veterinary visit if ears look red or smell bad. I have a new preventive ear product I really like that is all natural, called Zymox Otic Enzymatic Solution (ask your veterinarian).

Finally, play it safe. Even good swimmers can get in trouble, and dogs do drown, especially short-muzzled dogs that are front heavy (like Pugs and Bulldogs). If in doubt, purchase a pet life vest that can keep even the most leaden canine above water. Avoid swift currents, extra-cold water, and beaches with riptides and sharks. In some areas, you can subscribe to puppy pools for swimming in a man-made place, and many cities and park districts have started offering a swim day for dogs in public pools—usually as a fund-raiser for shelters before shutting down facilities for the winter.

Special for Small Dogs

Although little dogs can participate in all the activities above, their compact size opens up a whole new world of exercise opportunities you can create on their small scale. For ideas, visit the preschool section of your local superstore. Something as simple as a fabric tunnel and a step stool can be turned into an in-home agility course for your pint-sized pup. Games that allow your small dog to jump, tunnel, roll over, or seek and find all offer plenty of exercise and great opportunities for you to have fun together.

Of course, this doesn't even begin to scratch the surface of all the organized, competitive activities designed for dogs. Those are covered in Chapter 15.

All Hail the Tennis Ball!

Yes, I said the tennis-ball play needs to be surpervised. That doesn't mean it has to be limited. In fact, if there's anything more versatile than a tennis ball, I can't imagine it. One afternoon I just sat down with a pad and started jotting down all the things you can do with a dog and a tennis ball. Play tennis? Not even on the list. Here's what I came up with:

1. **Fetch.** Toss, return, repeat. You know the drill. This is the game by which all dog activities are measured, and sometimes there's just nothing better than the classic.

2. **Find.** Hide the tennis ball, then let your dog find it. For dogs who are already retrievers, this game is remarkably easy to teach. Hide the ball in plain sight a couple times so she'll know what you want her to do, then watch how easily she can find it anywhere.

3. **Herd.** Fetching uses one ball, but if you've got a herding dog, try tossing out a few and giving your dog a place to gather them all together. Since this game works with your dog's natural instincts, most pick it up very quickly for a treat reward.

4. **Get wet.** Water dogs love nothing more than the chance to go after a favorite ball *and* get wet. What more could a pup want?

5. **Monkey in the middle.** Got kids? Got a dog? Amuse everyone with the classic schoolyard game, with the dog playing monkey. Pass the ball by tossing, rolling, kicking—whatever works—and give Rover a small treat each time he intercepts it and gives it back.

6. **Flyball.** This one is a real sport, and one tennis ball–loving dogs live for once they learn to play. Your dog launches a ball by stepping on a trigger board (look for flyball classes in your area to get access and help in training). Add obstacles, jumps, and someone to compete against, and you've got a fast-paced, wildly entertaining game for both people and pets, participants and spectators.

GUIDELINES FOR EXERCISE (AEROBIC EVERY DAY)

All dogs need exercise, but to figure out how much your own dog needs, first consider his breeding (or, if he's a mixed breed, the predominant breeds in his family tree). Keep in mind that recommendations for aerobic exercise mean the kind of exercise that gets your dog panting and making a good physical effort. It bears repeating that besides daily oral care, getting a dog panting tired every day (and thus keeping him near his ideal body weight) will keep him healthy and living a full life.

The Super-Energetic Breeds

All dogs need exercise, but there are some with requirements that put them in a class all their own. Consider three of the most overwhelmingly energetic breeds: the Australian Cattle Dog (also known as the Queensland Heeler), the Border Collie, and the Jack Russell terrorist (ahem, I mean Terrier, also known as the Parson Russell). All three breeds are superior athletes, and all were bred to be triple threats: energetic enough to run all day long in the field, clever enough to manipulate and predict the actions of other animals, and sufficiently independent to do their jobs without direct human supervision. Combine all three traits and you get an autonomous dog who requires extreme exercise for both body and mind every single day—not the kind of pup to sit around and watch the clock while you're at the office.

When given sufficient stimulation and exercise—a bare minimum of an hour of aerobic work daily (more is better)—triple-threat breeds can be fantastic pets. When their needs are neglected, however, smart, athletic dogs get bored, and they dig, bark, chew,

climb, scratch, bite, and generally wreak havoc on their environment. Energy—mental *and* physical—has to be burned, and these
dogs have it in spades. It takes a special kind of dog owner to com-
mit to the effort an independent, athletic dog needs, but for the
right person these pups bring inspiration and boundless energy to
everyday life.

Sporting Dogs

Setters, retrievers, spaniels, and pointers were developed to work long,
hard outdoor days without complaint, injury, or strain. They live for
two things: exercise and your companionship (though food takes a
close third place). These dogs need thirty to sixty minutes of aerobic
exercise a day (or at least most days) to satisfy their needs for physical
and mental stimulation.

Herding Dogs

This group of dogs, including collies, sheepdogs, shepherds, and Corgis, are bred to be fast, smart, and able to work all day. Without sufficient exercise, they're notorious for finding other, less acceptable ways
to entertain and exhaust themselves. Like the sporting dogs, herding
breeds do best when they get thirty to sixty minutes of aerobic exercise daily. They do best when they have the opportunity to really run
and get tuckered out—a casual stroll around the block is almost never
enough for a healthy, strong herding dog.

Hounds

There are two major groups of hounds, and their exercise needs are
quite different from one another. Scent hounds, including Beagles,
Foxhounds, and Coonhounds, are designed to scent and follow prey.
They need nearly as much exercise as the sporting breeds—thirty
minutes a day of aerobic work if you can manage it; thirty minutes
every other day at a bare minimum. Sight hounds such as Greyhounds,

Afghan Hounds, and Deerhounds were bred to run in short, intense bursts, and so they don't require quite as much exercise as the scent hounds. Despite their reputations as the runners of the dog world, many of these dogs are surprisingly calm and low-key. A short daily walk coupled with more intense, twice-weekly gallops will keep them happy and healthy. When these dogs aren't in a secured area, they need to be kept on leash because they tend to take off when there's something to chase, and they're notoriously difficult to teach to come when called.

Working Dogs

Some dogs in the working group, including Mastiffs and Rottweilers, were bred to work as guard dogs. These dogs don't require an extreme amount of exercise. A short walk daily or even every other day will do. Other working breeds, like the Portuguese Water Dog, the Alaskan Malamute, and the Siberian Husky, were developed to do strenuous physical work for long days, and they need aerobic exercise nearly every day to stay healthy and happy.

Terriers

If you've ever spent much time with a West Highland Terrier, or a Jack Russell, or a Scottie, you've seen that many terriers manage to get quite a bit of exercise without any help at all from their owners. These busy dogs have energy to burn. Thankfully, because of their small stature, a brisk walk for thirty minutes every other day is enough for most terriers. But more is even better.

Toy Dogs

Toy breeds need aerobic exercise just like all other dogs, but thanks to their small bodies and short legs, giving them the workout they need should be easy for you. A short, brisk walk, indoors or out, will satisfy most toy dogs' exercise needs for the day. If you can get your toy dog to fetch, you can accomplish this workout in a space as small as a patio or hallway.

Nonsporting Breeds

This is the little-bit-of-this dog grouping, lumping together breeds as diverse as the Bichon, Bulldog, Chow Chow, and Poodle. Some in this group, including the Dalmatian, Poodle, and American Eskimo Dog, require as much exercise as most of the sporting breeds. Others, like the Bulldog, Pug, and Boston Terrier, not only don't need extreme workouts, they can be endangered if overexercised. When in doubt about the amount of exercise your dog can handle, start slow and work up to a level you're both comfortable with. Remember, all dogs should be happily tired, but never excessively panting.

EXERCISE CAUTIONS: PUPPIES, HEAT STROKE, LAMENESS

The beauty of exercising your dog is you'll rarely—okay, never—have to talk him into it. Almost all canine companions are all too happy to get in their daily workout. Most are also willing to go an extra mile, or two, or ten. In fact, many dogs get so jazzed up about exercise that they won't stop when they've had too much. For every dog who will hold up at the brink of overdoing it, there are probably nine who'll eagerly go over the edge. Veterinarians see these dogs every day—the ones who collapse from heat exhaustion, the ones who wear the pads off their feet, and the ones who run until they're lame and then can hardly move.

Since your dog may not have the good sense to cry "uncle!" when he's worn out, it's up to you to look for signs of trouble and be aware of the dangers of overexertion.

Puppy Pace

Even though puppies, especially bigger and older ones, may seem open to all the exercise in the world, it's important lay off the heavy running until they're fully grown. Puppies who run excessively, especially on pavement, can injure their still growing and strengthening bones. In general, jogging should be saved for after your dog turns two. In the interim, plenty of walks and play in the yard will get you both through.

Pug Problem

Dogs with very short muzzles and rounded heads are called brachycephalic, and their abnormal anatomy works against them in the exercise department. Pugs, Boston Terriers, and Bulldogs should really come with a label that states "EXTREME CAUTION: Handle with Care." These breeds can all have difficulty breathing when they get winded, and because they can't pant efficiently, they are extremely intolerant of heat. Rather than take any chances with your pug-nosed dog's good health, choose cool temperature times for workouts. If you live in a hot climate, improvise by exercising your dog early or late, or indoors. Choose moderate, regular exercise instead of intense exertion for these dogs. In their case, slow and steady really does win the race to health and happiness. Because the "design" of these dogs is so compromised, they can have not only lifelong breathing issues but also digestive issues. Veterinarians with expertise in the health problems of these dogs are now saying their problems are so severe that they need surgical intervention at a young age—typically at the time they're spayed or neutered. Surgery will open up their nostrils and remove the barriers to breathing their elongated palates present. Such early surgeries are sometimes the only chance these dogs have to live a normal life—or even a normal life span.

Wheeling to Good Fortune

When my daughter, Mikkel Becker, completed her certification as a dog trainer, she brought a new kind of expertise to our family of animal lovers. I thought I'd seen everything until I observed some of the creative and unconventional methods Mikkel has come up with to exercise her beloved black Pug, Willy. Since Pugs easily overheat and get out of breath, their workout time needs to be handled with care. Willy uses an indoor hamster wheel-type machine called a GoPet to keep his exercise climate controlled. He races in place like a pro, always happy to get in and cheerfully tired when he gets out.

When it's time for Willy's dinner, he has to earn it, military style. Mikkel has taught him to do puppy push-ups. This little pug has to follow orders for "down," "sit," "up," and "down" again, ten times, before his meal is served. You may never have seen a dog so delighted with the world as Willy is on that tenth push-up. Thanks to his own personal in-house trainer, this dog is a lean, never-mean, exercise machine. And yes, a lean, athletic pug, not the typical pudgy pug, is possible! I can't wait to see what he learns next.

Hot Dog

One of the biggest health threats to any dog is overheating. Dogs don't have as much ability to regulate their own temperature as people do, and so once they get overly warm, it can be tough for them to cool down. Dogs with dark coats (like Rottweilers and Dobermans) or dogs with cold weather coats (Malamutes, Huskies) are of special concern, since their fur absorbs or retains a lot of heat. Frantic panting, seeking shade, lying down frog-legged, glassy eyes, drooling, and confusion are all classic signs of overheating. If you recognize these symptoms in your dog, use cool (not cold!) water to help cool him off, and get him to a veterinarian immediately. (More on canine emergencies in Chapter 18.)

Trouble Afoot

Most dogs are so blasé about walking on any surface, in any weather, it's easy to forget that they're barefoot all the time. While the pads on dogs' feet are somewhat resistant to heat, cold, and friction, they are not immune to danger. A dog who walks daily on pavement has tougher footpads than one who walks on dirt or grass, and a dog who spends his summers in south Texas likely has more comfort on hot pavement than one from rural northern Idaho. Any dog, though, can suffer injury to a footpad if you don't take care to consider his experience and the surface. Footpads can burn on hot pavement or hot sand. A good measurement of tolerable heat is to put the palm of your hand on the pavement, concrete, or sand; since your palm has about the same sensitivity as a dog's footpads, if you can take it so can they. The pad can be worn right off if a dog undertakes more than his usual exercise or runs on a particularly rough surface. In the winter, dogs can pick up irritating salt and other chemicals from roads and sidewalks, so keep the hair clipped short between the toes and wash off with water after a walk. Check your dog's feet regularly to make sure they are uninjured, and anytime you make a change in your dog's exercise routine, be sure to keep good foot health in mind. And don't forget to check between the toes for hitchhikers, both ticks and spike-like grass awns. When in doubt, get booties!

Too Much, Too Soon

As the saying goes, the road to hell is paved with good intentions. Starting an exercise program with your dog is almost always a good idea. Starting an exercise program with your dog by going all out on the first day is a bad, dangerous idea. Just as you would never launch a workout regimen for yourself by running a marathon on the first day, so you need to ease your dog into any exercise program. Dogs who go all out without easing in to exercise suffer many of the same health problems people do in the same circumstances: pulled muscles, torn ligaments, strains, and sprains. As a general rule, if your dog is normally sedentary, start him off with gentle exercise for fifteen minutes a day—or four blocks (or four hundred feet) per ten pounds of body weight, adjusting for the fact that some dogs of similar sizes (such as the Pug and the Jack Russell) naturally have very different levels of exercise tolerance—and increase about 5 percent each week until you reach his workout goal. Or if you go back to the panting-tired rule, as the dog gets in better shape, it will take a little longer each week to get your pet panting-tired (and you, by extension, on the road to better health, too).

Jostling Joints

If your dog has arthritis or hip dysplasia, he can still reap the benefits of regular exercise—perhaps even more so than some healthy dogs. Exercise can help gradually ease mobility and take off extra pounds, easing the pressure on sore joints. The key to exercising any dog with joint problems is gentle, regular workouts with no running or heavy strain. Swimming is ideal for arthritic dogs, but walking is a great option as well. If your dog experiences soreness after walks, talk with his veterinarian about the possibility of a regimen of pain medication alone or in combination with special joint diets, supplements, or both. The veterinarian can help you find a way to make exercise both enjoyable and pain free for your pup. All veterinarians will tell you that the number one way to help an arthritic pet is to get rid of some of the excess weight. More on mobility help for older dogs is in Chapter 20.

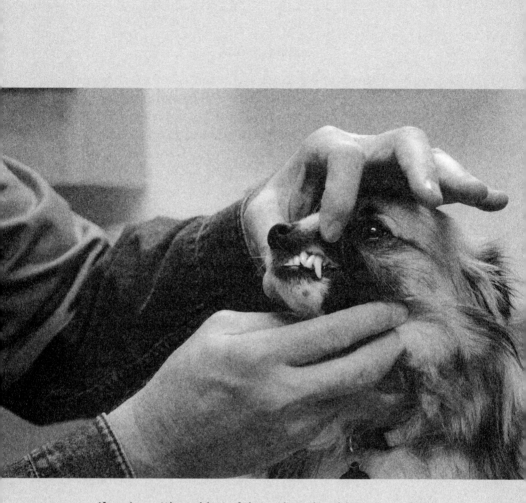

If you're getting a blast of doggy breath, odds are your dog has a health problem that's making him miserable and shortening his life. Anyone who has ever had a toothache knows it's nothing you'd wish on your canine companion. Good dental health starts with a thorough examination by your veterinarian and continues with following his advice, both for procedures to get the teeth and gums in the shape they should be, and for follow-up care at home, including brushing.

Chapter 8

GROOMING AND DENTAL CARE BASICS

When veterinarians talk about the importance of shiny fur and healthy teeth, I suspect many dog lovers tune out. After all, what is this, a beauty contest? Sure, everyone wants a clean dog, but what will it hurt if his nails are long or he goes a while between baths? And brushing his teeth? You're kidding, right, Doc?

No, I'm not. Good grooming is essential to your dog's good health, and paying attention to keeping up those appearances is the foundation for keeping him healthy, comfortable, and long-lived. You'll benefit, too, since a well-groomed dog is one you'll want to be with, huggable and kissable.

Good home-care routines also give you the chance to catch any unusual lumps, bumps, lesions, or skin problems before they become serious issues for your dog.

So the next time your dog's veterinarian starts talking about wielding a toothbrush, the importance of daily oral care, or giving regular baths, take a deep breath and listen closely—you and your pup will both be better for it.

Clients also ask me: "Do you brush your dog's teeth?" They know I'm an honest man, and that I will not lie to them. And so I'm not lying to you. My answer is always the same: I smile like I'm eating a banana sidewise, showing off my own big smile. And then I tell them, "Yes, you bet we do!" Because if my wife, Teresa, doesn't do it, I do.

And so should you.

SMILE, PUPPY!

Doggie Details

While we tend to think of dentistry as a cosmetic issue, it's much more than that. Decaying teeth give bacteria an in to your pet's body. Besides creating a stench that's hard to live with, those bacteria can wear down your dog's immune system, weaken his internal organs, and even infect his heart, taking years off his life. Starting a simple dental cleaning or other daily oral health-care regimen for your dog today can not only cure his chronic halitosis, it can contribute to his lifelong health and well-being.

In Part Four I share what your veterinarian's role is in maintaining your pet's healthy teeth and gums (see page 223). Once all those issues that can be addressed only by your veterinarian have been taken care of, it's time to start your home-care dental regimen. (If you have a puppy, just jump right in!)

BRUSH BRUSH BRUSH THOSE CANINES

Once your dog has had her teeth scaled, polished, and repaired, she's starting off with a clean dental slate. Keeping those chompers in good condition is best done by cleaning them at home at least twice a week—daily is better. Getting the right supplies will help you start off with success. Here's a step-by-step guide:

Choose Your Tools

Dog toothpaste may just be the thing that gets your dog thinking this whole toothbrushing thing isn't such a bad idea. You can pick her favorite flavor: chicken, beef, parsley, salmon, peanut butter, vanilla—you'll find plenty to choose from. Next up, a toothbrush. Again, you'll find a wide choice, including a three-headed version that can brush back, front, and bottoms of teeth in one swipe. Other options include glove-like finger covers with brushing nubs on the end, dental wipes, and good, old-fashioned gauze with toothpaste. A soft child's toothbrush is also fine. Experiment to see what your dog—and you—like best.

Start Small

A small minority of dogs will be happy to just open up and say "Ahh" when you decide to brush their teeth. Most, though, are going to require some convincing. Instead of tackling the whole process at once, ease your dog into it. First, choose a time of day when she's usually calm and content, such as when her tummy's full or she has had a good long walk. Next, put her up on a counter, if she's a small dog; if she's larger, get down beside her with your cleaning tools. Try three things to start familiarizing your dog with what's up: first, touch her gums and teeth with your finger—nothing too invasive, just a quick tap to prove you mean no harm. Second, show your dog the dental hygiene products and let her take a whiff. Third, put a tiny dab of the new toothpaste on your finger, and let your dog sniff it and take a taste.

Routine

Stick to a routine of time and place, and gradually work up to actively brushing your dog's teeth. Always wrap things up with a "Good Girl!" a hug, and a treat (we double down on our daily oral care by giving a dental treat), so she associates toothbrush time with cuddling and comfort.

Braces for a Dog?

You could call it the Rin Tin Grin—braces on dogs. Though it seems crazy to use orthodontia for animals, there are cases—therapeutic ones, not cosmetic ones—where braces are just what the doctor

(Continued)

orders. A couple years ago, I had a dog come in to my veterinary office with terribly deformed teeth. He had a tooth that was digging into his palate instead of lining up with his upper jaw like it was supposed to. The poor guy would sleep with a stuffed toy in his mouth because it was painful for him to close his teeth. That dog was a perfect candidate for orthodontia. And in case you're wondering: Braces for dogs look a lot like human braces but require anesthesia to install, adjust, and remove. They need to be kept on for only a few months—versus a couple of years for people—and they cost a lot less than human braces.

PROPER CHEWIES FOR DENTAL HEALTH

Some dogs are crazy chewers, while others aren't much bothered once they pass their puppy and young-adult chewing stages. For those dogs who live to chew, you need to make sure what they're chewing is good for them. Left to choose their own chew toys, dogs have notoriously poor taste. Some will chew the leg off a chair, some will chew through your slippers, and others will pick something inexplicable like, say, a rock. Aside from the obvious damages inflicted by these chewers, there are also consequences to their mouths. Dogs frequently crack their teeth, get splinters in their gums, and cut their mouths on inappropriate chewing objects. Once those objects get into a dog's digestive system, there's no telling what other harm they might do.

Provide your dog with a selection of veterinarian-recommended chew toys to keep him busy. For dental health, rope toys, rubber chews with nubs on them, and digestible dental chews (the ones I like include Greenies, C.E.T. products, Pedigree Dentastix, or DermaPet DenTees) can help prevent tartar from forming on teeth. In general, it's best to stay away from chews that are hard enough to potentially break a tooth. A veterinarian's rule of thumb: don't give a dog any chew toy that's so hard you wouldn't want it to hit you in the knee. Chew objects that give veterinary dentists nightmares (and also provide them a lot of business) include cow hooves and hard nylon toys. If you have a big, determined chewer, you may find he has a habit of quickly busting up chew toys that are supposed to entertain him for hours—and, worse yet, swallowing the pieces. For this type of dog, choose a chew toy that is too large for him to get his mouth around. He'll have to settle for scraping his teeth against it—and that will satisfy his desire to chew and help clean his teeth in the process. Choosing toys for determined chewers—such as black Kongs, which are even more chew resistant than the red ones most pet owners are familiar with—stuffing them with bits of treats or soft food (such as peanut butter or canned dog food), inserting a pencil rawhide fuse, and then freezing keeps many a tough chewer busy. Yes, give it to him frozen: it's harder to chew and makes a cool treat.

A FRONT-TO-BACK GROOMING GUIDE

The goal of good grooming is a huggable coat that's free of dirt, debris, mats, and parasites, a dog that doesn't have excessive shedding, is not greasy or dry, and smells good. In short, a dog you'd like to have sitting next to you on the couch, or what I call a huggable coat. Forget the stories you might have grown up with or read in old pet-care guides: you cannot groom too often. With the right soaps, conditioners, and grooming tools, you can bathe a dog every day if you want or if advised to by your veterinarian for a condition such as environmental allergies. And considering what some dogs like to roll in and how many of them sleep on their owners' beds, that's not such a bad idea.

Choosing the Right Tools

The equipment you need to groom your dog depends mostly on his breed, if you have a purebred. If you have a mixed breed, choose based on the kind of coat he has. In general, buying a good-quality brush, comb, and nail trimmer is a far better investment than purchasing cheapish ones and then having to keep replacing them. Choose your brushes and combs based on your dog's coat type:

- **Short and smooth.** Breeds like Rottweilers, Dobermans, Labs, and Pugs are easy to take care of. Just run a comb over them once a week and you're done.
- **Medium and smooth or wavy.** Golden Retrievers and setters fall into this category. Comb and brush to keep burrs out. For dogs with a similar coat but more of it—or lots of it on the bottom half of their bodies—such as Cockers, regular brushing and regular trims to keep the coat short. For our Golden, Shakira, we couldn't live without a shedding tool, such as the Furminator (found everywhere) or Mars Coat-King (found online or at dog shows, typically).
- **Wiry.** Wiry-coated terriers and Schnauzers need to be both combed and brushed weekly using a slicker brush, and they benefit from a clipping every couple months. If you're not too vain about your dog's appearance, you can learn to clip him at home using your own clippers.
- **Curly.** Poodles and curly Labradoodles (not all Labradoodles inherit a curly coat) fall into this category, and they are as high-maintenance as dogs get. They need to be brushed almost daily with a slicker brush, and they need regular clipping to look and feel their best.
- **Silky and medium coats.** Afghan Hounds, Maltese, Yorkies, and Golden Retrievers all require weekly combing and brushing to stay in shape. Use a natural bristle brush on these dogs to keep from breaking their fine, hairlike fur.
- **Long and double coats.** Corgis, collies, Pomeranians, Shetland Sheepdogs, and all the other breeds with thick, bushy fur fall into this category. These are major shedders who easily get dirty, matted, and messy. The only way to keep this kind of coat under control (and keep the shedding down to a minor crisis level) is to brush and demat them frequently and well. Twice a week, brush your double-coated dog first against the grain (toward his head) and then down toward his tail to get to both coats. You'll brush off enough fur to build a whole new dog. Just remember, fur removed during grooming is fur that doesn't end up on your carpet, bed, and couch. And while it may horrify those who love the long-haired look, there's no

reason not to cut these dogs short to keep things clean and manage-
able. In fact, the dog who sheds the least of all is a long-haired dog
cut short—it's true!

In addition to a comb and brush, you need a nail trimmer to keep
your dog's tootsies in good walking form. Choose a clipper designed
for your dog's size. Or you can try grinding your dog's nails instead.
Professional groomers and breeders have known for years that using
a Dremel-type rotary tool to grind a dog's nails is sometimes easier
and more effective than cutting them with a clipper. Now there are
grinders especially designed for dog's nails (Dremel makes one, and
so does Oster). These can be especially effective tools for owners of
big dogs—those nails can be very thick and difficult to clip in the
best of circumstances. If you're going to introduce a grinder into your
dog's life, take it slow! A quick tackle with a noisy grinder and contact
with his toes could ruin your chances of making this tool work, ever.
Instead, show your dog the grinder a couple times and give him a treat.
Move up to turning the tool on, holding it close, and finally working
the nails. Take it from me, make sure you don't stay too long on a nail
without a break or it can overheat. Think of yourself putting your finger on a hot burner; you wouldn't want to repeat it and neither will
your dog. (Grinding nails is really easy once you know how to do it,
but it can be hard to do unless you've seen it done. So go on Google
and search "dog nail grinding." You'll find some great instructionals
online.)

You'll also need some blood-stopping powder, just in case you hit
the quick. And don't forget the vet's secret of dipping a cotton swab
into the powder and applying it to the bleeding nail for a virtual cork
to put in the bleeder.

Trimming nails is about cutting off the dead part without hitting
the live part—the quick—which in white nails can be seen as a darker
area in the middle. In black nails, you need to use a light to find the
quick—a penlight is fine. (There are even nail trimmers that come
with lights on them.)

Have your veterinarian, one of the techs, or a groomer show you
the best technique. And then clip nails frequently. When your dog is
standing, the nails should not touch the ground. If you see your dog's

toes splayed out from excessively long nails or hear a *rat-tat-tat* on hard floors, your pet's nails are too long and need to be trimmed. A good routine to get into is to do a nail or two a night every night, taking just a little off to keep nails short. If you're starting with long nails, take just a little off every few days. The quick will recede, and over time you'll get where you need to be. Another tip: if you have your dog anesthetized for any reason, a dental for example, ask the veterinary hospital to cut the nails back, way back, as the dog won't feel anything under anesthesia and pain meds, and you'll have a much better chance of keeping the nails near their ideal length.

Why Your Veterinarian Shouldn't Do Your Pet's Nails

Dog owners hate trimming their pets' nails. So they put it off. And then they botch it, which means the dog pitches a fit, there's blood everywhere, and there is no way on God's green earth they are ever going to do that again.

So they figure their veterinarian will do it. Once a year.

Every veterinarian has seen dogs with nails so long the dog can barely walk, or with dewclaws—the nails that are the equivalent of a thumb in dogs, but up their leg and not very useful—so long that they loop around and dig into the flesh. Ouch!

But here's the problem with dumping the problem on your veterinarian: your dog will hate your veterinarian for the pain she or her staff has had to dole out, because your veterinarian will have to cut way back to make you happy, and that means she'll have to make your dog hurt and bleed. This is not a good way to build a good relationship, and it may make your dog so vet-phobic over time that he'll be horribly stressed out when he really needs help. So learn to do nails at home after seeing it done by your veterinarian, a tech, or a groomer, and do them often. Your dog won't be hurt, and your veterinarian won't become his enemy.

One exception to this rule: If your pet is scheduled for a procedure that requires anesthesia such as a dental, your veterinarian may be okay with "quicking" the nails while your pet's unconscious. Your pet's paws will still hurt, but he won't blame the veterinarian or the techs for it. And once the quick recedes, you can keep the nails short more easily.

HOW TO BATHE A DOG

Oh, c'mon, everyone knows how to bathe a dog, right? You'd be surprised how many people don't. Or who think they do but aren't doing it right. So here's the rundown:

Brush your dog before every bath. It'll help the shampoo reach all his nooks and crannies and make it possible for you to work out any mats before they get set in by the water.

Stock your station. Nothing good ever comes of starting to give a dog a bath and then realizing the shampoo/brush/bucket/towels are on the other side of the room. Unless you enjoy playing tag with a soaking wet pup, get all your supplies together before you bother bringing in the dog. Here's what you need:

- **Three-towel trick.** Have one towel to put in the bottom of the tub to provide traction and prevent slipping. The second towel is the antishake towel that you drape over a wet dog (between washes or before rinsing) to prevent a dog from shaking and covering you and the walls with water. The third towel is the drying towel.
- **Drain.** Put a piece of steel wool in the drain to catch all that dog hair and prevent it from plugging your drain.
- **No more tears or wet ears.** If you're going to bathe your dog's head, ask your veterinarian for some bland eye ointment and have him show you how to apply. Also, put a small cotton ball gently and not too deep into each of your dog's ear canals to prevent them from getting wet; just make triple sure you don't forget to take them out after the bath is over.

❧**Nonslip surface.** This can be just a towel in the bottom of the tub or shower, or a nonskid rubber mat. Always put something down on the washing surface so your dog can get his footing. Nothing stresses out a dog more than fear of falling, and giving him something to sink his toes into will help ease his anxiety about the whole bathing experience.

❧**Dog shampoo.** Shampoo designed for people—even baby shampoo—has a different pH than what's best for your dog, and it can dry out both his coat and his skin. If your dog has skin problems, ask his veterinarian for a recommendation so you can get a therapeutic shampoo that will help soothe his skin.

❧**Warm water.** Go ahead and fill the tub or sink with warm water before you bring in your dog. The sound of the rushing water will just add to his stress if he's not an enthusiastic bather.

Bring on the dog. Use a leash if you have to, but lead your dog to the water, offering good cheer and a treat along the way. Don't lose your cool if your dog resists—if he already dislikes bathing, he'll hate it even more if he associates it with your angry voice. Wet your dog completely, then start shampooing him at the neck and work your way down his body to tail and toes. If the dog has external parasites, putting a sudsy barrier up on the neck at the base of the skull prevents itchy, icky critters from beating feet out of Dodge (read the dog's body) and heading for safety (your dog's head or ears). Praise him as you wet and shampoo him.

While you're at the tail, if you're feeling brave, you should empty your dog's anal glands. These pesky little organs—which if you think of your dog's anus like a clock dial are at the five and seven o'clock positions—produce a stinky fluid that dogs use to mark their feces like gang colors and identify each other. Unfortunately, if they're not emptied from time to time, they can become impacted and infected. To do this job at home, suds up your dog's bottom and your hands. Place your thumb and forefinger on the outside of each gland, on either side of the anus, and gently squeeze inward and together. The goo will be released, and you can wash both your hands and your dog's bottom thoroughly before moving on. If you're not comfortable doing this at home, your dog's veterinarian or groomer will take care of it for you. If your dog has a lot of problem with the glands, talk to your veterinarian: many anal gland problems are the result of food and environment allergies—as are ear infections. Rather than treat the symptoms (sore, plugged anal glands or ears), treat the root problem (finding a hypoallergenic diet or treating atopy by more frequent bathing and medication); many skin and integument problems are greatly diminished or disappear completely.

Rinse, rinse, rinse some more. Rinse your dog with clean warm water from the tap. Be sure to get all the shampoo off his body, or it can cause skin irritation. Don't pour dirty water from the tub back over him! When you think you've rinsed enough, rinse more. And more. Getting all the soap out will keep your dog clean longer.

Dry before release. Here's a little tip from your dog to you: he thinks that the expensive shampoo you buy for him smells like crap. He really dislikes whatever fruity, flowery, or musky scent you've chosen, and he'd like to get it off him as quickly and completely as possible. To prevent an immediate muddying up of all your hard work, don't let your dog outside until he's completely dry. Throw a towel over him, horse-blanket style, and use a second one to dry first the face, then the ears, and then the feet. You can use a hair dryer to speed

Stop the Shake by Holding the Nose

If you're a good sport about giving your dog a bath right up until the moment of "the big shake," you're not alone. We all bargain on getting a little damp during a dog bath, but nobody is happy when that just-clean dog decides to quake from head to toe and transfer that water onto Mama. Here's a simple trick to keep your pup from soaking you after his bath: hold his nose. Your dog won't shake while you've got him by the schnoz. Take a minute to dry him the best you can, put him in the Shaking Allowed zone, then let go and let him have at it in his typical frenetic whipsaw motion.

things along if you like, but a lot of dogs despise the noise they make. Dryers made for dogs blast room-temperature air. They make drying go more quickly by blowing the water out of the coat so it can air-dry. If you have a long-haired dog, these are a pretty good investment in saving time.

MORE BATHING TIPS

The Skunk Crisis Bath: When your dog has a run-in with skunk scent or any other particularly noxious scent, it's time for an emergency bath. Here's the solution to skunk pollution:

One quart of 3 percent hydrogen peroxide to 1/4 cup of baking soda to 1 teaspoon of liquid soap, such as Ivory. Mix and immediately apply to the stinky pet. Rinse thoroughly with tap water.

You can't mix these ingredients until you're ready to use them, as they will bubble up and burst any container. Though it seems a little nerdy to be brewing up this kind of homemade concoction for a bath, this mix truly works and is a lifesaver. Mix it up just before you put it on the dog; the chemical reaction is what grabs the smell. Then follow with a regular soap-and-water bath.

How often is enough? That's up to you. Most dogs can get by on monthly baths, but weekly is better if you're living with a house dog, or if your dog has or is at risk for environmental allergies, which are caused by the absorption of dust, mites, pollen, and so forth, into your dog's skin. *If you use a good soap and conditioner and rinse well, a daily bath is fine.*

There are even some new twists, with tools that mix soap and water for a single spray that's faster and gets to the skin more easily. A couple different companies make them—Bamboo and Jarden—and some people use a simple dedicated hose-end garden sprayer for dogs who love the mud and don't mind a cold-water outdoor cleanup (typically retrievers or other water dogs). If your dog has skin problems, cool daily baths may be more than optional: they may be necessary. Talk with your veterinarian about how often to bathe and what products to use.

GROOMERS CAN BE GODSENDS

Do-it-yourself bathing is an important part of any dog's home routine, but many dogs really do need professional attention. For dogs with high-maintenance coats—like Poodles, Cockers, and terriers—you need to consider grooming a regular part of your dog-care budget.

A leash and collar is your dog's best friend, the sure way to keep him safe and allow him access to many fun places where ill-mannered dogs can't go. Teaching your dog to walk on a leash is one of the most important skills you can provide him; if you're having problems, ask your veterinarian for a referral to a dog trainer who can show you the right tools and techniques.

Chapter 9

AVOIDING PREVENTABLE CATASTROPHES

L ife is full of surprises, both the kind that delight us and the variety that stop us in our tracks. No one can ever plan for everything, but as a good dog owner, you do your best to anticipate dangers to your canine companion and head them off at the pass. In the words of every Boy Scout: Always Be Prepared.

Not only will an ounce of prevention possibly save your dog, it will also most certainly save you money. No one ever starts the day saying, "Today I'm going to let my dog be hit by a car or get attacked by another dog." It's an accident, sure. Too often, though, such calamities are preventable.

The time to prevent them is now. Or better yet, yesterday. So make a list and do what you can to keep your dog out of trouble. You'll sleep better for having done so, I promise.

LEASHES AND LOCKED GATES

Some of the biggest dangers to your dog are the ones he may face if he gets loose and has to manage on his own. Real threats like turf-guarding dogs, traffic, predators, and weather extremes are all circumstances our dogs don't know how to handle. So part of your job is to make sure your dog doesn't find his way out into the wild without you.

Leashes are a dog's best friend. Unless your dog has 100 percent recall reliability (you say, "Come!" and he runs right to you, every single time, and you never doubt that he won't), he should never be allowed to roam off leash unless there's a fence to confine him. Fenced dog parks and backyards are great places for dogs to run free. Open parks, friendly looking neighborhoods, and country roads are not.

Your best bet is a comfortable six-foot leash you can hang on to in almost any circumstance. Nylon and rope is sturdy and durable, but hard on the hands if your dog's not well trained. Retractable leashes? These are never to be used with dogs who are not trained. Stick to a leash. A real one.

Reels Are for Fishing—or Fully Trained Dogs

Every now and then you'll run across a product so useful, you don't know how you ever lived without it. The retractable reel-type leash (the Flexi is probably the best-known brand) is one such product. But every product has its limits and its rules for safety, which need to be understood. These leashes are no exception. Read the instructions, and don't risk injury to yourself or your dog by using this product in a way for which it wasn't designed.

The Flexi is not designed for use with an untrained dog. A dog who pulls at the leash or refuses to come when called back from the end of the leash is at risk of injuring himself, his owner, or an innocent bystander. This is not the fault of either the leash or the dog. It's an error on the part of the dog's owner in choosing the wrong piece of equipment.

Some dogs have hurt themselves hitting the end of the long leash at full speed and not having it give way (which is also pretty tough on the human holding the handle). Other dogs have bitten people or other pets, or have hurt themselves, after getting too far away on the leash before the handler has had time to reel them in.

And some dogs have pulled the leash out of their owners' hands when they reach the end of the line.

Users should always be aware of where the line is. Don't grab it with your bare hands. And be careful that it doesn't wrap around fingers or legs (yours or the dog's)—it can cut or burn if it's moving quickly.

As bad as those risks seem, even riskier behavior is using a slip or choke collar or a head halter with a reel-type leash. A dog hitting the end of a line at a run wearing these training tools can really be hurt.

Beyond the safety of the leash, your dog should be secure in your yard. A good fence is low enough to the ground to prevent digging under, high enough to deter jumping over, and secured with a latch your dog isn't smart enough to open—and a lock so no one else does. It sounds simple, but if you have a Houdini dog (or call them Houndini), you know it's tough. Some dog owners even have to resort to double fencing to keep their pups in. Install a self-closing spring on the gate to have it close automatically, and make sure your kids get in the habit of closing gates and doors behind them. After all, a fence with an open gate is described first in a single word: freedom. Your first feeling upon finding them gone is panic. And too often these scenarios have bad outcomes, so make sure the gate is always closed. We have dog runs at our Almost Heaven Ranch, and besides shutting the gates we use a carabiner to lock them tight.

COLLAR CONCERNS—RIGHT CHOICE, GOOD FIT

Your dog's everyday collar should be one that won't slip, tighten, come undone, or irritate his skin. A nylon collar with a snap closure or a leather one with a traditional buckle will work fine. If your dog has allergies, be sure to check under a new collar daily for the first week of wear to make sure it isn't rubbing him or making him itch. A properly fitted collar will sit snugly around your dog's neck and you should be able to slide two fingers between the material and your dog's skin.

In addition to a regular collar, your dog may need a specialty version for walking, training, or behavior modification. None of these collars should be worn full-time. They are all designed for specific, limited functions:

- **Slip or choke collars.** This kind of collar is not recommended for most dogs, or rather, for most dog owners. If you aren't experienced in using one of these collars that tightens when either you or your dog pulls, you can do more damage than good. If you think your dog would benefit from the use of a slip collar, schedule at least a couple lessons with a dog trainer to learn to use it properly. In the hands of a wise, capable trainer, both of these collar types have practical uses, but they are definitely not for the novice dog handler.

- **Martingale or prong collars.** These collars tighten with a limit. Unlike slip or choke collars, they tighten a little around the neck, but cannot go beyond a certain, safe point. Regular martingales, which look like normal, "flat" collars except for the adjustable section, provide plenty of control for walking many dogs. Prong or pinch collars have blunt tips that press into the neck when tightened, but they look a lot worse than they are and can be a decent choice for a dog with a heavily muscled neck.

- **Top-clip harnesses.** With a D ring for attaching the leash on the back between the shoulder blades, this kind of restraint is reserved mostly for dogs who have medical issues or are recovering from injury or surgery. Some harnesses are specially made to help support the weight of a dog who can't fully walk on his own. Others are recommended for dogs who have had trauma or injury to their necks. Unless your dog has some special circumstance that makes this a veterinary-recommended option, the harness is probably not an ideal choice for routine walking.

- **Head halters.** This kind of collar is also specifically for training uses—not for full-time wear. Even though head halters resemble muzzles, they do not muzzle a dog, inflict pain on him, or keep him from barking, eating, or drinking. The halter is used in a way that's very similar to a halter on a horse—it guides your dog's head and keeps him in check with gentle pressure behind his ears and at the bridge of his nose. This kind of collar can be a very effective tool in teaching a dog to walk politely on leash. Anyone can easily learn to use one. After the walk or training session, though, it should be put away until the next round.

✤**Front-clip harnesses.** These relatively new walking tools use the dog's own forward motion to correct pulling, and they're very effective at ending the behavior. And many dogs find front-clip harnesses easier to adjust to than the more common head halters. Front-clip harnesses have a ring in the front on the dog's chest where the leash attaches, so you get the same turning effect as with the head halter. The pressure is on the shoulders, not the nose, so many dogs find it less objectionable. When I recommend this to a client I tell them they're about to install power steering on their dog. Since 60 percent of a dog's weight is on his front legs, by controlling his forward momentum you control his movement.

✤**Electric collars, sound-emitting collars, and chemical-spritzing collars.** Like slip and prong collars, these behavior modification tools are really only as good as the supervision and direction of the owner who chooses them. If you just put an anti-bark collar, or an electric fence collar, on your dog and don't put in the time to train him how it works and why it works, you're doing your dog a terrible disservice. Punishments that your dog doesn't understand are cruel and unfair. While these training methods have their place, they're overused and should never be used routinely except under the supervision of an experienced dog trainer. Frankly, there are almost always better training options for most dogs and most owners.

You may choose to have your dog not wear a collar at all in the house, especially if you have more than one dog and they love to play. Dogs can get hung up on each other's collar, and the results can be deadly. Going naked is a tough call, though, since if your dog gets out he'll be without a collar and an ID. (Remember, even if your dog is microchipped, he'll likely be found by a neighbor who does not have a scanner.) Evaluate what's riskier, and make your best judgment accordingly. One option to consider: a breakaway collar, similar to those used for cats. If these collars get caught, they are designed to give way. If you have dogs who love to play rough with each other, a breakaway collar is a good option. (They turn into no-escape collars by clipping the leash to D-rings on either side of the breakaway juncture.)

GETTING LOST, AND FOUND

Countless dogs go missing every year, lost because of open gates, broken collars, doors left ajar, and a host of other explanations. Some pups walk through an open gate, and others are just natural escape artists; some get spooked by a thunderstorm, fireworks, or gunfire, and take off in fear; others just meander away after a sight or a scent and end up getting too far from home. Giving your dog a safe, secure home and always keeping him on leash when you're out can help avoid

GPS for Dogs? Don't Laugh—It's Coming

Among animal shelter workers, there's a wry standing joke that a strangely high percentage of dogs seem to get lost right after their baths; after all, what else could explain so many dogs ending up missing without their collars on? When the technology to microchip pets came along, it became a great hope for shelters—a way to quickly identify collarless dogs and reunite as many as possible with their owners.

In the last couple of years, the amazing, mysterious world of gadgetry has taken one giant step beyond the microchip: inventing dog GPS. The folks who made us all competent navigators by bringing global positioning to our cars are slowly bringing it to our dogs, too. GPS collars are still developing and improving, but in the long run, the ability to simply activate a tracker in your dog's collar and easily find him yourself may one day make the "lost dog" poster and the anxiety and worry that go with it a thing of the past.

this potential tragedy, but sometimes even the most carefully protected dogs get loose, and you need to know what steps you can take to
ensure your dog's safe return if this ever happens to you.

Collars, tags, chips, and more: The best way to ensure a happy
reunion with a lost dog is by making sure your dog is easily identifi-
able as a member of your family. Your dog should have an identification tag attached to his collar with his name and your phone numbers.
Cell phone is best because then you can be reached anywhere (home,
work, around town, or on vacation). Since ID tags sometimes come
detached, also use a permanent marker to write that same information directly on your dog's collar. You can mail-order collars that are
permanently printed with your dog's name and phone number from
companies like L.L. Bean, Foster and Smith, and Orvis.

Perhaps even more important than any outward label is a permanently implanted microchip that will identify your dog anywhere in
the world, even if he gets lost with no collar at all. If your dog has
not been chipped, ask your veterinarian to perform this two-second,
nearly painless procedure. The microchip—the size of a grain of rice
and with antimigration features—is inserted between your dog's
shoulder blades, and this is no more painful than a routine vaccination.
Once it's been implanted, if your dog is picked up by animal control,
or taken to a veterinarian or an animal shelter, the shoulder blade area
can be scanned for the chip and your contact information retrieved
from it. Since a third of dogs are lost at least once in their lives, there's
a fair chance that one day your dog's chip "will come in," and you'll
have the technology to thank for your joyful reunion.

HOW TO FIND A LOST PET

If your dog does get lost, it pays to know how to launch a quick, effective search.

✤**Act fast.** Don't waste any time before calling your neighbors, dis-
   tributing your flyers, or enlisting the help of family or friends to
   help find your lost dog. Missing dogs are very rarely stolen—they
   are just lost and need help getting home. The vast majority of pets

that are lost are very near their home, so that's where to concentrate the initial search; get help and do it fast and furious. The longer your dog is gone, the harder it may be to locate him and get him back, so launch a search the minute you discover he's missing.

❧ **Have pictures on hand.** In the age of the digital camera, it takes only a few seconds to take a couple good pictures of your dog. You could do it right now. Don't forget to update your photo yearly, as the image of a ten-month-old puppy looks far different from the same animal at age ten years.

❧ **Make signs that work.** The most effective "lost dog" sign is simple, eye-catching, clear, and legible. Assume anyone who sees what you post is going to look at it for only a few seconds. Make it effective by making your sign extra large (buy a poster board at any pharmacy or superstore), extra bright (choose a neon color), and clear (use ten words or less, all in large print letters, to ask for help). Enlarge a photo of your dog and display a copy on every poster. Blanket your neighborhood with flyers at every intersection, and have a friend hand-deliver them to every veterinary office, animal shelter, convenience store, and post office in your area. Also ask your mail carrier and the local UPS and FedEx drivers to keep a lookout.

SAFETY FIRST, FOR ALL

Every year, more than four million people in the United States are bitten by dogs, with children being by far the most common victims. In fact, one out of two children is bitten by a dog by the age of twelve. Eight hundred thousand people seek medical treatment for dog bites each year, according to the American Veterinary Medical Association, and the majority of those individuals are bitten by a dog that belongs to their own family or that of a neighbor. As a dog owner, you have a responsibility to both your dog and others to make sure you don't contribute to this problem. Your role is twofold: First, ask yourself if your own dog could be a biter, and if so, what you can do about it. Second, educate your family, especially children, about dog-bite prevention.

> **Doggie Details**
>
> The top three ways to prevent children from being bitten are: Don't let them near the dog while she's eating or is with a treat or favorite toy. Let sleeping dogs lie. Never allow a child to pull a dog's fur or body parts or bend down over it in what the dog thinks is a menacing manner.

AN AGGRESSIVE DOG

Have you ever felt afraid of your dog? Have you ever worried that your dog might inflict harm on another person or animal? If you answer yes to either of these questions, you've taken an important step—acknowledging a potential problem. Far too many dog owners are so enamored with their canine companions that they can't see the danger right before their eyes. If you've ever been on the receiving end of a throaty growl, an aggressive stance, or a stare-down contest with a dog while the owner insists, "It's okay! He doesn't bite," you know what a big issue this is.

If your dog has a potential issue with aggression, there's a good chance he can be rehabilitated. Start by making an appointment with the veterinarian to make sure there's no medical condition, such as cognitive disorder syndrome or extreme pain, causing bad behavior. Next, if you have a male dog and have been putting it off, make an appointment to have your dog neutered. The majority of dog bites are dished out by unneutered males. Next, ask for a reference for a reputable dog trainer or behaviorist. Most aggressive dogs need professional help to change their habits.

Whether you have an aggressive dog at home or not, teach the children in your household how to handle a testy dog when they meet one. Since most kids are bitten by dogs they know, teach your own children and any who visit your household that they should never disturb a dog who is eating, sleeping, or chewing a favorite toy. Dogs who have backed themselves into a corner are not to be bothered, and kids should never try to inflict a big hug on any dog without permission from the owner.

Plan for the Fourth before the Rocket's Red Glare

Every year, animal shelters and veterinary offices get a rash of calls and visits on the fifth of July. Why that date? Because dogs who are terrified by the noise of fireworks go a little crazy on the Fourth, and far too many of them escape and end up lost or picked up as strays or have injured themselves trying to escape. It doesn't have to be this way. If you know your dog has a phobia for loud noises like fireworks, take him to the veterinarian and ask for a small dose of anti-anxiety medication in advance of Independence Day. (I also prescribe generic Xanax for thunderstorm phobias, around the start of hunting season, or for dogs that are terrified of other noises such as road noise or snow sliding off roofs.) I'm happy to provide this for my clients with anxious dogs. Occasional small doses of these medications for fearful dogs have virtually no complications or side effects. They simply keep your pup calm and quiet while the world goes nuts around him. I have also started recommending the *Through a Dog's Ear* CDs, which are scientifically developed to calm a pet.

Another noisy holiday: New Year's Eve. For some reason that defies common sense, firing guns in the air has become a widespread way of "celebrating" the New Year. Stupid? You bet, and I say that as a man who has grown up in the country, around hunters who'd never be so irresponsible to mishandle firearms this way. Seems to be a city-slicker thing, but it's a bad idea. I can't change it, but I can advise you to look out for your pet.

Your Mother's an Ugly Dog!

It never ceases to amaze me the way a little dog will pick a fight with a big, burly one, as if size were really not an issue in a brawl. Some of the smallest breeds can be among the most aggressive—and if you've ever seen a Chihuahua bark and badger a big ol' Lab or a Golden Retriever into submission, you know exactly who I'm talking about. Sadly, in my veterinary practice I've seen too many small dogs who learned the hard way that they may be able to pick a fight, but the big dog will be the one to end it. While in their minds they're ten feet tall, in a fight they discover too late that they're only a fraction of that.

To keep your small dog out of tussles, don't make a habit of carrying him everywhere. Little dogs who spend their lives seeing the world from a person's height seem to quickly forget that they are, in fact, small. Let your dog get down and walk as much as possible. In addition, don't give your small dog a pass when it comes to training. It's too easy to look at the little guy and think there's no real reason he should have to obey—after all, you can always control him. But every dog should master the basic commands of "sit," "stay," "come," and "leave it." The first time you successfully get your ten-pound dog to "leave it" when "it" is a hundred-pound Rottweiler, your investment of time and energy in his training will be fully repaid.

If you or your child encounter an aggressive, unconfined dog, follow these steps to get safely out of the situation.

* Don't run away. This is the worst possible escape tactic. Dogs are genetically programmed to chase, and if you take off, an aggressive dog will follow.

(Continued)

🐾 Hold still and "be a tree" or "lay like a log." Teach kids to stop, bring their hands and elbows in, lower their eyes, keep calm, and hold still (!) around any aggressive, unfamiliar, or overexcited dog. Most dogs are smart enough to see that this posture is both boring and not threatening and walk away. If a child is on the ground, he should lie like a log (still) and cover his face with his hands.

🐾 If you have a bike, purse, or backpack, hold it between you and the aggressive dog.

🐾 If you, your child, or your dog are bitten by a dog, be sure to get medical attention.

Both people and dogs may need antibiotics after a dog bite to prevent infection. And call animal control even if you have a clean getaway, before someone else gets hurt.

DISEASE SHOULD NOT BE SHARED

Zoonoses (diseases transmissible from animals to humans) have gotten a lot of attention lately, thanks to one very confusing flu season that saw concerns about transmission among birds, dogs, pigs, and people skyrocket. In reality, zoonoses are a very small but necessary concern for most dog owners. The most dangerous zoonotic diseases that can be transferred from dogs to people are rabies and leptospirosis. If your dog is routinely vaccinated for both of these, the risk to you is miniscule. As long as your family and your dog are all reasonably healthy and up-to-date on your shots, your only significant worries about disease transmission between you come in the form of parasites.

Several nasty parasites can also be transferred from your dog to you, though the risk is pretty small. By routinely deworming your pets and keeping your yard picked up at least every three days you drop the risk to near zero. There's also that other "worm," ringworm, which is really a fungus and not a worm at all, that can be spread from pets to people. Avoiding these diseases is not difficult at all: heed the lifelong advice from your mom and wash your hands often and well with soap and warm water. Always wash your hands after grooming your dog. Scrub them scrupulously after picking up poop in the yard or on walks. Keep in mind that small children, who not only aren't great about scrubbing their hands but also actually eat dirt from time to time, need your help and supervision to achieve this goal.

If you or anyone in your family is immune compromised, talk with your doctor about the specific health risks dogs can pose. There's no need to banish the dog, but you need to be more careful than a person with a healthy immune system, who can fend off more diseases. The number one rule: wash your hands after petting your dog and after preparing his meals. Frankly, you just can't wash your hands enough these days—and teach your children to do the same.

Good preventive care, financial planning, and pet health insurance will help keep your bank account intact while offering the best care to your dog. Your veterinarian is also a key component, and every veterinarian is aware of financial constraints and is prepared to discuss what you can do to spend your money wisely throughout your pet's life.

Chapter 10

MAKING DOG CARE DOABLE— SAVE TIME AND MONEY

Every dog owner has to make lifestyle compromises for a four-legged friend, starting with the fact that dogs simply can't live everywhere (dogs aren't allowed in many rentals and some condominium communities). We can't just pick up and race off on a spontaneous weekend without making sure pets are welcome or arranging for boarding or a pet sitter.

And then there are the specifics, some of which change over time. Some of us get up every night to let out the old dog with the tired bladder. Most of us have had to toss out chewed-up shoes, clean mud from our cars, and scrub carpets on our hands and knees to get out pet stains at one time or another, especially after raising a puppy. Whether the sacrifices are great or small, they are something everyone in the society of dog owners knows and accepts as the price of unconditional, irresistible love and as a sign of our dogged devotion.

While compromises are inevitable, there are some aspects of a dog owner's life where it pays to maintain some control. Managing your pet-related spending and maintaining order in your clean, comfy home are the two areas where this might matter most of all.

FINANCIAL PLANNING FOR PET CARE

The good news about veterinary care is that almost all the advances in the medical world over the past two decades are now available in animal medicine, although of course not all practices will offer everything that's available. This means diagnostic tests, surgical and nonsurgical procedures, and medications are all far better and more effective than even just a few years ago. The downside? These advances cost more, and the sticker shock is severe for people who have had pets for years, even decades. Even though procedures in veterinary medicine are a fraction of the cost of most comparable procedures in human medicine, it doesn't feel like a bargain when you're paying the bill (versus a third-party payment from a health insurance company), and you're looking at options that are recommended but you simply cannot afford.

Americans spend more than $10 billion a year on veterinary care for their pets, and that number continues to increase as costs, options, and even the esteem in which most people hold their dogs all grow. That's a lot of money, but the fact is that countless pets don't get even the most basic care. While sometimes those dogs are victims of neglect, sometimes it really is about money—people who don't have it or who strongly believe that a pet is worth only so much and not a penny more.

Veterinarians call the point where a sick pet and the inability or unwillingness to pay for treatment meet "economic euthanasia"—the owner's choice is to humanely put the pet to sleep to spare the animal suffering rather than to treat the illness or injury. In most cases, these situations are heartbreaking conditions for both dog owners and veterinary professionals who do everything they can to serve their clients and keep costs under control.

Veterinarians Need to Make a Living, Too

I realize that I risk sounding whiny, or greedy, or even heartless. I know a lot of people think we veterinarians are all of those things— and incompetent, too!—because, like you, I spend a fair amount of time on the Internet and I see what people write when they won't say something face-to-face or put their name to it.

Your veterinarian lives in the same world you do and is well aware of what it costs to make mortgage or rent payments, keep clothes on the children, keep the car repaired, and, yes, take care of pets, because we all have them, too. What a lot of veterinarians have that you may not, though, is a crushing level of debt they signed on to so they could get through school. The average student debt coming out of college should be about one year's salary ($65,000 for a vet), but it's currently running about $125,000; put another way, student debt should run about 10 percent of a monthly salary, but it's about 25 percent for veterinarians. So never think that your veterinarian was drawn to the profession for the love of money or the easy hours. It's because of a love of animals. That's typical of younger veterinarians, who often are working for the practice you go to—they don't own it. Those who own practices are dealing with the same things all businesses do: employees' salaries and benefits, insurance, taxes, loans on the property and equipment, inventory, and much more.

Almost every client wants the most modern care for a pet, but they want it at 1980s prices. That just can't happen.

Your veterinarian usually cannot donate the goods and services, or carry you while you make payments. Veterinarians will always work with you on options or solutions, but giving it away isn't either. They simply cannot pay their loans and stay in business, and that's why in this chapter I want you to plan now for emergencies, so you have more options when something happens—and believe me, it will.

Planning ahead for your dog's future veterinary care makes good financial and emotional sense. The last place you ever want to be is standing in an urgent pet care clinic, turning down a lifesaving procedure for your beloved dog because you can't swing the expense. With a little luck, your dog will live a long, happy, emergency-free existence, but just in case, consider these options for if a crisis comes up.

For the best coverage, it's probably better to have all of these options in place. A special savings account can never be a bad thing: after all, if your pet lives a long, happy life and you never tap that savings account, you are ahead on the next pet. And a dedicated amount of credit that doesn't cost you anything (or anything much, anyway) is always a good safety net. But really, the one thing you probably need to consider more than anything is pet health insurance.

Here are your options:

Savings accounts. Americans are bad at savings, and I'll leave the why to sociologists and psychologists. My wife and I both come from families of savers, and savers we have always been. But there's no doubt it takes commitment, discipline, and the ability to turn down temptation to make this work. But work it does, and very, very well. Every dog owner should have a savings account for emergencies. Every one. There is simply no downside to this strategy.

It's simple to open a dedicated savings account and have your bank put whatever amount you want into it, at any interval you choose. Easiest plan? If your employer offers direct deposit, have part of your paycheck routed to your pet's emergency account. What you don't see, you'll never miss and never spend.

Even better: since few veterinarians take pet health insurance as payment, a savings account can complement insurance perfectly. You can pay your pet's veterinary bill, put in your insurance claim, and then put the money back in your account when you get the check. (Some insurers even offer direct deposit, so it can go back in without a thought!)

Pet health insurance. Fewer than 2 percent of Americans have health insurance for their pets. And that's astonishing, considering the cost of veterinary care and the very grim options for those who cannot afford care at any level.

But the industry is growing and changing, with more choices than ever before, and pet health insurance is picking up steam as people realize its benefits. When consumer advocacy groups look at pet health insurance, they inevitably point out that most people won't make money on the insurance plans—that paying cash for care is less expensive over a pet's life than paying insurance premiums.

While that's true, that's simply the worst way to look at the cost and the benefits. Insurance isn't supposed to make you money. Just like insurance on a home or car, it's supposed to help you with unexpected expenses that you cannot cover. Consider that if you're lucky, you'll never win the jackpot on your homeowner's insurance by having your home burn down, but that doesn't mean you don't want to be covered regardless.

The increase in pet insurance companies and the variety of plans they offer means that you can no longer rule out insurance without investigating all the plans. Read carefully. Some plans cover a percentage of reasonable costs that may not be disclosed. Some plans will not cover hereditary defects common to the breed you choose. Chronic preexisting conditions may not be covered; a healed injury or resolved illness may be covered after a set waiting period. It is also important to consider that veterinary costs are usually higher on the coasts and in major metropolitan areas because the cost of doing business in these areas is higher.

In a way, it's helpful to think of pet health insurance more like car insurance than human health insurance. If you have health insurance, you are generally covered for everything, less your copays. Your maintenance and your accidents are both covered. By contrast, when you choose car insurance, you're not looking for someone to pick up the cost of your oil changes, tire rotations, or even the occasional paint-scraping run-in with the garage door frame.

Instead, you're looking for some peace of mind that if you ever do wreck your vehicle, you won't have to go into hock to deal with the consequences.

Many veterinary health insurance companies offer both kinds of policies: the ones that cover everything under the sun, and the one that is just there in case your dog has a severe illness or injury. The latter is less expensive, especially if you choose a higher deductible— again, a cost you can plan for, with the use of a savings account.

No matter which plans or companies you consider, I hope you will consider one of them for your dog. Because having to euthanize a pet we could have saved is the worst part of what we do. Help us help you and your pet.

Give me credit. We've all seen the problem with credit, and it's safe to say the era of easy credit and a mailbox full of great deals on credit cards is long gone, and probably just as well. So, too, is the idea of using your home like an ATM machine—those people who had equity credit often find those lines have disappeared along with their equity.

That doesn't mean you can't use credit to help in a pinch, although it's probably not the best of your options, especially not traditional credit cards or putting your home on the line.

But then there are credit-line programs that may work for you, ideally with advance planning. The best known of these programs is offered by a company called CareCredit that partners with veterinary offices to offer short-term, low-interest credit for veterinary costs. The time frames for these arrangements vary, but generally clients have six to twelve months to pay back the cost of treatment, and as long as you make your payments and beat the payoff deadline, you don't have to pay any interest. Of course, if you do miss a payment or the payoff, interest rates are punitive, so be sure you can see this kind of plan through before you agree to it. Your veterinarian's office may also have its own version of this line-of-credit financing. Ask about it at your dog's next visit, so you know what might be available if you ever need it.

Bottom line: ask now. Make a discussion of the what-if a part of your pet's next wellness exam so you are not caught making decisions that are based on your lack of money, not your pet's lack of options for a cure. When the time comes to step up and say, "Yes, Doctor, do everything you can to save/treat my dog," you won't even hesitate.

SAVING MONEY: WHAT CORNERS CAN BE CUT?

Everyone loves saving money—and we all should be doing more of it. But there are two areas where you shouldn't try to trim expenses, since it'll catch up with your dog, and your wallet, sooner or later:

🐾 **Don't skip your regular wellness exams and preventive care.** The cost of a checkup, even with basic diagnostics, is a fraction of the cost of treating any major health problem. And consider: the vast majority of health problems that are identified in their early stages are far cheaper and easier to treat than those that are left to fester and worsen before they're discovered.

🐾 **Don't lower the quality of your dog's food.** Good nutrition keeps your dog healthy and strong. Please don't mess with his diet to save a buck or two. In general, pets need larger portions of low-quality foods anyway, so any savings is a wash once your dog's been fed.

Some other tips:

Work with your vet to cut costs. If your dog is sick, ask the veterinarian for suggestions or treatment options that are less expensive, even if not the gold standard of care. Surprisingly, the answer is often affirmative.

If your dog requires medication, shop around for the best price. Most veterinarians are used to being asked to write scripts, and you may well find considerable savings at a pharmacy, especially ones that offer new low monthly options for generic drugs. If you choose to use a catalog or Internet pharmacy for pet-specific medications such as heartworm preventive, check into the reputation of the company and choose one that requires a written prescription—in other words, not one that spams you with e-mail promising name-brand drugs for next to nothing. Don't be scammed. In fairness, once you've found the best price, you should ask your veterinarian to match it; they almost always do. Plus many veterinarians now utilize a nationwide Internet pharmacy that serves the profession and their clients at extremely competitive prices.

Convenience: From Your Veterinarian's Office to Your Computer

Cutting-edge care is about more than your veterinarian keeping up with the latest and greatest techniques, equipment, and medications. It's also about helping make it easier for you to keep up, too.

I'm happy to see my profession using the Internet for their patients' benefit. More and more veterinary hospitals and clinics are making it easy for you to re-order prescriptions, make and keep track of appointments, and stay up-to-date on care trends using high-tech solutions that are just a few clicks away.

(Continued)

Vetstreet is a great example of a new, high-tech way to stay informed. The company offers online communication with your veterinarian through free private, secure web pages. Once you've set up your pet's pages, you can:

🐾 Receive e-mail reminders about examinations, vaccinations, and other services your pet needs;

🐾 Get instant notification of pet food and medication recalls;

🐾 Request appointments with your veterinarian;

🐾 View your pet's medications;

🐾 Refill medications through your pet's online store (and have them delivered free);

🐾 Receive reminders when it's time to give medication;

🐾 Note your pet's food brands and other dietary needs; and

🐾 Access and learn about pets' health-related issues, in the care-guide section.

Such twenty-four-hour access makes it easier to care for your pet. We all have busy lives these days, so I'm thrilled to see companies like Vetstreet make good care for great pets so much easier for us all. I can't wait to see more growth in this area of veterinary care.

Keep your dog lean and fit. So very many serious veterinary health problems stem from a dog's excess weight and lack of conditioning. Keeping your dog at a healthy weight—on the lean side of average, ideally—and giving him regular exercise will improve both the quality and quantity of his life and save you money.

Do it yourself. Everyone loves having someone else do the hard, time-consuming, or messy work, which is why when the economy was booming, so were services from doggy day care to yard cleanup. Cut out or cut back on these services after analyzing their cost-to-benefit ratio. (Sometimes having someone else perform a service may free you to make more money than if you'd taken the time to do the work yourself.) Dog walking, grooming, tooth brushing, nail trimming: if you're on a tight budget and not already doing these things yourself, now's the time to start. Most people can learn to handle any basic grooming task at home. If your dog really needs professional maintenance, try stretching the time between appointments by a week or two to thin the costs.

Make a deal. Why not trade pet-sitting time with a friend whose dog you love? Or if you have a skill or product others need, barter! Bartering with your time or special skills for the goods and services you need is a tradition as old as human history, so why not make it work for you?

Shop smart. Buy your dog's food in bulk and store it in an airtight container, preserving the label with contact information and lot number in case there's a problem. Work with other dog owners to buy larger sizes of product at lower price and split it—this can really work if you and your couple of friends have Chihuahuas and you have no way to use (or even store) a Great Dane–sized bag of food. And don't forget that you don't need to buy everything new. Whatever you need, you can often find it used at a greatly reduced prize at tag sales or through online classifieds. Do realize, as well, that "cheap" isn't always the best value. Consider that buying high-quality items that last may be a better deal in the long run.

Home Health Checklist

Want a cheat sheet to make sure you don't miss anything? This is the one I share with clients. If you use this on a monthly basis, you can help discover many problems early on, before they cause unnecessary pain, expense,...or worse.

If any answer below is no, please call your veterinarian. It's important to your pet's health.

My Pet:

1. is acting normal, is active, and is in good spirits.
2. does not tire easily with moderate exercise.
3. does not have seizures or fainting episodes.

(Continued)

4. has a normal appetite, with no significant weight change.

5. does not vomit or regurgitate his food.

6. has normal bowel movements (firm, formed, mucus-free).

7. doesn't drag his bottom or chew under the tail excessively.

8. has a full, glossy coat with no missing hair, no mats, or excessive shedding, and with skin free from dry flakes; is not greasy; and has no bad odor.

9. doesn't scratch, lick, or chew himself excessively.

10. is free from fleas, ticks, lice, and mites.

11. has a body that is free from lumps and bumps.

12. has ears that are clean and odor free.

13. doesn't shake her head or dig at her ears.

14. has eyes that are bright, clear, and free of matter.

15. has normal hearing and reacts as usual to her environment.

16. walks without stiffness, pain, or difficulty.

17. has healthy-looking feet and short nails.

18. breathes normally, without straining or coughing.

19. has a normal thirst and drinks in the usual amount and frequency.

20. urinates in the usual amounts and frequency; color is normal.

21. has a moist nose, free from discharge.

22. has clean, white teeth, free from plaque, tartar, or bad breath.

23. has gums that are pink, with no redness, swelling, or offensive bad-mouth odor.

24. has no offensive habits (biting, barking, digging, chewing, scratching, spraying).

25. is well house-trained, and there is no offensive household pet odor.

Again if any answer above is no, please call your veterinarian.

KEEPING PET MESS DOWN SAVES MONEY, TOO

There's a reason why real-estate agents ask their clients to send their pets to live with friends and relatives when a house is for sale: because pets bring down the value and the perception of a home—and often cause greater wear and tear on a property than a coat of paint can hide. That's also true of cars, of course, which is why pet damage is often charged at the end of a car lease, and why car rental agencies that allow pets require pet deposits.

But even if you don't care about any of that, you probably don't want to live in a dog house. You don't want to replace or reupholster furniture frequently, and you don't want to spend your leisure time mopping up messes. My wife and I deny our dogs nothing—they have a bigger share of our bed than I do, and that's the doggone truth. But we also love a clean, comfortable house. Don't care about that? Keep it nice for your dogs! Some tips:

Keep it covered. One sure way to keep your house neat is to choose washable surfaces whenever possible. If you're making big choices— like for furniture or flooring—pick surfaces that are scratch resistant and easy to wipe clean. Tile and vinyl flooring are pet friendly, as are leather and microfiber furniture. Steer clear of natural fabrics in furniture, decorations, and rugs. Nothing soaks up the scent of a dog and holds it better or longer than wool or cotton. Synthetic fabrics repel scents and stains much better.

No matter what flooring or furniture you have, it'll stay cleaner and last longer if you make use of covers. Throws and slipcovers are terrific tools. Choose washable materials only, then put them through the laundry once a week or even more often. This is easier by far than trying to clean the surface of a chair or a couch.

Throw rugs are a dog owner's best friend. Secure them with double-sided tape and use them anywhere you have heavy dog traffic, including over existing carpets. Rugs are much more easily cleaned than carpets—especially those that fit in high-capacity front-load washers—and they're also much less costly to replace when they get stained or worn out.

Washable mats can waylay a great deal of a dog's mud, muck, drool, and general mess and keep it from the rest of your house. Put mats both inside and outside the doors your dog uses to catch as much dirt and grime as possible as he goes by. Also use a mat under your dog's food and water dishes to keep spillage and droolage under control.

Brush, comb, and clip: your dog is going to shed X amount of fur in an average day, week, month, or year. Since all dogs are going to shed, you want them to shed at a time and place of your choosing. The portion of that fur that ends up on your furniture and floors pretty much depends on how much of it you comb, brush, and wash off somewhere else. A one-minute, daily, outdoor brushing for heavy-shedding dogs in the summer or in a garage or an easily cleaned room in the winter can save you an hour of housework. Bathing your dog—weekly is just fine, and forget that old nonsense about waiting for months, yuck!— cuts down on the need for heavy cleaning, too, since a dirty dog mucks up his whole environment plus puts his own health and that of the human family (who might have allergies or asthma) at risk.

If you already have a double-coated or long-coated dog, you're in for his lifetime of shedding. If you want to choose a low shedding dog somewhere down the line, choose a small, long-haired dog and keep the fur clipped short. Long-haired dogs lose hair less frequently than short-haired-ones—true! You may laugh, but putting clothes on your dog (shirts and body suits) can also keep the shedding down, and may well be worth it if someone in your family has allergies.

Fur Heaven's Sake, Cut Back, Collect, and Contain

Shedding is one of the biggest of all dog-owner pet peeves. However much we love our furry friends, we'd prefer to keep their fur on them and off us—which means off our clothes, our furniture, our carpets, our floors, and the upholstery in the car.

Fortunately, you can help keep the flying fur under control with a number of proven solutions. I'm talking about the "3 Cs"—cut back, collect, and contain. By taking your dog to a place of your choosing, such as outdoors or the garage, and using a tool like the FURminator (see page 58) to brush out as much loose coat as possible, you'll drastically cut back on the amount of hair your dog will shed in the next several days.

Use an electrostatic sheet to mop and dust. The advent of electrostatically charged products like the Swiffer is a gift to dog owners everywhere. These sheets attract lint, dust, and pollen and hold on to them. By quickly picking up all those small particles, you not only keep a cleaner house, but you keep that debris off your dog. Considering that many long-haired low-to-the-ground breeds are not unlike Swiffers themselves—gathering dust and dirt with their coats as they move along—getting this stuff out of your dog's way will not only help keep your house clean, it'll help keep your dog from picking up dust that will make you sneeze. And don't forget the benefits of a powerful vacuum. Some companies—notably Dyson, Bissell, Eureka, and Dirt Devil—are so aware of the need for routine pet cleanups that they have models designed for and marketed to pet owners that clean pet debris off floors and upholstery easier and better. (And remember: vacuums are great as part of flea control!)

Keep dog toys and dishes clean. Nothing spreads drool around the house better than your dog's beloved squeaky toys. It almost seems like they were designed to add slime to household surfaces. Many dishes (especially durable stainless steel) and toys (such as hard plastic or Kongs) and food puzzles can be run right through the dishwasher. Hot water and soap works on most everything else, and soft toys can go right through the washer and dryer.

For equipment such as crates, scrub, then rinse with a half cup bleach to a couple gallons of water, and air-dry. Better yet, to clean dishes, kennels, and runs ask your vet for a small size of Novalsan. This chlorhexidine cleaner used by almost every veterinary practice is pleasant-smelling and powerful.

Mess be gone. Of course, no matter what you do, there will be messes, from one end of the dog or the other. Products specially designed for cleaning up pet-made messes contain enzymes that don't just mask but remove odors and break down organic wastes—Nature's Miracle is one such product, as is Anti-Icky-Poo. (Any pet supply store will have these brands, and others.) These products are perfect for cleaning up house-soiling accidents and often yield better results than all-purpose cleaners.

Products that contain ammonia are poor choices for cleaning up pet messes. The ammonia smells a little bit too much like urine to be a safe scrubbing agent. Left to deduce this particular chemical smell on his own, your dog might come to the unfortunate conclusion that he's discovered a convenient new potty place.

Whatever you do, don't procrastinate. If your dog has a house-soiling accident, if his muddy paws track through, or if he manages to dump a house plant and get dirt on the floor, don't wait to start the cleanup. Carpets get first cleanup priority, as they can be permanently stained by almost any soiling agent that's left sitting around. Even wood and tile floors, though, fare better if you clean them up right away. Keep cleaning supplies stocked and ready, and be sure to jump on a muddy pawprint—or any pet mess—before it can set.

PART THREE
THE SOCIAL
ANIMAL: TEACHING
GOOD BEHAVIOR

We love our celebrity dog trainers—heck we love our celebrity everything: chefs, talk-show hosts, designers, ministers, doctors, and even—or should I say "of course"?—veterinarians. Sometimes we love these people because they're just fun to watch. We share their passion, and we wish we could make everything look as easy as they do. A sprinkle of spice, a splash of color, a few wise words of medical advice, and, when it comes to dogs, the apparent magic that only a celebrity trainer knows. These folks swoop right in and take over, and the dog pays attention. Bad dogs "cured" instantly, a happy family, a happy ending, and good ratings.

Do these "supertrainers" have some kind of magic at their disposal? Well, yes and no. They do have a gift for timing and for reading a dog's body language. They know how to train. And even more so, they seem to be expert at reading dog *owners*. And take it from me, clever editing can go a long way toward showcasing the end result while glossing over mistakes, missteps, or outright disasters that never make it to air.

But really, we know so much about training and behavior now that you don't have to end up with a bad dog in need of reform-school tactics. If you've chosen the right breed or mix, from a reputable shelter, rescue group, or breeder, and set up a framework in which your puppy or dog can succeed, you'll have a wonderful companion. If you're not quite there, some common sense and basic knowledge will help.

While very few puppies will get the kind of socialization this one did with me on the set of *Good Morning America*, you can turn your puppy into a star with early training and socialization.

Chapter 11
PUPPY BASICS: BEHAVIOR AND BONDING

s there nothing we won't forgive a puppy? A puddle, a chewed-up shoe, a nip, and a run down the street with thong underwear for the neighbors to see? Puppies are born cute, and it's pretty easy to make the case that their very adorability is the best protection ever. It's easier to laugh at a puppy than deal with the destruction.

But the fact is that there's a mind behind those adorable eyes, and let me tell you, the wheels are spinning. Every time you let your puppy do something you wouldn't want him to do when he's grown up, he makes note of it for future reference. And before you know it, those bad first steps become a road to ruin from which it's very hard to recover.

Puppies grow up incredibly quickly, and you don't have much time to make the most of the easiest period for problem prevention. Just as in medicine, it's easier to prevent a problem than to fix it. And the best part of all? Puppy training is great fun, because puppies love to learn.

Plan for success. If you've done well in working with a shelter, rescue group or reputable breeder, you already have a puppy who has been primed to learn and maybe even knows a few things. He has been started toward house-training, knows a sit, been on a leash, and been exposed to dozens of different sensory sensations.

If you have this kind of puppy, take a minute to congratulate yourself, but no more. You have to keep the momentum going. And if your puppy had a little rougher start, don't worry. You can set things right, and turn your youngster into a canine Einstein—or at least a happy, well-mannered family companion.

It's not that complicated, really. Your puppy wants to be part of your family, and he craves loving leadership. The goals of puppy raising:

- Bond with your puppy.
- Socialize your puppy.
- Never let your puppy do anything you wouldn't want a grown dog to do.
- Teach your puppy using positive methods; make training fun.
- Realize your puppy will make mistakes, and don't get angry when he does.
- Remember that preventing bad habits is always easier than fixing them later.

BONDING

When you take a puppy into your home, you are asking her to accept your family in exchange for the canine one she was born into. And she will, quite happily and with amazingly few problems, if you hold down your end of the deal—provide her with companionship and show her a proper place in the social order, otherwise known as your family.

She cannot find her place in your family unless you make your

Doggie Details

One of the easiest ways to promote a fast, tight bond with your puppy is to have her sleep in a crate at the side of your bed. It's almost like cheating: you sleep, she sleeps; but as she sleeps, she bonds. She smells your wonderful smell (the bedroom has the highest concentration of your scent) and hears every sound you make, all night long—and she won't mind your snoring! When your puppy's all grown up and perfectly behaved, you can invite her on your bed if you like. But for now...the crate's a better place.

puppy part of your life. Simply put, a puppy cannot bond with people she barely knows.

Bonding isn't hard to accomplish. Spend time with your puppy. Talk to her. Sing to her. Put your hands on her. Use baby gates instead of closed doors if you don't want her in certain parts of the house, so she can hear you and see you and feel part of the crowd.

You are the only family she has from the time you take her home. Make her part of that family, and she'll be a better pet.

SOCIALIZING

You simply cannot expose a puppy to too many new things—people, places, and other animals. And yet this is one area where puppy owners undo the good work of many reputable breeders. When a puppy is not continually exposed to new things, her social development stops—and in many cases regresses. The goal is a confident, outgoing dog, not a shy or an aggressive one. The way to accomplish this is through socializing. Think of the goal as being a big canine cocktail party and your pet is the bouquet in the center of the action, not the shrinking violet in the corner.

We ask a lot from our dogs, a lot more than their wild cousins need for survival. Wild dogs and wolves need to learn to live in harmony with others of their pack and as important members of their ecosystem. There's one boss at a time, and they reflexively know the hierarchy. They share DNA with their own family, and they don't have to get along with members of other packs. No one ever asks them to live in peace with other predators, such as mountain lions, and the only relationship they have with prey animals is when one of them becomes dinner. Wild dogs and wolves know the seasons and the smells of their environment, and they know that it's prudent to run when anything unfamiliar turns up.

Contrast that picture to what domesticated dogs are expected to endure with good grace. We ask our dogs to form a family relationship with members of at least one other species. We ask them to live peaceably in this strange family, and we expect them to be docile with humans who are outside their pack. We ask, too, that they remain able to get along well with others of their own kind, both in the family and at such events as dog shows. We ask, further, that they abide the presence of a competing predator—the cat—and ignore the presence of what any wolf knows is good eating, although we call them pets: rabbits, birds, and other smaller animals. My coauthor, Gina Spadafori, even insists that her dogs get along with her pet chickens!

Although a wild dog or wolf never gets too far from his home turf— except in cases of human interference—we ask that our dogs be as mobile as we are. We take them when we walk to the store, we put them in our cars when we go on vacation, we place them on airplanes when we move across the country.

The world is full of scary things, especially to a little puppy. At times even the boldest of puppies is paralyzed with uncertainty when faced with something he's never seen before. Your response to his fear is very important. Do not soothe him. Petting him and saying "It's okay, baby" or something similar gives your puppy the idea that being scared is okay, that you're rewarding him for the behavior. Be matter-of-fact and encouraging. Rather than the "poor baby" look and language," be the Walmart greeter, upbeat and positive. Let him know that you think there's nothing to be afraid of. Let him work it out, and when he takes that step forward, praise him for his courage. And then move on.

CONSISTENCY

Puppies are adorable, even when they're naughty. Maybe especially when they're naughty. You catch your little fluffball with your slipper in his mouth, or halfway through the destruction of yet another roll of toilet paper, and, instead of being upset, you smile. And laugh. And head for the video camera and a YouTube upload.

Although this reaction is normal, it's definitely not the way to raise a puppy who knows to leave slippers and toilet paper rolls alone. If you want your puppy to learn, you need to be consistent about what's acceptable behavior and what's not.

But you know that, which is why sometimes you keep your face as stern as you can for as long as you can, until…well, who wouldn't laugh, the way that toilet paper's wrapped around his cute puppy body?

Look. I know it's hard. But you're going to be sorry a few months from now if you don't remember this one little rule: never let a puppy get away with something you wouldn't let a grown dog do.

Developing a consistent approach to naughtiness requires a little thinking and effort on your part.

Get That Puppy in Class!

My daughter, Mikkel Becker, is a dog trainer, an author, a TV personality, and the beautiful mother of the most perfect grandchild in the world. Can you tell I'm proud of her? As many times as she has given her mother and me reasons to pop with pride, I must admit that one of my favorites is watching her teach puppy classes. She is a natural communicator, with both dogs and people, and seeing those little puppies grow and learn while their owners do the same…well, there's just nothing I like better.

Now, if you're in northern Idaho, I'd sure recommend taking a class from Mikkel. But, of course, she hasn't room in her classes for every puppy in the world, and our winding two-lane roads wouldn't handle the crush of traffic anyway. But that's okay, because nearly every place big enough to have a four-way stop and a traffic light has a trainer who's offering puppy classes, and I can't recommend them enough.

These are not boot camp classes for problem pooches. The goal here is socialization and lots of fun. Big puppies play with little ones, and everybody gets to teach and pet everyone else's pup. And along the way, puppies pick up a few nice tricks—sometimes all the basic commands, taught in an encouraging, reward-centered way.

Puppy classes are good for your puppy and good for you, too. A puppy class gives you the opportunity to talk to a trainer every

(Continued)

week about difficulties you may be having at home and to get tips on how to keep puppy problems from becoming doggy disasters. And rather than feeling like a failure, you'll find other pet owners are having many of the same difficulties as you are teaching your pup the manners that will last a lifetime. For your pup, the class is a megadose of socializing, an ongoing lesson that learning is a pleasure, and the foundation for a lifetime of canine good manners. Ask your veterinarian for a recommendation.

PRAISE—AND LIMITS

You want your puppy to love you and respect you, to know his place in the family, and feel secure and happy in it. Achieving this takes encouragement and lots of loving praise.

Don't be stingy. When your puppy does something right, let him know it. The first time the little lightbulb goes off in his head connecting the word *sit* to the lowering of his rump—if you watch, you can see the workings of his mind in his eyes—be ready to tell him he's the most perfect, smartest, beautiful, and well-loved puppy in the whole history of the world the instant that little puppy butt hits the ground. Get as excited as the glee club teacher, televangelist, or motivational speaker, and watch your pet light up with joy and want to please you again and again.

Praise and treats are the foundation of training and a good relationship—use lots of both!

But what if your puppy needs to be punished? Never hit or yell at your puppy. Review what you might have done to allow the puppy to get into trouble, and put the puppy back on course without punishment. Some methods to do so are:

Switch focus. Especially useful for the young puppy, this technique stops a behavior you don't want and provides the puppy with one that's acceptable. For example, if your young puppy's chewing on your nice leather shoes, make a noise to startle and distract him—slap the counter or clap your hands—and then give him something you do want him to chew on, a toy. When he takes it, praise him!

Change direction. With older puppies, you can stop a bad behavior by asking for a better one. Tell the puppy who's jumping up no and then "sit"—and praise him for doing so. Tell him once, wait for his compliance, then praise and treat.

Crate time. This technique has two levels, and you need to pay attention to your puppy to choose the appropriate correction. Puppies thrive on your attention, even if it's negative. The time-out removes this reward and gives him a few minutes to think things over: *Oh, I can't stay with them if I do that!* he'll realize. This technique is especially good for a puppy who doesn't want to keep his mouth to himself, a bad habit for any dog to get into where people are concerned. When the puppy starts nipping, tell him no, then clam up, pick him up, and put him in his crate for five minutes. Ignore the cries and whimpers. After a few minutes, let him out without much fanfare and let him hang out with you gently for a while. This is just like a time-out you use for two-legged kids.

If your puppy has been running around for a long time and just seems bratty, he may be tired. If that's the case, put him down for a nap in his crate, along with a chew toy. Again, ignore his fussing. Chances are he'll be asleep in a few minutes.

If you're finding you want to punish, or if your puppy seems to be challenging you, discuss the situation with a trainer, and soon. You may have some big problems developing if you don't learn how to correct your puppy in an effective way.

BABY-STEPS TO A GOOD GROWN-UP DOG

No dog in the world has more freedom than one with good manners. And no dog is easier to live with. These dogs can go into stores and on vacation. They're welcome not only at the veterinarian's and the groomer's, but on the red carpet as well. Well-mannered dogs are helping to reverse the trend of antidog laws, including opening the minds in some communities to the possibilities of dog parks where good dogs can be rewarded by running... free!

About a million and six good reasons exist to train your puppy, and no good reason not to. So let's get the basics down.

Getting Used to a Collar and Leash

Your puppy can start wearing a buckled collar from the time you bring him home. By the time your pup's ten weeks old, you can introduce a leash for a few minutes at a time. Instead of using the leash to get the puppy to go your way, go his for a while, and then bend down and call him to you, sweetly. When he turns and heads in your direction, praise him and then get up and keep going, patting your leg and jollying him along. Introduce a command such as "walk on" or "let's go" so he will start associating it with the idea of heading in your direction.

A few minutes are enough. Try again later in the day, and maybe change direction once, saying "let's go" and praising when the puppy follows.

The leash can be an important bonding tool for both puppies and grown dogs. After your puppy's comfortable with the feel of the leash, try tethering him to you for a few minutes at a time. With a six-foot leash, slip the leash handle through your belt and snap it to the puppy. And then go about your business, hands off the leash. Doing so teaches the puppy to keep an eye on you, which in turn reinforces the idea of you as leader.

Puppy's first leash should be six feet long, slender, and light as possible, especially at the clasp. Even a length of lightweight cord tied to a light snap is better than a leash that's too heavy to start with.

Grooming

All dogs need to learn to be bathed and brushed, to have their nails trimmed and their ears cleaned out. Some breeds—Poodles, for example, as well as terriers and Cockers—need to be professionally groomed at regular intervals during their lives.

The time to start introducing your puppy to these experiences is the day you bring him home. Handle his feet and toes, lift and caress

Your Body Is My Body

All this handling may seem to be about good grooming, but it's really about gentling your puppy. Let your puppy know that he has to allow you to handle every inch of his body, from opening his mouth to fondling his toes. Make sure you handle every bit, with a firm yet friendly, matter-of-fact manner, and with lots of praise and treats. Your puppy will need to learn these lessons for life, because people will always be handling him, and he needs to be okay with that.

his earflaps, all the time telling him what a wonderful puppy he is. Keep the sessions short and always end on an upbeat note. Treats and praise!

For brushing and combing, put a towel on top of a high, solid surface like your dryer or a countertop—it's easier on your back, and because it's elevated your puppy may stay still—and hold him while you brush. If he wriggles and carries on some, don't let that stop you. Brush for a short period, and end the session with brushing in an area most dogs adore—their tummy. Then call it a day.

Expose your puppy to the concept of electric clippers by running an electronic toothbrush—or another small humming device—near him. Place the handle of it against him gently so that he can feel the vibration. Don't punish him for being scared: let him get used to it for a second or two, and praise him afterward for being so brave.

If your puppy is of a breed that needs professional grooming, make his first appointment as soon as he's done with his puppy shots—at fourteen to sixteen weeks of age—to minimize the risk of exposure to disease. Make sure that the groomer knows you're bringing in a puppy so she can take a little extra time with him. When you go in, ask your groomer about the potty path trim—taking the shears and making a clean path away from your pet's genital region so feces and urine have no place to stop on the way out. This trim will not only keep your pet cleaner, but it will also keep your home cleaner, too, since your pet won't bring back inside what you'd hoped got dumped outside.

Nail trimming should be done frequently from the time you bring your puppy home to avoid the fits many older dogs throw when faced with this necessary task. Ask your veterinarian to show you how.

Sit for What You Want

Teaching a puppy to sit is almost effortless. You don't need to lay a hand on him. All you need is his food bowl and the force of gravity. Here's how it works:

Call your puppy's name and hold his food dish over his head, forcing him to raise his muzzle high to keep an eye on it. Soon he'll lose his balance and his back legs will start to fold. The microsecond this starts to occur, say "sit." When his rump hits the ground, praise him and give him his dinner. Within a short time—if you're consistent in asking—he'll be sitting automatically for his food.

Once your puppy knows "sit," expand the situations in which you ask for it. Have him sit before you put the leash on, sit before you go out the door for a walk, sit instead of jumping up, and so on.

CURE FOR NORMAL PUPPY NAUGHTIES

Chewing, barking, and nipping are all normal for puppies, but they're not behaviors we humans approve of. The best time to tell your puppy so is as early as possible. And it's pretty easy to do so.

Chewing

Like babies, puppies have an oral fixation, and anything and everything goes in their mouth. All puppies chew, and chewing isn't bad. So would you if your gums drove you as crazy as theirs do, especially when their adult teeth start coming in, around four months of age. The trick here is to redirect the behavior by keeping things you don't want your puppy to chew on—what we call destructive chewing—out of reach and by giving her approved chews and praising her for using them—constructive chewing.

One of the oldest pieces of pet advice in the world is to not give your puppy things that are like the objects you want her to leave alone. In other words, don't give her an old athletic shoe to chew on and expect her to leave your new ones alone. Some objects—like table legs—are not capable of being picked up and put away. Discourage chewing on these by applying Bitter Apple spray (available in pet supply stores) to favorite spots—the taste is so horrible your puppy won't put a tongue on it again.

Remember that puppies must chew. If you catch yours chewing on something you don't want her to, don't make a big deal out of it. Clap your hands, give her an approved toy or treat, and cue her by giving her a short phrase to associate, like "good chew." Then praise her for using it.

Never give a puppy free run of the house, allowing her to make her own decisions on what is and isn't chewable. If you cannot observe her, put her in a safe area—a crate, ideally, but also a small area like a laundry room with a baby gate across the door. Make sure that you leave a chew toy or a food puzzle or both!

Think cool when it comes to puppy's painful gums. The indestructible Kong dog toy—truly a pet toy Hall of Famer—can likewise be stuffed with peanut butter and chilled. I also like the Squirrel Dude toy for stuffing and freezing.

Improper Greetings: Sniffing and Jumping

What do dogs do when they meet? They touch noses, then sniff under the tail and check out each other's privates. Doing so is natural, normal, and unstoppable canine greeting behavior, and yet we insist our dogs do not use it on us. We don't want dogs who stick their noses in people's crotches (along with our mouths, where the largest concentration of our scent is), and we don't want dogs who jump up to touch our noses. The former we consider merely disgusting; the latter could be downright dangerous, with children or people who are unsteady on their feet.

Of course it's not your dog's fault that he was born unprepared to deal with a species who prefers a handshake to a butt sniff, and whose noses are so far off the ground you just have to jump to be friendly!

These problems are fixed by redirection and consistency. When your puppy jumps up, ask her to sit and wait. Turn away to cut off the attention. When she sits, praise and treats!

Barking

Some breeds and breed types are noisier than others. Terriers and poodles and their mixes can be truly obnoxious yappers. Beagles and other hounds have a voice that is considered music in the field, but a nuisance in the home. Some barking is trained into puppies by owners who aren't thinking about what they're doing when raising their puppy. Puppy barks for attention, owners pick him up. Puppy barks for toy, or treat, and gets it.

Never yell at a puppy who's barking—he'll think you're joining in, too—and don't reward him for barking by giving him what he wants. One method that works is to put the barking on a switch—teach your puppy to bark on cue. When you know your puppy is probably going to bark, give a command and, when that bark comes, praise as if it's all a plan that came together. Your puppy will soon make the connection. Once that switch is installed, you control it. Get your puppy's attention and ask for a sit instead. A dog who sits for what he wants is a lot nicer to live with than one who barks for it.

Nipping and Biting

Nipping and biting are serious, serious stuff, and you need to take them that way. Like jumping up and sniffing privates, dogs display this behavior naturally with each other, roughhousing with teeth fully—but gently—in play. That's fine for playing with dogs, but not for playing with people—our skin's a lot more tender, and without a protective layer of fur. Puppies need to learn it's never, ever appropriate to use teeth on a human being. Not in play. Not ever.

All puppies nip, but some are worse than others. Those who were removed from their litters too young may never have learned how much those little teeth hurt and may be more inclined to use them than a puppy who was allowed to stay with his littermates for at least seven weeks. You can get this point across to the youngest puppies in the same way their littermates do—by crying out sharply and dramatically when those needle teeth touch your skin and stopping playing.

For some puppies, that may be enough. For others, you need to do more. Correct sharply with a no for nipping, stop play immediately, and put her in her crate to think about it for a while. If you can't seem to stop your puppy from nipping and biting—and especially if the behavior is accompanied by growling—consult a trainer right away. Private consultation early on can prevent a tragedy later.

Click with Your Puppy!

When you're looking for an easy way to train your pet, it doesn't get much better than clicker training. The no-force technique works on animals of all sizes, ages, and abilities. And that's true of the people who would administer clicker training, since it doesn't require strength or much coordination on the part of the trainer.

Best of all: it's fun for trainer and pet alike.

A clicker is a small plastic box that fits in the palm of your hand—a child's toy that's also called a cricket. To make the noise, you press down on the metal strip inside the housing and quickly release it—*click-click!*

The clicker itself doesn't have any magic powers. What it provides is timing—it allows a trainer working with a dog who understands the game to let the pet know that the behavior he's doing right now is the one that's being rewarded. And that means the behavior will be repeated. The clicking noise becomes a reward because in the early stages of training the sound is linked to the delivery of something a dog wants, most usually a tiny treat. Later, praise mostly with the occasional tasty tidbit.

(Continued)

Does this sound familiar? Like from a psychology class, perhaps? It should ring a bell, because the underlying principle of clicker training is scientific and is called operant conditioning (Pavlov's drooling dogs and all). But you can be excused if you don't want to know the ins and outs of the science and just want to cut to the chase.

After all, your pet just wants to get to the good part, too.

You start by teaching your pet that a click means a treat. Pick a time when your pet isn't sleeping (not just after a meal) and is a little hungry (a couple of hours before a meal). Choose a relatively small, quiet place you can work without too many distractions, and prepare a pouch or bowl of tiny, yummy treats. (Diced turkey hot dogs are popular, as are pieces of turkey bologna, cheese, or even bits of doggy jerky treats.) For the next few minutes, click and treat. One click, one treat. Again, and again, and again. Eventually your pet will show you he understands that the sound means food. For example, he may look immediately to the source of the treats after hearing the click.

When that happens, you're on to the next stage. But wait until your next session, because clicker training works best with a couple of short sessions—less than ten minutes—every day.

When you're all set up again, sit quietly with your clicker and treats—and wait. Your dog should start volunteering behaviors, everything from sitting to pawing to wandering in a circle. When your pet chooses one you like, click, treat, and wait again. Your dog will initially be confused but should eventually offer the behavior again. Be patient! When that moment comes, click, treat, and wait again.

Say you clicked your dog a couple of times because he finally got bored and sat. Soon your dog will sit to test his theory that sitting means a click-treat. When that happens, click and "jackpot" him with a handful of treats. When the pattern is firmly established, you can then give it a name ("sit") and make the food reward more random to strengthen it. (This is the principle that keeps you playing the slot machine.)

In future sessions you'll move on from the sit that your dog knows, waiting for more behaviors to click, treat, and name (such as down, roll over, speak), as you build your pet's repertoire of commands. More complicated behaviors are trained by "chaining"—training in pieces and putting them together. Sit, down, roll over.

One more thing: Never punish your pet for not getting it right. In gambling, the one-armed bandit never slaps you because you pushed the buttons wrong. Clicker training is all about the payoff, and once you get it mastered, there's no end to the things you can teach your dog to do.

Clicker training uses the science of operant conditioning to teach dogs small elements that are then linked together into ever more complex behaviors. The technique is easy to use once you master the basics and is so powerful that animals from chickens to dogs to marine mammals are trained in this way with no physical force.

Chapter 12

TRAINING FOR GOOD DOGS

Don't think of training your dog as a "you versus your dog" endeavor. Think instead about the two of you being on the same team, albeit in different positions. Consider yourself the quarterback, if you like: you call the plays. Maybe you've noticed that the quarterback doesn't get very far without folks to follow those plays. Winning is a team effort.

Of course, your dog has to learn the plays first, and you're the one to teach him. And this relationship is still not an adversarial one. You show your dog the things he needs to learn, and you do so with love and respect, which your dog will return in kind.

To bring your dog onto your team and show him the plays you'll be calling, you need to spend time with him. Bring him into your life. Let him sleep in a crate in your bedroom; practice his sits in the kitchen. The more opportunities for interaction and practice you have, the faster and more reliably your dog performs.

STARTING OUT RIGHT

Go in with the right attitude and you'll get a lot further with your dog. Forget about being dominant—training is about communicating and celebrating a partnership with your pet. Here are the foundations on which to build.

Be Positive

This tip goes back to having the right attitude, of course, but it's more than that. Praise and treats that are well timed and appropriate are essential to your dog's learning process. If all you ever do is tell your dog no, your relationship isn't going to be a very good one. How would you like to work with a boss like that or have had parents with those methods of child raising?

Praise is cheap—free, in fact!—so use it lots. Use praise when your dog tries to get it right. Use it more when your dog succeeds. Use it when your dog just pays attention to you, because as you find out in a moment, that's the first step in the training.

Treats! Which Ones and How Much?

Let your dog be your guide when choosing training treats. Use the most delicious food in the smallest amounts possible. Some dogs will work for little bits of carrots, some for slivers of boiled chicken, others get shivers for slices of lean turkey deli meats, while other easy keepers perform for their regular kibble or commercial treats.

Do realize, though, that you need to cut back on the overall portion you feed your dog when you're giving lots of treats, especially if you have a small dog. Otherwise, you're going to have a fat dog very soon!

Be Fair with Corrections

Make sure your dog understands what you want before you correct him for not doing it. And let the punishment fit the crime.

A correction should not be a release of anger, a clearing out of pent-up feelings by unloading them on the apparent cause of the problem, your dog. Instead, a correction is another way to communicate with your dog, to foster in him a clear understanding of his place in your human pack. As such, a proper correction is another way to strengthen the bond between you and your pet.

For many pets, the absence of praise is correction enough. For others, a verbal correction—*arrggh!* or *NO!*—and then an opportunity to do the right thing is right. Never, ever hit or hurt your dog. It's not necessary, and it's not called for. And it may well make a bad situation far worse. For example if you follow Grandma's advice and whack your dog with a newspaper or rub his nose in a house-soiling accident, the next time the dog has to go he might very well hide from you to do his duties so that he doesn't get punished.

Be Consistent

How would you do in your job if your boss kept changing the names of your tasks, asked you to do two things at once, and asked you to do the same task differently on a whim? Or had different rules for different places and times? It would drive you nuts, wouldn't it? And yet, that's exactly what people do to their dogs, all the time. Here are some things to think about:

Training consistency. Two things to remember: After your dog knows a behavior, use it the same way each time and never change its meaning. The most common of these is probably saying "sit down" to a dog when you really mean "sit." Now, you know when someone says that to you, it's the same thing as "sit." But if you teach your dog "sit" and "down" as two separate commands, you can understand why it's confusing. Which do you want?

Another kind of training inconsistency is when you never expect your dog to mind until you've repeated the command a few times. Instead of teaching your dog to mind, you teach her that she doesn't even have to pay attention until the veins start popping out on your neck. After a dog knows a command, always insist that she execute the behavior. It's not like being in a foreign country where speaking louder makes understanding easier. Don't repeat the command. Wait if needed. She heard you the first time.

Situational consistency. People who compete with their dogs in obedience trials have a word for dogs who know they can get away with disobedience in certain situations—they call them ringwise. Because the rules say you can't correct your dog in the competition ring, some dogs realize they can get away with murder. (*Hahaha, and she can't stop me, because that person with the clipboard won't let her!* thinks the dog.)

Like the ringwise obedience-trial competitor, a lot of dogs learn to recognize situations where they can get away with murder. They learn, for example, that you're timid about enforcing the rules in public, lest someone glare at you for correcting your dog. Or maybe that when you're in a hurry you'll shrug off disobedience: you're in a rush to feed your dog, for example, and when you say "sit," he doesn't. And you throw the food down anyway.

If "sit" doesn't always mean "sit," eventually it will never mean "sit." Don't put up with these games.

Build on Your Successes

Dog training succeeds by degrees and creativity. You continue to expand the length of time and the number of situations in which your dog will perform a behavior, and you look for new ways to use what he knows so you can continue to develop and strengthen the bond between you.

Ask your dog for what you want in a sensible, no-nonsense tone loudly and clearly enough for your dog to hear—but never yell. Don't whine a command—"Tiiiigerrrrr, ssiiiiiiiitttttttt, baayaaabbbyyy"— and don't say it angrily or rough. Ask once—a command, not a suggestion—as if you are confident your dog is listening, and she's more likely to do so.

Teach the Basics

How often should you train your dog? When you're trying to introduce something new, short lessons twice a day are ideal. You don't have to teach everything at once just because you're in a five- or six-week obedience class. Just do the sit twice a day for a week, if that's all you have time for. Then train the down, and so on. Just be—oh here's that word again—consistent. If you take up the same lesson for a day or two and then drop it for two weeks, you'll never get anywhere. After your dog knows the command, look for every opportunity to practice—and praise.

Walk this way. Walking on a loose leash is one thing all pet owners want from their dogs. All dogs may go to Heaven, but it's a sure bet that only the ones who walk calmly on a leash get to go to many places here on Earth.

It's natural for dogs to pull, but this can be dangerous for both pet and owner. Pulling on the leash can injure the dog, hurting his neck, shoulder, front legs, and more. And people have suffered broken bones and strained muscles trying to control untrained dogs. Humans pull away from pressure but dogs pull against it. It's called the oppositional reflex and works great if you're a sled dog in the Iditarod. If you're a dog in suburbia, it's a one-way ticket to the shelter.

Traditionally, training a dog to walk on a loose leash required a show of strength, perfect timing, and a willingness to teach the dog that the consequence of pulling was pain. Today, trends in training emphasize a less physical, more dog-friendly approach that encourages and rewards cooperation.

Start with the dog sitting in front of you on a standard six-foot leash attached to a buckled collar. Put a treat in front of your dog's nose and back up so he follows it. After a few steps, turn so that you're walking forward with the dog at your side. Take a few more steps, stop, have the dog sit, and give him the treat. Any time he charges ahead, back away and offer the treat again so he turns and follows.

Certain products can help with control. Many trainers, for instance, recommend front-clip harnesses (which I love!), which use a dog's own momentum to impede his forward progress and stop the pulling. Head halters may help dogs with more complicated problems than mere pulling, such as excessive barking and hyperactivity.

Sit. Take the slack out of the leash with your right hand, but don't tighten it. Then, spread the index finger and thumb of your left hand and place them on either side of your dog, just in front of his hip bone, with the underside of your finger and thumb resting on his back. Say "sit" and exert gentle pressure inward and down. He should fold up like a folding chair into a sit to avoid the pressure, and when he does, even if only for a minute, praise.

Some trainers prefer to tuck, and that's fine, too, if this method works for your dog. Slide your hand over his rump and apply pressure to the back of his legs right at the bend, tucking his legs and tail comfortably beneath him. Praise and treat!

If you're using the clicker, you don't even have to touch your dog. Eventually your dog will sit, and you can click that behavior to establish it.

Sit is the number one thing all dogs know; even most shelter dogs who have no other training know it! What's great about sit is that you can use it to steer your dog away from other problems. Ask your dog to sit before you give him a treat, a toy, open the door, put on a leash. Ask him to sit instead of jumping up. It's magic!

Down. Down builds on sit. Make sure your dog is cool with that first. Start with the dog sitting at your left side with the slack taken out of the leash. Take a treat and hold it between your dog's front legs, asking for a down. When he follows the treat to the ground, praise and reward.

Wait. This is different from stay because the dog is not required to hold a position, just not cross an imaginary line of your choosing. To teach this command, position your dog in a doorway, call his name, say "wait," and draw your hand from frame to frame in front of his eyes. Walk back into the room and allow him to move around, and then step back out through the doorway. If he follows across the imaginary line, give a voice correction, repeat the command and hand signal. When you're done, give your release word, let him cross the line, and praise.

This command has many uses. Your dog should wait when you open the car door, so he doesn't jump out into traffic. Dogs wait before entering people's homes or leaving their own.

Go to your bed. This one builds on down, but is not so formal. It means "go there and plant it, pal," and is a great command for getting your dog out from underfoot. Call your dog's name, tell him to "go to your bed," lead him there, and tell him "down." With practice—and consistency, the down becomes automatic.

"Bad" dogs can usually be turned around with training, exercise (of mind and body), and the substitution of an acceptable behavior for an unwanted one, such as asking a dog to sit instead of allowing him to jump up on people.

Chapter 13

FIXING A "BAD" DOG

Dogs don't know guilt. They don't know a behavior is bad until you teach them so, and they don't know how to be spiteful. They're just being dogs. They live in the now, and revenge is not in their gene pool. Barking, chewing, and digging are another story: they're natural, normal behaviors, part of every dog's DNA.

Which means a lot of the motives some people attribute to dogs for their behavior just can't be. They don't chew because they're mad at you for leaving them. They chew because they're stressed about being alone; chewing fills the time and makes them feel better.

You're the one with the big brain and opposable thumbs. Don't lose your temper and don't punish your dog. Read up, and fix the problems.

TAKE STOCK AND TAKE ACTION

Talking to your veterinarian is always the best place to start when you're struggling with a behavior problem. That's because the first step to solving a behavior problem is to make sure that it's not a health problem, especially if nothing has changed in your life except suddenly you have a dog problem. For example, a dog who starts throwing fits when you try to brush out the mats that form in the feathery hair behind his ears may have a painful ear infection. Two more examples:

some kinds of chewing can be attributed to nutritional deficiencies, and some house-soiling problems can be the result of a chronic or metabolic disease that needs to be managed or a curable infection that needs to be treated. It's not uncommon for a dog to start house-soiling because hidden arthritis-of-the-back problems make it too painful to climb steps or go outside to potty.

Don't guess at the problem and throw a home remedy at it. See your veterinarian. You'll probably save money in the long run, and you'll certainly spare your pet some misery.

After your dog checks out okay on the medical front, you need to start addressing the other necessities of his life:

❧ **Mental exercise.** Training is for life. Your dog needs to keep learning and keep using all he has been taught. That doesn't mean, however, that you have to make formal obedience sessions a permanent part of your life. Think instead of creative ways to expand your dog's working vocabulary and integrate the skills he has learned into your life together. When you play fetch, vary the routine: Make him do a sit or down before you take the ball from him. Put him on stay, throw the ball, then send him. Have two family members play recall games with him in the house: one calls and praises, then the other does. These games keep him engaged, and they also help enforce his place in your family, which makes him feel confident and secure.

❧ **Physical exercise.** Probably one of the biggest contributors to dog behavior problems is that dogs don't get nearly enough exercise. (Lack of exercise is also a big contributor to health problems: too much food and not enough exercise make dogs fat.) By enough exercise I don't mean a walk around the block, stopping and sniffing at every shrub, streetlight, and fire hydrant. These outings are important, too, for your dog's mental health, not his physical one.

Your dog needs thirty to forty minutes of aerobic exercise that gets his heart pumping, and he needs it three or more times a week to stay fit, burn excess energy, and alleviate the stresses of modern life, which for many dogs starts with being a latchkey pup. This kind of exercise is especially important for dogs with a working heritage such as sporting or herding breeds. They need to move!

MANAGING THE ENVIRONMENT

Sometimes the answer isn't training the dog; it's training the rest of the family. If you have a dog who keeps getting in the trash, the behavior is so rewarding that retraining may be very difficult. Instead, getting a lidded can or putting the can in a cupboard is the easy way to fix the problem.

Sometimes doing things a little differently just makes sense with a dog in the house. If you don't want your dog retrieving your dirty laundry, keep it in a closed hamper. If you have allergies and need your bedroom to be a no-pet-zone, keep the door closed. Not that I want to add even more to the toilet seat wars that rage in some households, but if you want to know how to keep your dog from drinking out of the toilet, how about trying the obvious: close the lid. (Come to think about it, that solves the human gender war over this issue, too.)

Some adjustments are forever, some not. When you have a dog who goes nuts when you leave her alone, the answer—while you're building up her confidence and taking care of her exercise needs, of course—is

Litter Off-Limits

Another problem where an adjustment is in order: dogs who love to snack from the litter box (which is most of them, really). As veterinarians we call them "litter-box crunchies" or, my favorite, "Kitty Rocca." Put your cat's litter box in a place where the cat has access and the dog does not. One of the cleverest things I've seen in a long time is the AirCatditioner, a product that looks like a window-unit air conditioner but is really a clever hideaway for a litter box. You can also find furniture—some of it very attractive—that hides the litter box so you can't see it and your dog can't get into it!

not to give her more choices, but less. That may mean putting her in a crate with a chew toy while you're gone and then slowly building up the space available to her, room by room.

SWITCH BEHAVIORS

Instead of jumping on your dog for what he can't chew, show him what he's allowed to chew and praise him for doing so. Make his toys more appealing than your shoes or the remote control. One tactic is to take an almost destruction-proof Kong toy and put Kong Stuffing (in a can like spray cheese) or a little wipe of peanut butter inside it. Your dog stays busy for hours.

Another kind of substitution is to put an activity you approve of in the place of one you do not. For example, teach the dog who jumps up on people that sitting, not jumping, gets her the attention she's looking for. And be consistent: if you don't want your dog to jump up in greeting, don't ever let her. No fair saying that jumping is okay when you're in jeans but not when you're dressed for an evening out. It's also not ever acceptable to jump up on a UPS deliveryperson and not on your neighbor or visiting relative.

LET THE LESSON COME FROM ELSEWHERE

You can help steer your dog away from inappropriate behavior by making the objects you want to protect do their part to discourage your dog. You can do so in three ways:

1. Make the object taste bad. Coat the object with something dogs find hateful, such as Bitter Apple, available in any pet supply store. Tabasco sauce is another disagreeable taste to dogs. No matter what you choose, remember to test it on a small area first, in case the product you use causes a staining problem.
2. Make the object startle him. Balloons, shake cans (soda cans filled with a few pennies or small stones), and mousetraps make sharp noises that startle your dog and help him decide that maybe he'd

better leave the booby-trapped area alone. Some products give off a piercing noise when motion is detected near them, and these can work, too. (The mousetrap won't hurt your pet: it's the noise of it snapping shut and the motion that scares him.)

3. Make the object shocking. Vinyl mats and strips that give off a tiny static shock can be very effective in teaching dogs to stay off furniture and countertops. If your local pet supply store doesn't have them, search online pet retailers. The Scat Mat is one such product.

A QUICK TAKE ON THE BIGGEST COMPLAINTS

Ready to problem-solve? Let's see how your new skills apply to some of the things that really endanger dog's lives by putting them at risk for needing a new home.

Barking

This one puts your dog at risk from the people in your neighborhood. The purchase of barking deterrents that make an unpleasant noise if a neighbor's pet barks or, worse yet, the poisoning of a nuisance barker is all too common. Even if your neighbors aren't the kind to take things into their own hands, a barking dog can run you afoul of the law, and not dealing with the situation marks you as an irresponsible and inconsiderate dog owner.

Dogs bark to express a variety of emotions: anxiety, boredom, territoriality, aggression, playfulness, and hunger, to name a few. In addition, barking sessions can be triggered by certain conditions in the dog's environment. For example, a dog who barks a warning when strangers are near will bark constantly and frantically if one side of the fence in his yard separates his area from a well-traveled, public sidewalk. Likewise, an intelligent, high-energy dog, neglected and bored in a lonely backyard, often rids himself of that excess energy by indulging in barking sessions that can last for hours, day or night.

Breed characteristics factor in, as well. Expecting an arctic breed or mix not to engage in an occasional howl—or a hound not to give voice when on the trail of a squirrel or rabbit—is unrealistic. Some herding dogs drive livestock by nipping and barking at their heels, and even their suburban relations many generations removed from the farm may still yap joyfully at the heels of the family's children at play.

Figure out the kind of barking your dog indulges in. Is he a fence runner, trading insults with the dog on the other side of the back fence? Consider reworking the yard to deny him access to that activity. Is he a bored outside dog? Make him a part of your life, bring him into the house, and make sure that the needs for physical and mental stimulation are being met. Another advantage of having him in the house: many of the sounds that trigger barking are masked inside. (You can help this masking even further by leaving a radio on when you leave.)

Train him not to bark by teaching him the "quiet" or "enough" command. Allow him a bark or two—let him get his point across—then say (don't yell) "enough" and put your hand over his muzzle. Praise him for stopping. If he's loose, you can also get the point across with a shot from a spray bottle. Allow him a bark or two, say "enough," squirt, then praise him for stopping.

It's not a quick fix—you still have to address the underlying problems of boredom, stress, and inactivity—but one kind of training collar offers real promise in fighting the battle of the bark—the spray collar. Unlike traditional collars that deliver a small shock, a spray collar shoots a blast of citrus scent, which is both annoying and distracting.

Digging

Filling up the holes and putting an inflated balloon or the dog's own feces inside is one oft-touted solution that can help—assuming your dog's not into eating stools; many are—but digging is a classic case where looking at the bigger picture is essential. If your dog is left outdoors while you're gone—or all the time—and never gets worked or exercised, he'll destroy your yard. Add to that the fact that some dogs—such as terrier types (terrier comes from "terra," or "earth")— simply live to dig dirt, and suddenly that your yard is as hole-y as Swiss cheese becomes no surprise. Northern breeds such as huskies are also notorious diggers.

Three things that can help: Work and exercise your dog. Limit his unchaperoned access to the parts of the yard you'd like preserved. And give him an area where digging is okay or even—dare I say it?—rewarded with praise or treats.

Destructiveness When Left Alone

This is the classic problem with the dog you adopt as an adult. He's had his heart broken once and his hopes rekindled, by you. And then you leave him and he copes with his anxiety—will you ever return?—by going nuts and chewing, most typically on or near the area you left from (exit doors and door frames are common targets). We call it the Unwanted Extreme Home Makeover!

You help build his confidence by getting him into a routine and by training him. You relieve some of that excess energy by exercising him. And finally, while the cure is working from the inside out, you minimize the damage potential by confining him to a crate or small space.

A few other tips for dealing with separation anxiety:

* Feed your dog his biggest meal before he's about to spend his biggest chunk of time alone. What dogs do after they eat is sleep, and if you're lucky, he'll sleep most of the time you're gone.
* Give him something special to chew on just as you leave. Have a really good chewy that's just for his alone time, and hand it to him as you leave. He may even become a little glad to see you go!
* Leave a radio on to mask outside noises. Something soothing, please. Classical music. Your dog's anxious enough without having to listen to talk radio.
* Desensitize your dog. There are almost always triggers that cause a doggy destruction crew to rev up, including but not limited to: putting on your work shoes or coat, grabbing a briefcase, taking out the car keys, grabbing your travel coffee mug. Take out your keys, walk around, put them back. Put on your shoes and coat and just walk

around the house. Even fill your coffee mug, go out, and start the car, but rather than leaving you come back in the house.

☙ Also practice no-fuss comings and goings. Some people unwittingly make matters worse by making hellos and good-byes high drama. New rule: no pats. When you leave, tell your dog "guard the house" and give him his special chewy—it makes him feel important. When you return, tell him to "sit," and then praise slightly—I mean very slightly—and ignore him for the next ten minutes. Read your mail, check your answering machine, visit the bathroom. And then sit down, call him to you, and tell him how your day went. The message here is that all this in-and-out is no big deal, so chill already.

In some cases, behavioral modification and exercise are not enough. In fact, I have a shelter rescue, Quora, who needs medication (a doggy form of Prozac called Reconcile) along with vigorous exercise and behavior modification to keep her from morphing into Emelda Barkos (shoe fetish), a furry wrecking ball when we leave. Ask your veterinarian.

BITING

Aggression in dogs has both genetic factors and learned ones. Some dogs are born with the potential to be aggressive, and that potential can be fully realized in a home that is either encouraging aggressive behavior or ill-equipped to cope with it. Other perfectly nice dogs can become unreliable because of abusive treatment.

If you think your dog will bite, you're probably right. If he has bitten, he'll bite again. A dog who has killed another animal or has threatened or bitten a human is not a candidate for home training. Talk to your veterinarian immediately for a referral to a trainer or behaviorist who can evaluate your dog and outline your options.

Aggression never goes away on its own. You need help, now, before your dog seriously injures somebody and you face a loss of insurance or an expensive lawsuit.

Get Help, Already

If you're finding yourself getting frustrated to the point of giving up your dog, you're past the stage when you should have asked for help. There have never been more dog trainers than there are now, and the trend has long been toward not punishing dogs but teaching owners how to praise and treat their way to good behavior, including how to set limits and manage for success.

Ask your veterinarian for a referral to a trainer or behaviorist at the first sign of a problem, not at the breaking point. You may not want to spend the money, but getting help is cheaper than replacing your couch, and a far better option than plastic surgery after a bite.

Trainers can handle most problems, especially those that need some basic lessons in dog management for you and basic good behavior for your dogs. A couple in-home sessions can help get you and your dog on the right track.

For more difficult problems, you may be best served going to a veterinarian trained in solving behavior problems. These veterinary specialists will lay out a program for you and your dog to resolve a specific issue, and may prescribe medications for the short-term to bridge the gap, or the long-term to help manage a problem for life.

In either case, ask your veterinarian for referrals.

The better your dog's manners, the more likely you are to make him a part of your life, including taking him everywhere with the rest of the family.

Chapter 14

OUT AND ABOUT

One of the best things about living with a dog is doing things together. Having a dog is the perfect path to an active life of play, walks, hikes, games, and more. People who have dogs exercise more, stay in better shape, and have more entertaining social lives. I want you to get the most out of your relationship with your dog, and one of the best ways you can do that is to have fun with him, as well as to help him have fun when you're not around. Here are some of the best ways to do that.

DOG PARKS: THE GOOD AND THE UGLY

Who doesn't love a dog park? A wide-open grassy space where dogs can run and play freely while their people sip lattes and exchange advice on care and behavior of their furry four-footers. Dog parks have many benefits, but there's a lot to consider before you turn your dog loose in one.

First, the advantages. Regular playdates with other dogs are a great way to keep your dog active and entertained. That's especially important if you have an only dog. Park playdates help your singleton learn proper canine etiquette from his peers.

If you don't have much of a yard, or any yard at all, a nearby dog park is a super substitute where your dog can leap after a flying disc, fetch tennis balls until your arm gives out, or just plain run flat out. More sedate or scent-oriented dogs will enjoy meandering along, sniffing the pee-mails left by previous canine visitors.

Some parks are divided into areas for big dogs and little dogs. That means you don't have to worry that your petite Petunia will be pummeled by more active dogs who don't even notice that they're about to run her down. Other positive features include a fence, trap gates to prevent escape, and trees or other shaded areas.

What's not so great about dog parks? For one thing, they can be reservoirs for disease. Kennel cough and canine influenza are just two of the diseases that can spread rapidly through a dog park population. If your dog frequents a dog park, ask your veterinarian about vaccinations for Bordetella and canine influenza. You may also want to look for a dog park that requires people to apply for membership and supply proof of vaccination for rabies, parvovirus, distemper, and adenovirus-2 (hepatitis and respiratory disease). Avoid dog parks until your puppy has completed his vaccinations at sixteen to eighteen weeks of age.

Some dogs are not suited to dog park visits. They are unfriendly, untrained, or were poorly socialized as puppies. They don't know how to interact properly with other dogs or people, and taking them to a dog park won't magically cure their aggression or shyness. And certain breeds, such as flock-guarding dogs, are territorial, even with socialization. They just don't play well with others. They can enjoy dog parks as puppies, but once they hit adolescence, most owners curtail the visits.

Dog Park Manners

The rules of etiquette aren't meant to restrict the behavior of people and dogs but to make everyone happy and comfortable. Follow some simple guidelines to help keep interactions friendly, fun, and healthy.

- Take only friendly, well-trained dogs to the park.
- Keep your dog on leash until you are inside the park and for a few minutes afterward until you assess what the other dogs are like and how he gets along with them.
- Limit your dog's play to friends of her own size. Your little Stella might be used to running with the big dogs, but in a group things can go south in a hurry. You never know when a dog with a high prey drive will decide that Stella looks like a bunny.
- Skip the park visit if your female dog is in season.
- Bring water for your dog so he doesn't have to use a communal water dish and run the risk of exposure to disease.
- Don't lose sight of your dog while you're talking with others. You should always know where he is, what he's doing, and who he's with.
- Pay attention to canine body language, and don't let rough play get out of hand. Pinned ears, a lowered tail, and raised hackles are signs that trouble is brewing.
- If your dog behaves aggressively or starts a fight, apologize and take him home.
- Pick up after your dog and dispose of the waste in a trash can.
- Leash your dog before exiting the park. Even the best-trained dogs can unthinkingly give chase if they see something interesting.
- Keep your dog at home if he's not feeling well, especially if he is coughing, vomiting, or has diarrhea. Spreading disease to other dogs is not cool.

TIME FOR A ROAD TRIP

Have you ever seen the way a dog's face lights up when you ask him if he wants to go for a ride? That tail becomes a blur and he starts doing a furry tap dance in the canine body language that means *Yes! Yes! Yes!*

Most dogs love to travel. My theory is that it's a throwback to the days when people and dogs migrated from place to place, following the herds in search of food. Maybe deep down in their genetic code, dogs still think that going somewhere ultimately results in a good meal. Whatever the case, they are usually up for a car trip or other journey— especially if it means they get to spend time with their beloved people.

Lots of us travel with our canine pals to competitions or simply on vacation. Here are some tips for taking your dog along. Follow them, and airlines and hotel managers will welcome you back any time.

Get Packin'

Don't leave home without food and water dishes, a couple of your dog's favorite toys, essential grooming tools, and treats. You'll also need plastic bags for picking up waste, and it's always a good idea to travel with a supply of paper towels and your favorite enzymatic stain and odor remover.

If your dog likes sharing the furniture with you, pack several large flat sheets to throw over the bed or sofa so he doesn't embellish them with dog hair or drool.

Take enough dog food, plus a little extra, to get you to your destination. If your dog eats a boutique brand, check the company's website beforehand to find out where you can purchase it on the road. If you feed a frozen diet, call and ask if there's a refrigerator in your room or if the lodging will store your dog's food elsewhere for you until you

Doggie Details

Changes in drinking water can upset your dog's stomach and lead to diarrhea. Fill a jug with water from home and gradually mix the water from your vacation spot with the water from home so his gastrointestinal system has time to adjust. If it's summertime, you can even freeze a couple of gallon jugs of water and put them in the car for the dogs to curl up around to keep cool or for a drink of cold water along the way.

need it. Don't forget measuring cups for scooping kibble into a bowl or a spoon for serving up canned food.

Bring any medication your dog needs, plus a copy of the prescription in case you need to get a refill during the trip. In case you're asked, have a copy of your dog's vaccination records or a letter from your veterinarian confirming that his immunizations are up to date. Scout out veterinary emergency hospitals at your destination beforehand, or ask your vet to recommend a colleague in the area. Being prepared with this information will make things easier if your dog unexpectedly becomes ill or injured.

For safety in the car and confinement in the hotel room, bring your dog's crate. In the car, attach a crate fan to help keep your dog cool. Older dogs and dogs with flat faces can quickly succumb to extremes of heat and cold.

When bringing a crate isn't possible, consider purchasing a doggy hammock or car seat. It gives your dog a comfy resting spot, protects the car's upholstery from dog hair, and doubles as a bed in the hotel room. Choose one that allows you to protect your dog by restraining him with a canine seat belt.

Think you're ready to go? Wait just a doggone minute. Is your dog wearing the latest in identification? In addition to his high-tech microchip, your dog should wear an ID tag engraved with your cell phone number. If you lose him during the trip, anyone who finds him will be able to reach you right away, wherever you are.

On the Road

If your dog has a tendency toward motion sickness, don't feed your dog before the start of the trip. Also, there is a powerful new antinausea medication called Cerenia that I have found to be of great benefit. Ask your veterinarian if it's a good choice for your dog. Giving your dog a ride with a view can also help. Being able to see out the window and feel the breeze often stifles a dog's tendency to upchuck.

When you're driving with a senior dog, schedule plenty of stops so your golden oldie can shake out his legs, especially if he has been riding in a crate. Puppies also need frequent potty breaks.

Jet-Set Pets

Flying to your destination? Be sure the carrier you choose is airline approved. It should fit comfortably beneath the seat with your puppy or toy dog inside it.

Unless he can ride in the cabin with you, flying your dog to a vacation destination may not be the best idea. Dogs riding in cargo can overheat or become chilled, depending on the weather. Short-nosed dogs can suffer breathing difficulties and even die. Many airlines prohibit shipping dogs during summer, when the belly of the plane can overheat. And dogs in cargo run the risk of loss or mishandling by airline personnel.

When travel in cargo is unavoidable, think twice and then again before giving your dog a tranquilizer to keep him calm. Tranquilizers blunt a dog's ability to deal with temperature extremes. They can also have a paradoxic effect, causing pets to become even more anxious than they would have been without the drugs.

One more thing: if you have a short-nosed dog (Bulldog, Pug, Puggle, etc.) I just can't recommend putting your pet in cargo. These dogs account for about half the deaths reported by U.S. airlines. These dogs find it difficult to breathe under normal circumstances, and the stress of air travel is too great for them. If you have a brachycephalic dog and he's not small enough to travel in a carry-on with you, don't put him in cargo. The elevated risk isn't worth it.

Summer Camp

Remember how much fun you had going to camp when you were a kid? Swimming in the lake, going hiking, taking archery lessons? Relive the good times with your dog at a place where both of you can learn some new tricks: dog camp!

During your weeklong stay, you and your dog can try out all kinds of activities, including agility, clicker training, dock diving, freestyle, flying disc play, lure coursing, rally, tracking, and trick training. More laid-back campers can enjoy barks and crafts, power lounging, massage lessons, and canoeing or walking together.

Camp should be fun for both of you, so make sure the accommodations and food match your comfort level and that trainers are enthusiastic and use positive techniques.

Agility is one of many sports open to all breeds and mixes, and it's also one of the most popular. The top dogs work joyfully as a seamless team with their owners. This sport, based loosely on show-jumping in the horse world, has also proven to be a hit with spectators.

Chapter 15

COMPETITION'S FOR FUN

One of the best things about living with a dog is doing things together. Having a dog is the perfect path to an active life of play, walks, hikes, games, and more. People who have dogs exercise more, stay in better shape, and have more entertaining social lives. I want you to get the most out of your relationship with your dog, and one of the best ways you can do that is to have fun with him, as well as to help him have fun when you're not around. Here are some of the best ways to do that.

DOG SPORTS: THE JOY OF ORGANIZED PLAY

Playing with a dog used to mean a game of tug-of-war or fetch. These days, canine sports are televised on ESPN or other networks, and they draw big crowds of spectators. Agility, dock diving, flyball, freestyle, obedience, tracking, and more—there's an activity for every dog.

Canine Good Citizen

Run by the American Kennel Club (AKC), the Canine Good Citizen (CGC) test is where every dog should start his canine sports career. In fact, it's something that every dog, athletic or not, should be able to achieve. The CGC title is awarded to any dog who can demonstrate the manners that make him a great companion and ambassadog for his species.

To earn a CGC, a dog need only pass ten simple tests:

- Respond politely, not maniacally, when approached by a friendly stranger.
- Sit for petting without being either shy or rambunctious.
- Present a healthy, well-groomed appearance (this is more of a test for the owner) and permit the judge to go over him with a brush or comb.
- Walk nicely on a loose lead.
- Walk nicely through a crowd.
- Respond to the sit, down, and stay commands.
- Come when called.
- Behave appropriately around other dogs.
- React calmly to distractions or unexpected noises.
- Stay calmly with a stranger while the owner is out of sight.

During the CGC test, you can pet and praise your dog, but no incentives such as treats or toys are allowed. That's all! Ten easy pieces to what can be your dog's first title.

The CGC is more than a title, by the way: it can help you get rental housing, by showing the property owner that you're a responsible owner.

Get Going, Any Way You Can

I've showcased some of the dog sports that are most open to newbies, but there are dozens of others, including very breed-specific ones such as field trials for hunting dogs or herding trials for, well, mostly Border Collies.

Many people make these competitions their life, and some get quite good at them as a team with their dogs. They end up investing in lessons with coaches, seminars on how to get better, special vehicles for gear, and even lots of gear, such as an entire home agility setup. Of course, I love anything that makes for a closer bond between pet and owner.

But you don't have to do anything organized to have active fun with your dog. You can go on a long wilderness hike in a national forest. Or camping. Or even just get an RV and be snowbirds with your dog, heading south during the winter and north during the summer—it's a life many retirees enjoy and is made better for having a dog along.

The truth is, anything you do with your dog is better than doing it without him. So get active. You and your dog will thrive for it!

Agility

Think of agility as a canine obstacle course with jumps, A-frames, teeter-totters, open and closed tunnels, weave poles, and dog walks (like the balance beam in a gymnastics competition). Agility trials test physical skill, control, patience, and teamwork, and demonstrate canine athleticism, versatility, and speed.

Racing against the clock, dogs directed by their handlers must navigate a challenging course. In each of five height divisions, the winner is the dog with the fastest time and a run free of faults such as knocking over the bar of a jump or missing the contact zone when coming off an obstacle. Any breed or mix can compete in agility, and just about every dog breed has, but medium-sized dogs who are quick and nimble usually do best.

Dock Diving

Splash! For some dogs, there's nothing more fun than running and jumping into a body of water, whether it's a swimming pool, a pond, a lake, or the ocean. Not surprisingly, that love of water has been channeled into competition. It's called dock diving, and it's one of the wettest, wildest dog games around. Your water-loving dog of any breed or mix can compete in three events: Big Air, Extreme Vertical, and Speed Retrieve.

Big Air dogs go for distance. The dog with the longest jump off the end of a dock is the winner. In heats known as waves, the dog runs down the dock, the owner throws a toy out over the water, and the dog jumps in after it. The distance he jumps is measured at the point where the base of his tail hits the water. Each wave consists of two jumps, and the dog has ninety seconds to complete each one. The longer of the two jumps is the official score for that wave.

If you say "Jump" and your dog asks "How high?" Extreme Vertical might be his game. In this event, the dog races down the dock, then leaps up to grab a bumper suspended ten feet above the water. The winner is the dog with the highest-measured jump.

Speed Retrieve is a timed event that calls for the handler to release the dog when a green light comes on. The dog races down the dock, jumps in, and swims to a toy suspended at the end of the pool. When he grabs it and pulls it down, the timer stops. As in Big Air, dogs get two tries, with ninety seconds to complete each run. The fastest of the two runs becomes the official score.

Some dogs are triathletes, competing in all three events. They can earn points toward the Iron Dog title.

Flyball

This simple relay race involves four hurdles and a tennis ball. Two teams race each other over a fifty-one-foot course lined with four jumps. At the end of the course is a spring-loaded box that ejects a tennis ball when the dog steps on a trigger. Catching the tennis ball in his mouth, the dog races back over the hurdles, crossing the starting line before the next dog goes. The first team to run without errors wins.

This is one sport where size doesn't matter. Shorty dogs like Chihuahuas or Papillions can even be an asset to a team. That's because jump height is determined by the height of a team's smallest dog. With a small dog on the team, larger dogs benefit from lower hurdles.

Speedy dogs and dogs who love to retrieve excel at this game, but any dog can play as long as he can learn to jump a hurdle and retrieve a tennis ball. Large and small dogs and dogs of all breeds and mixes can compete together.

Freestyle

Nicknamed "the tail-wagging sport," canine freestyle (also known as musical freestyle or heelwork to music) is a choreographed routine set to music that incorporates elements of traditional canine obedience exercises and the equine sport of dressage.

Almost any dog with a love of the limelight can do freestyle. Young dogs, old dogs, blind dogs, tripods; they're all capable of following in the footsteps of Fred and Ginger, once they've learned a few basic moves.

Freestyle builds on a dog's natural moves such as spins, rolls, jumps, and bows. Freestyle dogs learn to spin in different directions, to jump through or into their partner's arms, to bow before a waltz, to place their paws on an arm or on their partner's back. The only limitations are the dog's own abilities. For instance, breeds with short legs or long backs, as well as dogs younger than fourteen months, should avoid jumping. Once a dog is physically mature, though, freestyle is a great way to help him stay limber throughout his life.

For two-legged team members, it helps to have rhythm and an understanding of choreography. But even if you don't, freestyle is a great way to have fun with a dog right in your own backyard. Or to find a better dance partner than your spouse.

Hanging with the Pack

The world of dog sports used to be a closed-pack situation. Most people had show dogs, and the other sports were all about getting some extra titles or maybe about the challenge. Dog sports were regulated, cliquey, and, well, boring. Heel, sit, stay. Yawn.

But outside the world of the American Kennel Club, people were getting organized to have a lot of fun with their dogs. Agility, an

(Continued)

obstacle course for dogs, is fun for dogs, handlers, and spectators alike. And you'll even see the occasional celebrity: Olympic gold medalist Greg Louganis is a top agility handler, and it's no surprise that he's pretty competitive, although he also has a lot of fun, too.

Flyball, dock diving—these are all sports that started with some dog lovers just having fun. You didn't need pedigree papers to play. You just needed a dog and a good attitude.

The American Kennel Club seems to be catching on. They offer some of these new dog sports, and they're also opening them to mixed breeds. Good on them!

Obedience Trials

This sport tests a dog's abilities at various levels. Dogs competing at the novice level must demonstrate the manners every dog should know, such as heeling, coming when called, sit, down, and stay. More advanced skills include off-leash heeling, dropping to a down position on command, retrieving over a high jump, and a three-minute sit while the handler is out of the dog's sight. The highest level of obedience competition, known as Utility, calls for dogs who can carry out complex commands. They must be able to understand and respond to hand signals only, directing them to perform such actions as sit, stay, down, stand, and come; correctly choose an article with their handler's scent on it; and perform a jump and a retrieve at the handler's direction.

Top obedience dogs perform each exercise in a precise manner. Dogs and handlers must have mental discipline and stamina to be successful in high-level obedience competitions. The most successful breeds are those with a heritage of working closely with people, such as retrievers and herding and working breeds, but just about every breed has at least one representative who has done them proud in obedience trials.

Tracking

Thanks to their great and powerful schnozes, dogs have a natural ability to recognize and follow a human scent trail—or any other scent trail, for that matter. In this activity, the dog leads the way and the handler is only along for the ride. After all, only the dog can identify the presence of the scent and follow it to its conclusion.

The art of following a scent trail is one in which scent hounds such as Bloodhounds, Basset Hounds, and Beagles excel, but every dog has a good sniffer. It's not unusual to see other breeds participate in tracking tests, including toy dogs such as Pugs and Chihuahuas.

Tracking skills are developed through hide-and-seek games at home and practice on different surfaces, including grass, dirt, and asphalt. Dogs can earn tracking titles—Tracking Dog (TD), Tracking Dog Excellent (TDX), and Variable Surface Tracking (VST)—by passing a single tracking test at each skill level.

At the beginner level, the dog must be able to follow a track that is 440 to 500 yards long and between ten minutes and two hours old. A TDX-level track is longer and older, with more turns than a TD track. It may also require the dog to go over physical obstacles, such as fallen trees, or include mental distractions, such as the presence of false scent items along the trail. The VST track is not as long as one for a TDX test, but it goes over three different surfaces in an urban environment rather than a field. For instance, it may take the dog through streets and vacant lots and into buildings.

A dog who earns all three titles becomes a Tracking Champion. Now that's a dog who really knows how to use his nose!

PART FOUR
IN SICKNESS AND
IN HEALTH

I f you've chosen the right dog from the right source and practiced high levels of preventive care from the beginning, you probably won't be spending a lot of time with your veterinarian from the time your puppy is an adult until the onset of middle age.

And by that I mean you've given him nutritious, healthy meals and treats, kept him a nudge on the lean side of normal weight, exercised him regularly in ways that got his heart pounding and limbs moving, prevented accidents through training and by keeping the bad stuff—poisons, speeding cars—out of reach and the good stuff—fences, leashes—in good repair. You've socialized him, trained him, and worked toward a good relationship in which you trust and count on each other. You've kept him clean and well-groomed, with nails trimmed and ears and mouth smelling clean.

Regular checkups to make sure you're not missing anything, along with preventive care such as vaccines, parasite control, daily oral care, dental cleanings as needed, and routine grooming including brushing, bathing, and nail trims, will be all a healthy adult dog requires, for the most part.

"For the most part" is the important part of what you just read, because let's face it: things happen. Some of them are out of your control, written in secret code, which science has yet to decipher, on your dog's DNA—if it ever can be, that is. And what about the accidents—like when the ball takes a funny bounce, and your dog leaps after it, lands awkwardly, and gives a cry of pain that means something is broken or torn? Even "bad design" can throw you for a loop: the ears that hear so much better than our own have ear canals shaped like an L, a natural place for infections, especially when you throw in floppy ears that can make an inner ear like a bacterial petri dish.

Yes, no matter how carefully we try to keep our pets healthy and safe, I can tell you, both as a lifelong animal lover and as a practicing veterinarian, that bad things happen even to good dogs—and good dog owners. The trick to making the best of the bad is knowing when things are going wrong, finding the right veterinarian to help you, and working with that health-care professional to catch problems early, treat what can be treated, manage what can be managed, and lessen the suffering.

That's exactly what this final section is about: how to know when your dog is sick, whether it can wait a day or not, and how to work with your veterinarian to help him feel better. You know this is my life's work, and I want to help you work with a veterinarian who cares as much about your dog as I do!

Your dog's health is served best when you work in partnership with your veterinarian in a relationship where you feel comfortable asking questions and feel confident your concerns are being understood and addressed. Your veterinarian should also not insist on being a "lone ranger" and should refer you to specialists for specific health-care needs your dog has.

Chapter 16

FINDING A GOOD VETERINARIAN

Time passes at such a crazy pace—and if age creeps up swiftly on us humans, then it practically gallops as it makes its mark on our pets. By the time your dog turns two, he's passed through the canine equivalent of infancy, childhood, and adolescence. By age five, most dogs hit middle age. And at just eight years old, most dogs are seniors—not the kind found on a wild spring break, but the kind that gets the early-bird discount at restaurants.

Because dogs age more quickly than people, they may get illnesses earlier than you'd think. Making sure your dog has regular checkups with the veterinarian is the best way to catch and treat developing health issues before they become serious problems. I recommend twice-yearly wellness visits. Just as in human medicine, veterinary care has come a long way in the ability to detect health problems before they become symptomatic—and to treat many of those problems simply and effectively. That's even true of the thing that scares everyone the most: cancer, which is often very treatable if caught early. Does that surprise you? It shouldn't. The old adage about an ounce of prevention is just as true in your dog's life as it is in your own. Preventive, proactive veterinary care can add years to your dog's life and good health.

The place to start a good preventive-care regimen? With a good veterinarian, of course.

YOUR PARTNER IN YOUR PET'S HEALTH: CHOOSE THE RIGHT VETERINARIAN

Into every dog's life must come a relationship with a special person with some special letters after her or his name—DVM, VMD, or even MRCVS (for veterinarians trained in the UK). For some dogs, the veterinarian is just a vaguely familiar person who gives them treats and rudely palpates their privates once a year. For others, though, this is someone associated with all kinds of discomfort—strange and disturbing odors, barks and howls of unfamiliar dogs, and memories of pain from visits during an illness or following an accident. The veterinarian's office can be a scary place, indeed.

But it doesn't have to be that way, and in fact, it shouldn't be.

Making sure you and your pet have found the right veterinary practice can cut way down on the stress and strain of your dog's visits. Having a practitioner—and indeed a veterinary practice, from front desk to veterinary technicians and more—you can trust and count on when it comes to your dog's health care is essential to your dog having as long, healthy, and happy a life as possible. Because without a well-run practice, an expert team and great veterinarians, neither you nor your pet will be likely to go as often as you need to, and that means less than optimal health for your dog.

What makes a great veterinarian?

It starts with your level of confidence and trust and goes from there.

Does your dog's veterinarian put you at ease?

Do you feel comfortable calling or coming in with any question or concern? Are you taken seriously when you bring your dog in for something nonspecific, like overtiredness, a slight change in bathroom habits, or becoming snippy with the kids?

Does the veterinarian acknowledge your role as "Dogtor Mom" or "Dogtor Dad"?

A good practitioner respects the fact that you are her eyes and ears at home. You're the one who knows your dog's normal habits and attitudes, and you can be trusted to raise an alarm when something is outright wrong or your dog is just a little off.

Do you like the way pets are treated at the practice?

It's fair to expect to feel confidence in everyone from the receptionist to the surgeon in your dog's practice. Ask for a tour of the entire clinic before becoming a client. Beyond reception areas and exam rooms are the areas where the nitty-gritty work of the office takes place, and most veterinarians will be happy to show you around. Employee- and pet-only rooms should reflect the same level of care, compassion, and cleanliness as the ones out front. In fact, they must. I have a mantra that you should demand from veterinarians: that they treat your pet exactly as if you were standing there looking over their shoulder.

Leveling with You: Details Count

As you might imagine, I've seen a lot of veterinary hospitals and clinics, front to back and in every nook and cranny. What always catches my attention when I walk in for the first time is odor—or, better yet, the lack of it.

A veterinary hospital should be what I think of as "odor neutral," which is to say that if I walk in and can smell anything, it doesn't make me happy. I don't want to smell either foul odors or a strong fragrance. Frankly, if I smell something it makes me wonder about how much the hospital cares about its sanitary practices. When I owned veterinary hospitals, I never tolerated bad odors. And even now, when I'm just too busy to own my own hospital, the practices where I work when I'm not on the road are clean as clean can be— and I don't think I could work in them if they weren't.

(Continued)

> Now, I want to confess. Laugh if you want to, but I also can't stand it when diplomas and pictures are crooked in a veterinary practice or lightbulbs are burned out. No, it's not as big an issue as a problem with odors, which may signify a bigger problem with sanitary procedures. But I'm a firm believer that when a hospital's staff pays attention to the smallest of details, they're not as likely to miss things—big or small—when it comes to your pet's care.

Does the practice take your pet's discomfort seriously, whether the pain is physical or mental?

Dogs have huge ranges of pain tolerance and some are more nervous than others, but you want a veterinary practice that works to keep your pet comfortable and pain free. If it's consistent, your veterinarian's work to keep your pet physically and mentally comfortable will help your dog see a trip to the vet as something like a field trip rather than a forced march. When discussing any procedure, surgery, or chronic health condition, pain management should emerge as a priority issue. Ideally, your veterinarian will address both pharmaceutical options and "creature comfort" matters like bed padding or hot water bottles. And your veterinarian will be up-to-date on the new products, such a laser or stem-cell therapy for chronic arthritis.

Is the cavalry on call?

Your veterinary office doesn't have to house a host of specialists to provide top-notch care, but it does need to have good relationships with specialists and a willingness to ask for help if your pet's case gets complicated.

Is there a crisis plan in place?

Even if the office is open only bankers' hours, your practitioner should help you plan for emergencies. Where would you go and who would you call if your dog had an accident at midnight on a Friday, a holiday, or during a natural disaster? You and your veterinarian should be in agreement on how to handle an emergency right from your first appointment.

Does the veterinarian look at whole dog health?

Even if your visit is scheduled because your dog is limping a little or sporting a sore on his nose, a good doctor will take advantage of the up-close-and-personal time to perform a full exam, make a general health assessment, and update your dog's medical information. She will look past obvious problems—the entering complaint or something as obvious as a bleeding wound on a dog—and flip the lip, lift the earflap, check the eyes with an ophthalmoscope, feel the lymph nodes, listen to the heart and lungs with a stethoscope, palpate the internal organs such as the liver, spleen, and bladder, move limbs through their range of motion, and rub her hands on the curvatures of the body. A good vet will treat the problem you brought the dog in for. A great veterinarian will prevent problems when possible, detect other problems at their earliest phase, and always recommend everything you need but only what you need to keep your pet happy and healthy. Put another way, she is a pet advocate.

Does the veterinarian know your dog?

A health professional who knows and remembers your dog (name, sex) and his health and lifestyle is, as they say in the credit card commercials, priceless. Even if you choose a big veterinary practice, try to build a relationship with one person who can serve as a touchstone for your dog's health all his life. If you see your veterinarian away from the practice—at a grocery store, church, or sporting event—and he remembers your pet's name and asks about her, you've got a keeper.

Do you feel that your concerns are addressed, no matter what they're about—costs, billing, care, what food to buy at a place that's convenient for you, options for prescriptions, even waiting time?

While misunderstandings and disagreements are often unavoidable in life-or-death situations, you want to know that your veterinarian and the entire staff is interested in helping your pet—and keeping your business. In the practices where I work we have a philosophy that every client gets treated like number one.

If you're satisfied with all these factors, then congratulations! You've found a strong, capable advocate for your dog's well-being—in sickness and in health.

THE PLACE TO START: THE WELLNESS CHECK

As great as you may be in your role of Dogtor Mom at home, there's no substitute for your dog's regular wellness checks with the vet. When you consider these visits, think of your dog for a second as a trusty, well-loved car. You see it every day—and you know how it looks and how it sounds. But do you really understand what goes on under the hood? Your dog's veterinarian is responsible for checking your dog's internal systems and making sure he's "running right." Long years studying every aspect of animal health and learning the ropes of canine medicine make your dog's veterinarian the pro at not only diagnosing but also anticipating health issues and troubles. Veterinarians know what problems can be triggered at what age. They know specific breed problems to be on the lookout for and may even take steps to delay their onset or start treatment before much damage has occurred. For example, certain breeds of dogs are prone to kidney disease, and traditional kidney function tests detect a problem only after 80 percent of a dog's kidney function has been lost. If we know your breed is at risk we may run a specialized test (called E.R.D., for Early Renal Disease), put the pet on a special diet that requires the kidneys to do very little work, or both.

For most young, healthy dogs, an annual checkup after puppyhood should be enough. Your dog's veterinarian may order basic lab tests to provide baseline information on what's normal for your pet at the time your pet is spayed or neutered, then again at about age five for an early comparison. Some people think a spay/neuter is as routine as a lube/oil/filter change in a car. It's not! This is perhaps the only major surgery your pet will ever have, and it's important to test the function of the organs that will eliminate the anesthetic and catch worrisome problems early on. Every visit, your dog should get a nose-to-toes examination and an objective assessment of his general health and body condition.

If your dog's breed is prone to specific health problems, or if your dog is approaching his senior years, the veterinarian may recommend bringing him in twice a year for routine exams. These semi-annual exams can actually save you money and your pet pain, spotting problems early, and slowing or even stopping some problems of aging for a good long while. When you factor in any increased risk of health problems—be they breed specific or related to old age or environment—frequent wellness checks become the number one tool available to you in keeping your canine companion in good health and saving you money in the long run.

Help Your Pet Stay Calm

First of all, don't feed your dogs for twelve hours before going to the veterinarian. We want them hungry so they respond to food rewards and fasting in case we need to draw a blood sample.

If your dog gets apprehensive about visiting the veterinarian, there are a few tricks you can use to help him relax and even enjoy the experience. For starters, ask your veterinarian for or take a trip to your local pet supply store and pick up a bottle of dog-appeasing pheromones, or DAP. This product is kumbaya in a bottle for dogs and comes in spray bottles, diffusers, or impregnated collars. The scent is a match for a chemical a mama dog secretes to calm her puppies and settle them in to nurse. It's a scent deeply ingrained in your dog's psyche—something that tells him to rest easy and feel secure—and it works on him throughout his life. Dog-appeasing pheromone doesn't have any scent to humans, but you can put it on a bandana for your dog to wear on V-day (veterinarian day,

(Continued)

that is) to ease his stress. If you have a small dog, spritz his travel carrier, too.

In addition to using pheromones to help your dog relax, remember that he takes many of his emotional cues from you. Use your happy voice in the car and in the clinic. Encourage veterinary staff to get in on the act, too. Over time, you can help your pup learn to associate the veterinary office with comfort, not fear—a service you, your dog, and the veterinarian will all appreciate.

If a pheromone spritz, tasty treats, and encouraging words fail to calm an anxious dog, or if you can tell he just doesn't like the vet, don't be afraid to ask them to dim the lights or even switch personnel. At North Idaho Animal Hospital in Sandpoint, Idaho, where I work, if one of us can't win over a pet even with an effort worthy of *The Bachelor* or *The Bachelorette*, we tell the pet owners that we're going to switch with a veterinarian of another gender, and we dim the lights before the entrance. More than half the time the pet ends up being a happy camper.

SO WHAT IS YOUR VETERINARIAN LOOKING FOR?

Normal vitals. Depending on the practice, your veterinarian's technician may get some basic information first, such as if you've noticed anything that's odd or that concerns you. The tech will also get the basics, including weight, before you head into the exam room, then temperature and heart rate, body condition scoring, and dental health. He will also check the status of vaccinations and parasite control. All will be noted in the chart for your veterinarian to discuss with you further if there are problems.

Shiny on the outside. The first, simplest indication of canine good health is a shiny, healthy coat. Some dogs have a luster to their fur that's like a neon sign advertising their vitality. This "Healthy Dog

Here" sign is any veterinarian's first indication that a pup is being fed a high-quality diet and is getting good care and regular grooming at home. It's a low-tech health barometer that has nothing to do with your dog having a fancy 'do—a lustrous coat is still lustrous when it's actively shedding or sporting a smudge of mud from the dog park. It's the canine equivalent of a glowing complexion.

Signs of trouble in your dog's coat can sometimes be masked by normal shedding. Your veterinarian looks beyond the shedding, for lumps or bumps, bare patches, thinning areas, a lack of shine, and any visibly irritated skin. As the person who wields the dog brush at home, you point out any spots of concern.

Walk this way. A dog's gait can tell the story of who she is and how she's feeling. Your dog's veterinarian is looking for surefooted steps and balance. Symmetry is a clue that things are working properly. If your dog favors a leg, doesn't want to stand with equal weight on all fours, walks as if on eggshells, or adopts a bunny-hop gait, your veterinarian may want radiographs to help pinpoint the root of the problem.

An uneven gait doesn't always point to an orthopedic issue—it can also be the first sign of a neurological problem or a symptom of a severe ear infection. If you notice your dog having more difficulty rising to his feet, not wanting to exercise or play as much, not jumping up on the couch or going upstairs, leaning to one side or suddenly seeming clumsy in his walk, be sure to mention it.

Flip the lip. A healthy adult dog has forty-two permanent teeth. If those teeth and the gums and bone that support them are not cared for, the consequences are grim. A healthy mouth is critical for a dog's overall health and happiness because they use their teeth not only to chew but to pick up things (a dog's mouth is like our hands) or to hold their tongue in place while they pant. Not only will a dog with dental disease be in constant pain, but those infected gums become breeding grounds for bacteria that are sent through your dog with every swallow, putting strain on all internal systems. When your veterinarian looks at your dog's mouth, she'll first look for signs of periodontal disease including plaque, tarter (brown mineralized matrix adhered to the outside surface of the tooth), and red, bleeding gums. Then she'll rub her finger along the teeth and gums to feel for lumps and for the roughness that indicates periodontal disease. She'll check for healthy gums that are firm and colored the same as your dog's skin—black, pink, or spotted. Gums should feel equally firm on both sides of the mouth—bleeding or swelling in any area indicates a potential problem.

Doggy breath, believe it or not, should not be repellant—a healthy dog is kissable from nose to, well, just short of the tail, let's say. If your dog's breath makes you gag, you're already looking at dental disease that likely needs your veterinarian's attention, with full cleaning under anesthesia that will include dental radiographs for broken teeth and rotting roots, and may require extractions of teeth too far gone to be saved. Veterinarians not only use special machines to vibrate the tarter off the visible tooth surfaces, they go deep under the gum flaps to root out infection you can't even see with the naked eye. No dog would tolerate this if not anesthetized. Because cleaning leaves the surface of the teeth rough, the next step in a veterinary dental is to polish the teeth so that plaque has a much harder time adhering. The final step is to put a dental sealant on the entire dental arcade. If you've noticed your dog favoring one side of his mouth when eating, or drooling, or of course if he has bad doggy breath, you'll want to mention all these issues to your veterinarian. If you have a small-breed dog who is most at risk of dental disease, ask your veterinary about dental vaccines and a more robust daily dental-care program to help dramatically delay the times between professional cleanings.

The ears have it. Healthy ears are light pink and clean on the inside. A little yellowish or brown wax is normal, but any kind of crust, brown speckles, or the dreaded dark brown muck of an infection is a concern. When your dog's veterinarian checks the ears, he's feeling for abnormal warmth in the area, looking for discharge, and sniffing for abnormal odor. When you consider how advanced—and painful—ear infections often become before owners even notice the stench, you can truly understand how your veterinarian's trained nose can head off a problem before it really gets going. He's also checking for foreign bodies (such as grass awns or other weed seeds) that get down those ear canals. You'll want to mention any head-shaking you've noticed, even if it has stopped. Sometimes grass awns will stop irritating your dog as they soften, but it doesn't mean they've been shaken out—they need to be found and removed. Recent research has shown that many ear infections are caused by environmental allergies. Dogs with allergies to dust, mites, pollen, even human skin, itch and scratch, thus opening the skin up to secondary infections. My own mother-in-law's Pekingese/Shih Tzu cross, Shing-I, has environmental allergies, or atopy. I treat the root problem with a product called Atopica. Three times in the past ten years as I've been traveling, she thought Shing-I's ear, anal-gland, and itching/licking problems were cured, and she quit the medicine. Every time the ear and anal-gland problems flared back up, and the dog started scratching, chewing, and licking. We'd start her back on Atopica and the problems would disappear. She double-pinky-promised me three years year ago she'd never take her off the meds again. She hasn't. And Shing-I has not had the problems again.

Eye for good health. Healthy eyes don't have excessive tearing, are bright and shiny, and whites are white—not yellow. A yellow tinge to the whites of a dog's eyes can mean he has jaundice, which can be a symptom of a number of serious illnesses. The lining around your dog's eyes should be pink, not red or yellowed. When you look in your dog's eyes, you may one day discover cloudy spots on the lenses gazing back at you. Owners often self-diagnose cataracts and presume their dogs are losing their vision. In older dogs, though, the cause is often nuclear sclerosis—a natural aging of the eye's lens that changes its appearance. The good news is that nuclear sclerosis doesn't usually affect your dog's vision and doesn't present any health threat.

Any kind of irritation on or around your dog's eye is reason enough for a visit to the veterinarian, as untreated eye infections rarely clear themselves up. Ranging from extra eyelashes rubbing on the eye (entropion) to corneal scratches and ulcers and foreign bodies left to linger, they can lead to chronic, painful irritation or even vision loss. (And injury to your dog's eye, by the way, is an emergency situation that needs prompt veterinary attention.) Ask your veterinarian to show you how to reveal the third eyelid on your dog. I always show my clients this and tell them that when the dog is outside, sometimes a small bit of debris can become lodged there. I tell them to get somebody to help them, then just wet a cotton swab and use it to flick the offending substance out.

If your dog is a Pug, Boston Terrier, Pekingese, or other breed with naturally bulging eyes, you will likely learn a lot about canine eye care as you live together. These dogs are prone to all sorts of eye problems, everything from eyes being knocked out of the sockets, to other injuries because their eyes are not well protected, to a predisposition to glaucoma. The best thing you can do as an owner (short of having your dog wear goggles and a helmet) is be vigilant in looking for any out-of-the-ordinary eye issues and bringing them to the attention of the veterinarian ASAP.

Nose news. It's funny how often we turn to the nose as a barometer of a dog's health—and it is not particularly accurate. As a veterinarian I can tell you that not a day goes by in practice when a dog's owner won't point out a dog's nose to me, especially if it seems dry. That's what everyone "knows"—a dog's nose should be cool and moist. I often point out to my clients' astonishment that tears run from a dog's eyes out the end of each nostril (why our nose runs when we cry) and that as the tear exits the dog will alternately shoot out its tongue and wipe it across first one nostril then the other. The moist nose attracts more molecules of scent, something very important when you had to sniff out supper. Their dog's been doing this robotic act every few waking minutes its entire life, and they never noticed it or knew what it was for. Well, usually, but we veterinarians look for other things.

Dry conditions won't concern your veterinarian as much as when a nose is draining—a sure sign of something going wrong further up, such as an inhaled foreign object, or an infection. If the sound of the breathing through the nose is a wheeze, the concern is an obstructed airway. Your veterinarian will also look for cracks, lumps, bumps, and irritations, which can be symptoms of many different problems, including chronic disease having nothing actually to do with the nose. We even look for a loss of pigmentation, which may put a dog at more risk for skin cancer and require a waterproof sunscreen be used when he's out in the sun. But the bottom line is: it's not about the cool or the moist. If you've noticed sneezing, wheezing, pawing, or especially a rapid-fire series of sneezes that seemed to produce nothing, mention it to your veterinarian.

Checking the lymph nodes and internal organs. As your veterinarian continues the nose-to-toes-to-tail examination, she'll be feeling for abnormalities in areas you may not even know your dog has. The lymph nodes are an anatomical feature people have very much in common with their dogs. Just as your mom used to feel beneath your chin and along your throat when you were feeling sick, the veterinarian routinely checks a dog's lymph nodes for signs of illness. When all is well in a body, the lymph nodes are usually so small you can't find them unless you've got a medical degree. They're about the size of a bean and located under the jaw, at the collarbone, in the armpit, groin, and about midpoint of the rear legs. When something is wrong in the body, though, the lymph nodes swell as they help fight infection or injury. Swollen nodes can indicate a wound, a virus, an infection, or some other illness. For example, I've known a dog that had a hidden cheatgrass causing infection deep inside a leg, which I discovered just from my finding a single swollen lymph node. The swelling itself is a clear sign that something is not right. As with all lumps and bumps, be sure to point these out to your veterinarian.

Your veterinarian will also press into your dog's abdomen to palpate the internal organs, feeling to make sure everything is as it should be.

Give a listen. The heart is the most important muscle in the body, which is why your veterinarian will put on that stethoscope—no, it's not just for looking cool—and listen to your dog's heart, lungs, and for the sounds of normal digestion. When it comes to the heart, in particular, she'll be listening for problems such as murmurs that may be the sign of a chronic cardiac problem that will need lifelong management.

Bend over and cough. Yes, your veterinarian will do that, too, snapping on a plastic glove and going where neither veterinarian nor dog wants that finger to be. But again, your veterinarian is looking for internal structures that don't feel right, in order to catch a problem when it's small and treatable. Your veterinarian will also be checking the anal glands to make sure they are not enlarged, painful, or infected. Yes, the veterinarian's life is a glamorous one!

Lean and fit is best. Nailing down a healthy weight range for a dog breed, let alone dogs in general, is about as precise and simple a task as herding cats. There is no functioning height/weight chart for a species that includes both the bull mastiff and the greyhound, and there never will be. There is huge variability among the long, tall, short, big-boned, and slim-line dogs—and it's normal.

That means the best gauge of your dog's healthy weight is your veterinarian's assessment and the history of your dog's gains and losses over a lifetime. For this reason alone, your dog should get on that scale in the vet's office at least twice a year. Better yet, stop by and weigh him once a month—your veterinarian not only won't mind, he'll welcome you free of charge so as to better chart a dog's progress trying to attain or maintain an ideal body weight.

Veterinarians see fat dogs every day—it's estimated that more than half of all dogs are over their ideal weight—but they're sometimes loathe to say much, especially if the owner is likewise overweight (or if the veterinarian is!). But this is a discussion you must have. Here's how veterinarians determine ideal body weight:

🐾 **A look from above.** When seen from above, a dog should have a waist—an indentation between the ribs and hips, the shape of a modestly proportioned hourglass. A bulge between ribs and hips, however, is bad news on any breed—the equivalent of a potbelly on a person.

🐾 **A peek at the side.** A dog's abdomen should appear to tuck up behind his ribs like a furry wasp. If his belly makes a straight line from ribs to legs, or if (Heaven forbid) it hangs below, he's packing too many pounds.

🐾 **Ribs, what ribs?** You shouldn't be able to see your dog's ribs at first glance unless he belongs to one of the leanest of breeds (a Greyhound or Whippet, for example), but you should be able to easily feel the ribs and just a light layer of fat with your fingers when you touch his sides. If you have to push and prod through fatty padding to feel bones, chances are your dog is carrying too much weight.

No Bikini Season for Dogs

For dogs, there's no stick-thin dog models on TV, no favorite pair of jeans, or getting into last year's swimsuit. There's never a day when they spy their rear in a full-length mirror and cry, "Oh, no! My butt must be a mile wide!" And if your dog doesn't care, then why should you or I?

The simple truth is that keeping your dog at a healthy weight is like leading him to the fountain of youth and pouring him a long drink. Pets kept at a healthy weight live an average of 20 percent longer than those who are overweight or obese—an average of two years. Two years is a lot of life—countless walks to the park, snuggles on the couch, and panting greetings at the door!

If your dog is overweight, your veterinarian will have strategies to help you get him back where he should be, from an exercise plan to the "green bean diet"—using green beans to fill your dog up with fewer calories—to special diet foods to medication that may take the edge off the hunger. Remember: your pet's weight is yours to manage, since your dog won't be snacking or overeating if you don't let him. Food is not love. Good health is.

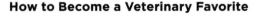
How to Become a Veterinary Favorite

Let me tell you an insider secret. There are certain people who call, or we notice on the appointment log, and we just grin and can't wait until we see them and their pets. What makes these clients VIPs? How do you become one, and what will you receive in return for your efforts? The more boxes you tick off this list, the higher your ranking as a veterinary VIP:

🐾 A tiny bit early for your appointment.

🐾 You treat the entire staff with respect, warmth, and good humor.

🐾 You come armed with a full history of your pet's medical problem, the more detailed the better (e.g., vomited three times yesterday; it was slimy, yellow, and contains bits of cardboard packaging).

🐾 You've trained your dog to welcome, not fear, a veterinary visit, and because you went through gentling techniques with your pet we can easily examine everything.

🐾 You accept our recommendations.

🐾 You pay your bills.

🐾 If we don't just meet but exceed your expectations, you recommend us to others with enthusiasm and frequency.

🐾 On occasion, for any or no reason, you bring us a plate of brownies or cookies to feed a tired crew.

In return you get:

🐾 People who fight to take your call and veterinarians who fight to win you as their vet.

🐾 A veterinary team who lights up even brighter when you walk through the door.

🐾 Somehow we find a spot on an overbooked schedule for you, or we find a place to board your pet during a holiday, even though we've been booked full for months.

🐾 We examine your pet even more closely and aren't afraid to pick up and call you or e-mail you with breaking information that could affect your pet's health.

🐾 We don't watch the clock as closely when it's your turn in the exam room.

🐾 Perhaps most importantly, you can call us 24/7/365 for help when you most need it, and we'll either pick up the phone to talk you through it, race to the practice to meet you, or refer you to someone else and tell them to take extra-special care of you.

Once your dog has gotten a thorough physical and a clean bill of health from your veterinarian, the discussion of how to keep him that way begins.

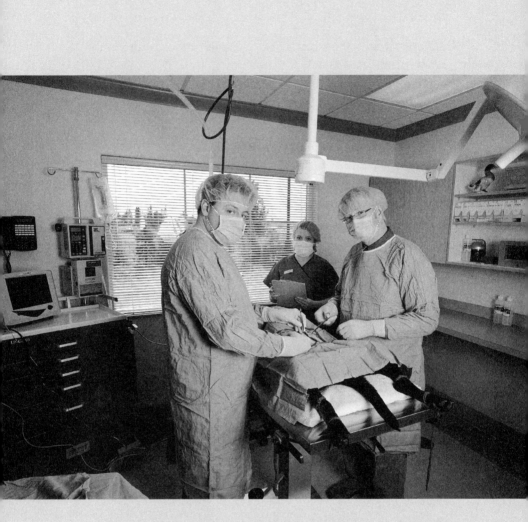

For most dogs, spaying or neutering provides important health and behavior advantages. While the temptation is to look on this surgery as minor because it is so common, make sure to use a veterinarian who tailors this and any surgery to your pet's individual needs in terms of timing (early spay/neuters can be a problem in some breeds), preop testing, and postop pain control.

Chapter 17

FOCUS ON PREVENTIVE CARE

When you first got a puppy or adopted an adult dog, chances are that one of the first things you did was visit your veterinarian for that all-important checkup. That's why the last chapter was about what your veterinarian does when going over your dog—what he's looking for, and why—and how regular wellness checkups with a good veterinarian are the cornerstone on which to build a healthy, long life for your dog.

But once that physical exam is over, the next phase of the veterinarian's work begins—helping you to make choices to keep the good health coming, with decisions that will focus on preventing illness in your dog.

That is, of course, if you have no concerns and your dog is healthy. If you or your veterinarian think there might be something wrong, that important conversation you'll be having will be about how to be thorough enough with the physical exam and tests to look past obvious problems to potential ones, detect emerging problems (such as respiratory problems, kidney disease, or metabolic diseases), restore health, or maintain a chronic condition so your dog's quality of life is preserved.

All my life I've heard (and, I admit, told) the little bit of humor that compared to veterinarians, doctors who treat humans have it easy. After all, veterinarians need to be able to treat 'em all—different species, all ages—and no veterinarian's patient has ever been able to explain where it hurts. Far from just seeing one species and specializing in one thing, veterinarians are internal medicine specialists, surgeons, radiologists, pharmacists, obstetricians, pediatricians, gerontologists, and behavior and grief counselors.

Yes, but fortunately, we have ways to make pets talk—or rather, to let their bodies talk for them. Today's modern diagnostic tools—from sophisticated laboratory tests on blood or other body fluids, to special dental radiology machines, to ultrasounds—take a great deal of the educated guesswork out of veterinary practice. And that's good news, because a correct diagnosis is the first step toward choosing the best treatment options. Even better news? Preventive care saves you money.

But before I get to all that, let's talk more preventive-care options that your veterinarian will be talking about with you.

THE SIMPLE "YEARLY SHOT" ISN'T EITHER ANYMORE

Safe to say that everyone knows dogs need shots, but that's about all they can say on the topic. Most people don't even know what they're vaccinating their pets against, much less how often those vaccinations are needed.

Vaccines are weakened versions of the very diseases they protect against, and they're placed in an animal (usually by injections with a sharp needle, but sometimes through other methods, such as squirting the medication into the nose) to teach the immune system to recognize and destroy a virulent, stronger attack of the disease. The system works because of antibodies, the body's warrior particles that surround and destroy viral and bacterial intruders.

In adult dogs, one dose usually offers immunity for a long time— more on how long next—but that's not how it works in puppies. While a challenged immune system gives grown, healthy dogs a fighting chance against disease, even strong, healthy puppies lack that ability because their immune systems aren't yet functioning fully.

Puppies are initially protected from disease by antibodies passed to them through their mother's milk. While this protection declines in the first few weeks of a puppy's life, it interferes with the preventive-care benefits provided by vaccinations. Since it's not economically feasible to pinpoint the moment when a vaccination will be effective, puppies are given a series of shots over the first few weeks of their lives. Most veterinarians now recommend a series of at least three combination vaccinations at three-week intervals starting at the age of six to eight weeks. These help to protect puppies against five to seven common diseases, and how many vaccines are in the shot will depend on your puppy's risk profile and how prevalent a certain disease is in your region. The final, separate vaccine in the puppy series is rabies, which protects both you and your pet, and is required by law.

Often the breeder or shelter gives the puppy her first shot, and your veterinarian administers the rest. For your pup's sake, follow through on your veterinarian's recommendations—if you stop at just one shot, you're leaving your puppy at risk for disease. Because of public health implications, you'll need to see a veterinarian for that rabies shot anyway, and receive certification that it was given. That's the law.

For all puppies and dogs, vaccines can be divided into two major categories: core and noncore. Core vaccines are the ones designed to protect against major, potentially fatal diseases that could threaten any dog. They are for rabies, parvovirus, parainfluenza, distemper, and hepatitis. Every dog should have the core vaccines as a puppy and then as the veterinarian advises in adulthood. In the past, most vaccines were given annually, at a dog's routine exam. (In fact, many folks mistakenly believed the vaccines were the only reason or the most important one for that annual exam.) However, recent research has revealed two important issues with that schedule: First, many vaccines are effective for longer than a year. Secondly, unnecessary vaccinations can carry health risks of their own, and a very small percentage of dogs do have bad reactions to their shots. Now, the core vaccines for parvovirus, distemper, and hepatitis are advised once every three years.

Rabies vaccination schedules are a little different—they're determined by the government. Because rabies can be transmitted to people and can be fatal, dogs must be vaccinated against it. The maximum time allowed between vaccinations varies from one year to three years. Your dog's veterinarian can tell you exactly what your state and municipality require—most are now on a three-year cycle.

I remember when I first started practicing as a veterinarian, dare I say it, thirty years ago, we robotically gave every pet that came in for their annual shots exactly the same thing. No more. Now we carefully evaluate each patient and look at breed, life stage, lifestyle, and emerging risks to determine exactly what vaccines and other preventive health-care measures are recommended. We call this a "personalized pet health protocol." Noncore vaccines are treatments you should discuss with your dog's veterinarian—and these vary by region and even in your own home, if one dog goes places the other dog doesn't. Each one addresses a specific health threat, and you can decide together whether that threat might be a danger to your dog. Noncore vaccines cover health issues ranging from dental bacteria to Lyme disease and giardia to kennel cough to flu shots. In some cases, your veterinarian can tell you whether a particular health problem concerns dogs in your geographic area (for example: Lyme disease). In other cases, lifestyle choices you make for your dog will determine if he needs a vaccination. For example, if you board your dog at a kennel or veterinary office, you'll be required to provide proof of a vaccination for highly contagious kennel cough before he's allowed to stay.

Vaccination recommendations continue to change and are always being debated. The key takeaway is that your dog should get what he needs and no more, and no more often than is necessary. Again, a personalized pet health-care protocol. Your veterinarian will discuss what she believes is necessary and why, but the final decision is yours—aside from the legally required rabies shot, of course.

What are the core vaccines, you ask? The veterinary code is DHPP, which stands for distemper, hepatitis, parvovirus, and parainfluenza. All dogs need these, along with rabies. Everything else is case by case, so talk to your veterinarian.

Don't Listen to the Anti-Vac Crowd

Just as in human medicine, there's a sizable camp of people who are convinced that vaccines cause more disease than they prevent. Some of them refuse to vaccinate their pets at all, counting on the health and vaccination status of other pets—so-called herd immunity—to protect their animals and avoid the small risk of vaccines.

Don't believe what you read on the Internet: a good, sensible vaccination program is key to your dog's health.

Just as in human medicine, contagious disease used to sweep through regularly, causing misery and death by the millions. Vaccines are one of the true success stories of modern medicine, a lifesaving measure of near-miraculous importance. Manage this risk with your veterinarian's help, vaccinate no more than you need to and no more often then you need to, and you'll be doing what's best for your dog and, by extension, helping all other pets in your community.

DON'T LET PARASITES BUG YOUR DOG

There are two kinds of parasites to worry about, and worry you should. Because not only are these voracious freeloaders—I call them heinous hitchhikers—a danger to your pet's health, they also put your human family at risk. That's right, several of the things that live on or inside your pet's body can also cause the human family harm, and chances are you can't even see them. That's why you need to keep on top of parasite control, both inside and outside your dog.

Let's start on the outside. Did you know that a single flea can multiply to a thousand fleas on your dog and in your home in less than a month? And that single flea can bite your dog up to four hundred times a day. One flea can make your dog's life miserable—have you ever even been bitten by a single bug of any kind and thought, *That doesn't hurt a bit—bring it on?* Of course not. Bug bites hurt! And if you don't get a burgeoning bug problem under control, it can make you pretty unhappy, too. Plus, if your dog has a condition called flea allergy dermatitis (dog is allergic to a protein in the flea's saliva), even a single flea bite can cause an explosive skin reaction in your dog that can be extremely painful for the dog and can be expensive to treat.

The best way to control fleas is to work with a veterinarian to make sure your dog never gets them at all. Modern medicine has come up with some pretty sophisticated flea and tick preventives. Topical products like Frontline, Advantage, and Revolution are able to keep dogs flea free if they are just consistently applied once a month. I also like newer products like Comfortis, a prescription tablet you simply give your dog to control fleas for a month. Ask your dog's veterinarian what management program would work best for your dog, and then stick to it. I can't stress enough the importance of lifetime parasite control for all dogs. Period. Exclamation point! That means once a month, for life. Your life, and your pet's.

A great low-tech, low-cost complement to prescription flea control is to use your vacuum and washing machine to remove fleas from your home before they can reproduce. Vacuum all carpeted areas and any upholstery your dog comes in contact with at least once a week until all signs of fleas are gone. Be sure to pick up cushions, lift furniture, and get in the corners. Fleas are most comfortable burrowed down in dark, sheltered spots—so you've got to really clean aggressively to get them out. And wash pet bedding—and your bedding, if your dog sleeps on the bed, as many do—weekly, as well. Getting fleas out of the environment is as important as killing fleas in the environment.

And while topical medications do help control ticks, they are not as effective against these nasty bloodsuckers as they are against fleas. Ticks can and do transmit some debilitating diseases to both pets and people, so it's essential to be proactive when dealing with these pests. If you're in a tick-infested area, be sure to go over your dog carefully immediately after walks to remove any ticks. Run your hands over her and check for small, telltale lumps. If you find one, part the fur to get a look at the skin and see if your dog has a hitchhiker.

By the way: if you think we're losing the war against ticks, you're right, but it's not because tick-control medications aren't working. Parasite experts say the reason there are more ticks in more places is because there are more deer in more places. And where deer go, so do ticks.

Removing a tick is a simple procedure you can do at home. Search for them after every outing, even if it's to a city park, and remember some species of tick are quite small. Using a pair of fine tweezers (a curved jeweler's tweezer is ideal) or a tick removal tool (Tick Key and Ticked Off removers are two on the market), firmly grasp the tick as close to the skin as possible and steadily pull. Don't twist the tick, or you may end up leaving part of it attached to your dog's skin. The tick will release its hold if you apply steady pressure. Never touch a tick with your own bare hands, and always dispose of them after removal. The best way to get rid of a tick is to submerge it in a small container of rubbing alcohol, then toss it out. Don't panic if you see a part of the tick left behind. Just check in a day or two for swelling and infection, and talk to your veterinarian if you see a lingering problem.

Always Follow Directions

I've been a practicing veterinarian for more than thirty years, and in that time I have seen a huge change in our ability to prevent parasites that once made our pets' lives miserable—and our own lives more dangerous. I remember all sorts of noxious bombs, dips, aerosol cans, yard sprays, soaps that practically required a respiratory mask (and definitely gloves) to handle. We used to alarmingly call it chemical warfare, and I remember all kinds of snake-oil suggestions that were sold (and, let's face it, are still being sold), to people who wanted fewer fleas with less side effects. Ultrasonic deterrents or magic crystals, anyone?

It was common to see patient after patient come in—usually for other reasons—but crawling with fleas. And while I'd be talking to the client, I'd notice flea bites on them as well.

Words cannot express how much better we have it today. While no medication is or can ever be completely safe, today's flea-control products are more effective and safe than we could have ever have hoped for or dreamed of when I was just starting out as a veterinarian. The biggest problems we have with them: people who don't follow directions and don't apply them as indicated, in dosages appropriate for their pet, or who bathe or swim their pet without reapplying, wait too long between doses on purpose or just forget, or use a medication meant for one species on another. Follow directions to stay safe, but be cheered: at least today's treatments are more targeted, less dangerous, and more effective!

And what about worms—the parasites on the inside? Dogs are hosts to a variety of worms, from the roundworms that virtually all puppies get and tapeworms, whose segments stick around the dog's anus, to hookworms and whipworms, to heartworms that are so dangerous once they mature inside your dog that the best cure is always prevention. Puppies are wormed routinely as part of their preadolescent health check series, to rid them of roundworms. If started on preventive medication as puppies, they don't need to be tested for these pests.

For adult dogs, your veterinarian will recommend tests and treatment for worms as needed: a stool sample for most worms and a blood test for heartworms. What is found will determine treatment and preventive care to keep these pests away. Typical wormers and many monthly parasite products take care of roundworms, whipworms, hookworms, and heartworms. If your dog has tapeworms, though, your veterinarian will prescribe a different medication, along with helping you fight fleas, which are the source of tapeworms.

THE KINDEST CUT OF ALL—SPAYING AND NEUTERING

Studies show that the vast majority of dogs are spayed or neutered. The constant drumbeat of those fighting pet overpopulation has been heard, and more than three-quarters of all dog owners alter their pets, or adopt them already spayed or neutered by the shelter or rescue group.

On balance, this is a very good thing. The near-total acceptance of spaying and neutering has helped to steadily drop shelter populations. The benefit of spaying/neutering for an individual dog and the family include reduced roaming, reduced tendencies toward aggression, and reduction in cancers related to the reproductive system. Altered dogs are just easier to live with.

It's not all good, though. Some recent studies have documented increased risks of some cancers when pets are altered, especially when it's done before puberty. And yes, it is true that spaying and neutering change a pet's metabolism, meaning that you must decrease food and increase exercise or your dog will get fat.

Taken on balance: the public health benefits, the individual health benefits, the inconvenience and difficulty of handling unaltered animals...well, for the vast majority of pet owners the decision still leans very heavily on the side of altering. But don't make it automatic: this, too, is a decision that should be made on an individual basis, after discussion with your veterinarian.

Spaying and neutering are the most common surgical procedures, but common doesn't equal easy. While neutering—more specifically, castration—of a male dog is a very easy procedure, spaying isn't that easy at all, especially if the female is in season, has other health risks, or is overweight, particularly if the animal is extremely obese.

Spaying—perhaps the only major surgery your pet will have—involves the removal of the female's entire reproductive system: the uterus, fallopian tubes, and ovaries are taken out through an incision in the abdomen. Your veterinarian may require you to return to have your dog's stitches removed after about seven to ten days, or he may use stitches that are absorbed into the body. Unlike with humans who milk a surgical procedure for all it's worth, recovery is fast, taking just a few days, during which you should limit your dog's activities—no jumping or boisterous play. Recently, this surgery has been made even easier on the animal with a new generation of anesthetics and the introduction of laparoscopic surgery, which requires not an incision but small holes through which surgical instruments are inserted. Recovery time is faster and pain is even less.

For dogs of breeds prone to gastric torsion (also known as bloat), a life-threatening emergency in which the stomach twists and must be surgically repaired to save the dog's life, a procedure called a gastropexy may be added at the time of spaying. This procedure fixes the position of the stomach to prevent it from twisting. It's routinely done as part of the lifesaving surgery following an incident of bloat, but now is increasingly recommended as a preventive measure in the large, deep-chested dogs such a Great Danes and Dobermans, who are especially at risk.

In neutering, the male dog's testicles are removed through an incision just in front of the scrotum, the pouch holding the testicles. Self-absorbing stitches are the norm, and your veterinarian will inform you if your dog needs any postoperative care. Many dog owners are surprised to see that their dog doesn't look neutered at first, since the scrotum remains in place and may be somewhat swollen. The loose skin will gradually shrink away over a few weeks. Some people don't like the neutered look, and for them (and it is for them, because a dog doesn't care) there's a product called Neuticles, which is an implant that fills the area where the testicles were, so a dog looks normal.

Behavior changes in males are more dramatic than those in females, but it does take time for the hormone levels to drop before these changes can be seen.

"Cheap" Surgery: You Get What You Pay For

Because spaying and neutering are common procedures, people tend to think they're easy ones, too. And while that's not too far from the truth with male dogs—who have thoughtfully arranged to leave their removable pieces hanging out like ripe fruit for the picking—that's not the case with females.

I understand the desire and the need to save money, but price-shopping for surgery really isn't a good idea. When you get rock-bottom prices, you're often getting only the most basic of care. Your pet is at more risk of an adverse anesthetic event if the function of the kidneys and liver isn't known and pain prevention and control either isn't a priority or isn't addressed. And while that's probably necessary for the clinics working to keep feral cat populations down, opting out of top-quality care may not be the choice you want to make for your own pet.

Don't make price the bottom line. If you're going to price-shop for surgery—and I don't recommend it, honestly and strongly—be sure you're comparing apples to apples. What sort of anesthesia protocol will be used? Will the anesthesia be monitored? Preop screening? Pain medications? Warm pads for recovery?

Again, an informed decision is the only kind to be making, and that requires knowing what's involved and considering all the options, not just knowing what your final bill will be.

DENTAL CARE: HEALTHY TEETH AND GUMS ARE KEY TO A HEALTHY DOG

Dental health is another of those areas where veterinarians' recommendations have changed a good deal—and for good reasons. We now know that the health of teeth and gums are important not only for quality of life but also for longevity. Periodontal disease (plaque on teeth; infected, swollen, bleeding gums) is the single most commonly diagnosed problem in veterinary medicine. A mouthful of rotting teeth and gums is home to bacteria that put stress on a dog's internal systems, and that stress leads to a shortened life span. Remember how keeping a pet at or near its ideal body weight helps it live 15 percent longer or an average of two years? Well, practicing daily oral care and having a healthy mouth will help your pet live another 15 percent longer. Taken together, a lean pet with a healthy mouth will live an average of four years longer! Seems the furry fountain of youth just may be found. Just put less food/treats in your pet's mouth, put more miles on his feet, and do something every day to keep his mouth healthy and take him to the veterinarian as needed for professional cleaning/care.

Yes, I'm aware that a lot of people my age consider dental care for dogs to be at best a joke and at worst a rip-off. Let me just say that those people haven't seen what veterinarians see every day and aren't aware of the suffering a mouthful of disease can cause. But let me bring this home: Have you ever had a tooth break? Had periodontal work? Needed a root canal? Did you enjoy waiting for those procedures or were you begging for pain medications? Nobody says, "That hurts like a hangnail." No, they say, "That hurts like a toothache!"

Now, consider that every day veterinarians see dogs who have not one of those problems but all of them—advanced dental disease. You can smell them coming by their doggy breath, and you can feel their pain and admire their stoicism. When I open their mouth their teeth are so loose I jokingly but pointedly say, "Your dog's teeth are like yellow piano keys." But mostly, as a veterinarian, what I really want is to not see dogs in that condition.

And that means preventive dental care.

Dental care starts with a veterinary exam that goes over the teeth and gums to spot problems.

If you're starting out with a puppy, or a dog with no plaque buildup or gum disease, prevention is easy—and very inexpensive. Your veterinarian or one of the technicians will go over home preventive care—brushing your pet's teeth daily and using pet-friendly toothpaste and rinses (unlike humans, pets don't spit—they swallow, and they abhor the minty tastes humans love but crave those on the meaty side). Your veterinarian will also advise on healthy chews—Greenies, DenTees, Dentastix—that clean the teeth with little chance of breaking one, enzyme-impregnated chews, dental scrubbing toys, and dental vaccines, and he may even suggest a diet that will help by adding an abrasive element with every bite. I call the latter "edible toothbrushes."

If there are already dental problems, however, your veterinarian will likely recommend radiographs and a more complete examination under anesthesia, along with treatment—and possibly removal—of broken teeth and scaling and polishing of the remainder. We also use dental sealants like OraVet. It's also likely that because of the bacteria issues, your dog will be started on an antibiotic before the procedure and continue on the medication after, possibly along with pain control medications.

After your pet's mouth is restored to good health, you can stretch the period between cleaning with home care, but do be aware that some dogs—especially small ones—are very prone to plaque buildup and will likely need regular veterinary care under anesthesia once or twice a year for life.

Groomers Aren't Dentists

I have nothing but respect for the hard work of dog groomers, and I believe their contributions to the health of pets are significant.

But they are not dentists, and that's why I cannot recommend so-called anesthesia-free dentistry in good conscience. It's a cosmetic practice only and has no benefit to the dog's dental health—but it will give you, the owner, a false sense of having done something beneficial for your dog, when all you did was make him prettier, for a while.

Scraping the teeth without being able to completely examine them and polish out the rough patches and grooves allows oral disease to go unnoticed and creates a matrix for the rapid recolonization of bacteria on the teeth. It also fails to get at the bacterial buildup where it's doing its damage, under the gumline. Can you imagine sitting still, in comfort, while somebody elevates your gums and scrapes the base of your teeth. Of course not, and neither should your dog.

Good groomers are worth their weight in gold. But so are good veterinarians. And when it comes to your pet's health care, you should no more trust your pet's health to a groomer than you should trust your own to a hairdresser.

Your veterinarian may also suggest a recently developed dental-health vaccine. The vaccine does not completely prevent tooth decay, but it does banish the most common types of oral bacteria from your dog's mouth and may help prevent bone loss in the teeth. Talk to your veterinarian about this important advancement.

One of the most common veterinary emergencies is poisoning, and one of the most common poisons a dog will get into is medication prescribed for either humans or pets. Be sure to secure all medications behind cupboard doors and to remind guests to do the same. Use medications only as prescribed, and if you have a concern about your dog's reaction to a medication, call your veterinarian right away.

Chapter 18

HOW TO HANDLE AN EMERGENCY

No matter how careful you are about providing preventive care, how much you've worked to control such things as your dog's access to poisons, or even making sure the gates stay closed, accidents happen. That, as they say, is why they're called accidents.

That fencing you double-checked for loose boards or a spot where the dog has been trying to excavate an escape route? One big windstorm can knock a bough off your neighbor's tree and take a section of fence with it. Your dogs could be trotting across a busy street before you know it, and you know that's not going to end well.

Or maybe you misjudge how hot it is when you take your dog out for a run. It might not be anything related to acts of God or human misjudgment. Your dog could tear ligaments in his knee jumping off your bed or twisting for a tennis ball, or suddenly show frightening symptoms of a disease that had been rumbling unnoticed. Seizures, collapse, dramatic changes in eating or bathroom habits, hair coming off in clumps, a dog crying out in pain, withdrawn and not wanting to play or go for a walk.

So what do you do?

It used to be that almost every practicing veterinarian was on call all the time. Great for the animals, but not so great for the veterinarian and his or her family. These days most veterinarians either share emergency on call with colleagues, or a community has a dedicated emergency-care facility. Not to mention the emergence of specialists in emergency and critical care.

But unless you're living with a veterinarian, chances are you're still going to be the first person to deal with the emergency pet health problem. You need to know what's an emergency and what's not, whom to call and where to go, and what to do before you can get help.

While I believe every word in this book can help to make your pet healthier and happier, this chapter can save your pet's life. Read it now, and know what you need to do before you need the information. Because the time to be looking in the index of a book (or checking the web) is not when a life is on the line and minutes count.

SYMPTOMS THAT SAY, *GET HELP NOW*

Those of us who've worked at veterinary hospitals have our own stories of the emergencies that weren't: The pet owner who was sure the animal's intestines were coming out the back end when even the greenest kennel attendant could tell you they were worms, not guts. The big dog who was brought in because he ate a tiny piece of milk chocolate when the toxic amount would be measured in pounds, not ounces, and dark chocolate's the bigger concern, anyway. The dog who is bleeding hasn't had an injury—she's in heat, so please schedule that spay, okay?

Yes, it's true there's a little dark humor going on behind the scenes at any veterinary hospital, but really, when you deal with life-and-death situations, if you didn't laugh sometimes, you'd cry. And the truth is every veterinarian would rather have you call or come in than dismiss a real emergency as something that can wait. Think about it. Have you ever experienced or heard of a veterinary hospital charging for knowledge or help they give out over the phone? No, it's free, especially if we're able to answer something over the phone. (In our neck of the woods, when somebody calls in the wintertime and says their pet is itching, the first thing we think of is low humidity. Absent of any other symptoms, we tell the caller to use a humidifier and add essential fatty acids to the food and give oatmeal baths. Problem solved inexpensively and over the phone for free.) Alternately, people often want to get the veterinary equivalent of "Take two aspirin and call me in the morning" when we know the problem is serious, painful, or even life-threatening and the pet needs to be seen immediately.

Knowing what's not an emergency can save you money, since after-hours care is almost always more expensive. But knowing what is really an emergency is going to save you something more important than money—it's going to save your pet's life.

Animals instinctively try to hide signs that they are sick or injured, for in the wild "sick is supper," and these sickly animals are quick to be preyed upon. For this reason, always treat any serious incident (like a seizure, no appetite—as you know healthy pets love to eat—bloody vomitus or diarrhea, being hit by a car, a fall, crying out in pain, limping, an eye injury, or a possible overheating) as something that requires veterinary care—even if your dog seems to be bouncing back. Internal injuries could be killing your dog.

Here are some signs that should have you heading for a veterinarian, day or night:

- Seizure, fainting, or collapse.
- Eye injury, no matter how mild.
- Vomiting or diarrhea—anything more than two or three times within an hour or so or anytime there's blood.
- Allergic reactions, such as swelling around the face, or hives, most easily seen on the belly.
- Any suspected poisoning, including antifreeze, rodent or snail bait, or human medications.
- Snake or venomous spider bites, or poisoning from licking or eating toads.
- Thermal stress—from being either too cold or too hot—even if the pet seems to have recovered. (The internal story could be quite different.)

(Continued)

- Any wound or laceration that's open and bleeding, or any animal bite.
- Trauma, such as being hit by a car, even if the pet seems fine. (Again, the situation could be quite different on the inside.)
- Any respiratory problem: chronic coughing, trouble breathing, or near drowning.
- Straining to urinate or defecate.
- Also watch for bloat: Attempts to vomit, or vomiting foam. Licking lips. Hunched up or "roached" appearance. Lack of normal gurgling and digestive sounds in the tummy, tight tummy, and anxiety.

WHAT TO DO BEFORE YOU CAN GET HELP

Being ready for an emergency is the next best thing to handling one. It's amazing how much better prepared a pet owner can become by spending just a couple of hours—put another way, about the time it takes to watch a movie—organizing a few documents and tools. When you do your emergency prep, keep in mind that another member of your family or a pet sitter might just be the one nearby if your dog has a crisis. Posting a single page with clearly written instructions for how to find help and where to find your dog's first-aid kit could one day save your dog's life. These are the main issues to address:

Emergency Contact Information

At the very least, every household with a dog should have an easy-to-find, clearly worded list of emergency contacts with phone numbers. Don't call 911 when your pet is sick: these emergency services are for people, and the operators are neither trained nor allowed to give you veterinary advice. Keep a current weight posted so in an emergency you can tell the vet or poison control, "My dog weighs—," then they can give you dosages accurately and quickly.

Your emergency-care sheet should include:

🐾 YOUR DOG'S VETERINARIAN: name, office hours, address, phone number

🐾 URGENT CARE OR VETERINARY EMERGENCY PRACTICE: name, address (directions if you've never been there), phone number

🐾 ASPCA POISON CONTROL HOTLINE: 888-426-4435 (There is a charge for this service, but in an emergency when your veterinarian is not available, it is well worth the fee.)

🐾 A TRUSTED FRIEND, NEIGHBOR, OR PET SITTER: name, phone number

Program all this information into your smartphone, as well, under the contact name "ICE"—In Case of Emergency.

Dog Identification

You should also keep good, current pictures of your dog from all angles with a clutter-free background, in case you ever need to make a "lost dog" poster.

First-Aid Kit

If your dog has a health crisis, the last place you need to be is digging around in the cupboards for a leash, a pair of scissors, or bandages and tape. Spending an hour now to prepare for an emergency later is the best way to ensure this doesn't happen to you. Besides, if you believe in Murphy's Law, you can rest easier knowing that once you've gone to the trouble to make the ideal emergency kit, you'll probably never need it!

If you have the space for it and if your dog's a traveler, a second kit to keep in the car will give you double the peace of mind. Here's what to include:

(Continued)

- A clearly printed label with your dog's name, your name and phone number, your veterinarian's contact info, and a note listing your dog's allergies, medical conditions, and weight.
- Leash and collar.
- A soft fabric muzzle (from any pet supply retailer)—be sure to get the right size for your dog. If you have a pug-nosed dog, choose a mesh one made just for his shape. A comfortable cage, or box, muzzle is also a good thing to have around, in case you're in a longer-term emergency situation, such as a natural disaster. These muzzles allow your dog to behave normally but do not allow a stressed-out dog to bite. In an emergency you can also use roll gauze, a men's necktie, or a bathrobe belt to muzzle a pet (wrap twice around muzzle, tie underneath chin once, wrap around back of head and tie in a bow so it can be easily released) or to create a tourniquet (leave loose enough so blood still seeps, not spurts, and release every few minutes to allow blood to flow).
- Disposable medical gloves.
- Antiseptic.
- A tube of K-Y gel.
- A tube of Super Glue.
- Styptic powder (from pet-supply retailers in the grooming section), to stop bleeding.
- Q-tips.
- Bandaging supplies: sterile gauze, cotton pads, first-aid tape, bandages, scissors.
- Tweezers.
- Flashlight.
- A bottle of 3 percent hydrogen peroxide solution.
- Pepto-Bismol.
- Over-the-counter antihistamine.
- 10 cc syringe for giving medicine orally (no needle!).
- Clean washcloth, towel, and blanket.
- Resealable plastic bags in different sizes.

THE SHARED MEDICINE CHEST

There are a surprising number of "people meds" that can be helpful in a canine health crisis. There are also a surprising number of people meds that can be quite dangerous, so when in doubt be sure to call your veterinarian to check about the use of any product from your own medicine cabinet. Don't give your dog anything that contains acetaminophen or ibuprofen—both of these pain medications are toxic to and potentially deadly for dogs.

The products listed here are all safe for occasional canine use. Always call your dog's veterinarian to let her know you are giving medication at home and to verify the dose. Don't treat symptoms at home for more than twenty-four hours unless you are following your veterinarian's specific directions.

Benadryl. This common medication can be a godsend if your dog is swelling from an insect bite or a sting. It can also provide relief from itching and irritation, even when you aren't sure what caused it. Veterinarians sometimes use this antihistamine to treat allergy symptoms, but don't give it for more than a day without approval from your dog's veterinarian. In a pinch, you can also use Benadryl as a sedative.

Dose: Once every six hours, give 25 mg for pets up to thirty pounds, 50 mg for pets up to eighty pounds, or 75 mg for pets over eighty pounds.

Pepto-Bismol. Dogs can take this medication for an upset tummy or diarrhea. Just as it does for people, Pepto-Bismol gives dogs a little relief when they're suffering from why-did-I-eat-that-itis. If your dog is vomiting, however, or the diarrhea doesn't stop in a day, you need to see your veterinarian.

Dose: A child's dose for every forty pounds your dog weighs. For example: if your dog weighs twenty pounds, give half of one tablet. For an eighty-pound dog, give two tablets. Follow the same guidelines for liquid Pepto-Bismal. Dogs can have Pepto-Bismol every four hours if needed.

Pedialyte. Another source of relief for dogs with gastrointestinal upsets is the same stuff you'd give a baby with tummy problems. Pedialyte is designed to rehydrate and restore the balance of electrolytes in a child's system after a bout of vomiting or diarrhea. It can help your dog bounce back from a sick belly by doing the same.

Dose: Give unflavored Pedialyte in small amounts—up to a quarter cup every half hour for a forty-pound dog.

Hydrogen peroxide. The first use that comes to mind is cleaning wounds, but hydrogen peroxide can also be used to induce vomiting.

Dose: Use a medicine syringe to give your dog 3 cc of hydrogen peroxide per twenty pounds of body weight. Do not repeat unless directed by a veterinarian. If you're concerned enough about something your pet ate to induce vomiting, you should be talking to your veterinarian to be sure your pet doesn't need to come in. To give any liquids to a dog, whether it's a household product your vet has told you to use or a liquid medication the vet has prescribed, *don't* try and put it on the tongue or the floor of the mouth like you do for children. The veterinary secret is to pull the corners of the lips straight out and pull the head up, creating a funnel; when you squirt the liquid there it runs around the gap behind the teeth, and voila! right down the throat and not all over you!

Aspirin. Your dog can occasionally have aspirin for pain as needed. Choose a buffered aspirin in 325 mg strength. As with any pain medication, talk to your veterinarian. If your dog is already on a prescription pain medication, never add another. And ask about an over-the-counter stomach-acid-reducer drug to protect your pet's stomach while on such pain meds.

Dose: One 325 mg tablet every twelve hours for large (more than sixty pounds) dogs; one-half tablet for medium-sized dogs (thirty to sixty pounds); one-quarter tablet for small-sized dogs (under thirty pounds).

Pets and People Meds Don't Mix

The number one cause of accidental poisoning in pets is people medicine. In 2009 alone, the ASPCA's Animal Poison Control Center (ASPCA.org/APCC) fielded more than forty-nine thousand calls regarding pets sickened by medications for humans. In many cases, the dogs dosed themselves. If you've ever seen a small child beg for a flavored vitamin or cough drop, you can imagine how a dog, capable of chewing through a plastic bottle in seconds might help himself to a whole bottle of either one. Likewise, any found item on the floor—be it an aspirin or a tranquilizer—is fair game for eating, as far as your dog is concerned. Always store your own medications, including cough medicines and lozenges, out of sight and out of reach of your dog.

And remind houseguests to do the same: it's typical for people who don't have pets and especially elderly visitors to put medications on the nightstand, or in an easily accessible purse or piece of luggage. When you have visitors, ask them about their medications, and put whatever they have behind secure cupboard doors or in a drawer. And ask them about sugar-free gum and candy. These, too, need to be out of range, because the common sweetener xylitol is deadly to pets.

WHEN A CRISIS HAPPENS

If you find yourself coping with a seriously sick or injured dog, you're going to have to dig deep and calm yourself before you can be much help. As first responders like to say, "Take your own pulse first."

That means take a deep breath, ask for help if you've got anyone nearby who can pitch in, and approach your dog's emergency step by step.

Later, when he's recovering nicely, you'll have time to allow yourself a little breakdown. You'll have earned it.

First Thing's First: Restraint

You love your dog. Your dog loves you. In the event of an injury that requires any of the following procedures, *any dog*, even yours, may instinctively lash out from pain or try to protect itself from further injury during first aid. The best way to protect both your dog and you is to use restraints. Snap on a leash, wrap your dog in a blanket or towel, and enlist the help of an assistant if possible. A blanket will help you to immobilize your dog during treatment. It may also help calm your dog so you can help him.

A good first-aid kit contains a soft muzzle, and you should put this on your dog to protect yourself. If you don't have a muzzle, you can make a quick one from a pair of panty hose, a necktie, or any soft fabric cut in a long, narrow strip. Fold the fabric in half, lengthwise, to find the midpoint. Put it over your dog's nose, with that midpoint on top of the nose. Wrap the fabric around your dog's mouth, crisscrossing the material under the chin. Take the two loose ends and tie them snugly in a bow—not a knot—behind your dog's head. Never muzzle a dog who is vomiting, and never tie a muzzle in a knot—you need to be able to take it off quickly if your dog has trouble breathing.

If you have a short-nosed dog, like a Pug or a Bulldog, you need to have a specialized muzzle in your first-aid kit. Make sure you buy one at a pet supply store and keep at home. It would very difficult to fashion an effective one at home without risking your dog's ability to breathe.

Bleeding

If your dog is bleeding heavily, your priority is simply to stop the flow. Use a clean cloth, towel, or gauze to push down on the wound. Once you start applying pressure, do not let up! Don't lift your bandage to look at the wound beneath or to replace it, as this can interfere with clotting and restart bleeding. Instead, if your bandage soaks through, put another one on top of it and keep applying pressure.

Open Wound

If your dog has an open wound but isn't heavily bleeding, rinse the wound with hydrogen peroxide, Betadine, or saline solution, and coat the area with K-Y gel. This will help keep dirt and infection away from the wound until your dog's veterinarian can treat it properly. If you have to bandage a wound at home, cover it with sterile pads and then secure them by wrapping the area in an Ace bandage. Bandaging a dog can be a complicated business—after all, your dog has a very different shape from the kind you've been giving first aid to all your life. Be creative—a clean sock pulled up over a leg bandage may keep it in place. A long-sleeved T-shirt can be wrapped around your dog's torso and tied together at the arms to help keep a temporary bandage in place.

Overheating

Overheating is one of the biggest hidden threats to dogs and one of the most deadly. Your dog can overheat in the car, in the house, or in his own yard. It can happen during a strenuous walk, or in the middle of a lazy afternoon. Dogs overheat much more quickly than people because they can't sweat much to adjust their body temperature. Instead, a dog's temperature can quickly rise with the conditions. As a watchful pet owner, it's your job to avoid the obvious dangers—like the inside of a closed car, even on a seventy-five-degree day. But it also falls to you to watch for the signs of overheating when the conditions aren't so obvious. If your dog is not accustomed to a temperature or an activity level, always err on the side of keeping him cool and protected.

The most obvious signs of overheating are frantic panting and wide, glassy eyes. Overheated dogs may also seem disoriented. If your dog is overheated, you are facing a true emergency. Start cooling him down with water immediately. Cool water on his belly will get his temperature heading in the right direction. You can use the hose, the shower, a soaked beach towel—whatever you've got. Do not use ice cold water or ice to cool an overheated dog: the water should be cool, not ice cold—the extreme of using ice on a hot pet actually stops the cooling and could send him into shock. As soon as possible, get your dog to his veterinarian. Even if he seems be improving under your care, he needs to be evaluated and treated by a pro.

Broken Bones

If your dog falls, gets hit by a bike or car, or otherwise breaks a bone, there's not a lot you can do at home to help him. You job is to try to immobilize the broken bone and get him to a veterinarian as soon as possible. A quick way to splint a broken leg is with a rolled up magazine or piece of poster paper. Wrap it around the wound and tape it. Transporting your dog may be easier for both of you if you carry him wrapped in a towel, a blanket, or a small rug, or better yet, get somebody else to drive so you can sit in the backseat comforting and securing him. The less your dog moves between the moment of the break and the time his veterinarian sets it, the better.

POISONING RISKS FOR YOUR DOG

It's amazing that a dog who might consume the contents of a trash can and live to tell the tale can be laid out by a little piece of gum, but it does happen. There are many items—both edible and not—in your dog's environment that can make him very sick or even kill him. Knowing the most common poisons will help you be more vigilant about your dog's exposure to them in and near your home:

❧Medications. Yours, your children's, your dog's. It really doesn't matter much what the medicine is if your dog helps himself to the whole bottle—he's in danger from any pharmaceutical in a large dose. Keep all meds where your dog cannot see or reach them at all times.

✿ **Poisons.** This one seems so obvious, but every year thousands of dogs are sickened or killed by poisons intended for other animals. Two of the most common culprits are mouse/rat baits (like d-Con) and insecticides. The easiest way to avoid this potential tragedy in your home is to not use poisons at all. If you do use them, check and recheck the dangers and then put them in places your dog cannot possibly reach, or use secure bait stations that can be filled with rodenticide accessible to mice but not pets, then secured so that dogs can't shake the contents out.

If you have any contractor who visits your home to chemically treat for insects or other pests, be sure that person understands you have dogs and are concerned about their health.

✿ **Food.** Many dog poisonings are the result of ingestion of food designed for people. Sometimes the problem is simply quantity— a dog eats more than he can safely process. Often, the trouble is that some chemicals that seem all right for humans are toxic to dogs. Among the foods to watch out for: sugar-free candy and gum, chocolate, macadamia nuts, raisins and grapes, onions, avocados, and caffeinated and alcoholic beverages.

✿ **Household chemicals.** This is a broad range of poisons, and many of them are ingested by dogs accidentally rather than deliberately. For example, your dog eats grass that has just been treated with fertilizer or, worse yet, a herbicide for weeds, or he eats insecticide for bugs; or he drinks from a toilet that's got a bleach disc in its tank. Most dogs have no interest in poking around your cleaning caddy looking for snacks (though, to be safe, the cleaning caddy should always be stored out of reach). When it comes to chemicals, you have to think one step further and consider your dog's access to their point of use.

✿ **Plants.** Many household and landscape plants are poisonous for dogs. Why they eat them, we couldn't say, but if you have a dog who's prone to chewing grass or nibbling from your garden, take extra care to limit your dog's exposure to the following commonly seen poisonous plants: azalea, tulip bulbs, cyclamen, crocus, chrysanthemum, peace lily, English ivy, yew, and Sago palm. Some things you've grown to fear over the years—most notably poinsettias—are a minor problem, but others you've probably never thought of can cause big problems. If we had to pick the single most dangerous plant (both because of its toxicity and popularity) we'd say the lily. I have a saying—"Lilies are lethal"—and I implore pet owners to forgo this plant entirely. If you'd like to look up any specific plant to see if it is dangerous for your dog, the ASPCA Animal Poison Control Center (ASPCA.org/APCC) has an extensive, searchable database online. They also offer a free refrigerator magnet with their phone number on it.

🐾 **Surprising things around the house.** Candles, potpourri, mothballs, underwear, rocks, children's toys, remote controls, pennies—the list of things a dog (especially a puppy) can and will eat is astonishing. Pet-proofing your home means looking at everything your dog can get to—and making sure it's out of the way. What you don't need to worry about, but that I get asked about all the time anyway: Swiffer Wet Jet and Febreze. It's an urban myth that they're lethal if injested; they're safe to use as directed around your pet.

Put It All Away, and Lock the Door

In my decades as a veterinarian, I've seen dogs do everything short of stand on their heads to get their paws on poisonous products. I've treated counter surfers who emptied their owners' pill vials, Houdini dogs who pried open cabinet doors to reach lemon-scented dusting spray, and rascals who went all the way to the bottom of the trash can to reach spoiled meat that could have been classified as toxic waste.

The best way to pet-proof the poisons in your house is to treat them with the same kind of full effort you'd use if you were toddler-proofing instead. In other words, assume not only that your dog might stumble upon these items, but that he might actually go looking for them. Store all potentially toxic products both *inside* a cabinet and *above* counter height. Also, remember that the garbage can is the land of opportunity for a curious/hungry/trouble-prone dog. Use a can with a snug-fitting lid—and if necessary, use a toddler-proof lock to keep it shut.

While the Internet can be a great source of research that can help you in discussing your dog's care with your veterinarian and even a good way to keep in touch with your vet, there really is no substitute for a face-to-face between your dog and your veterinarian. Don't guess what's wrong with your dog and treat a problem yourself based on that. You may well be wrong, and your dog may suffer for it.

Chapter 19

GETTING THE BEST MEDICAL CARE

Even the healthiest of dogs with the very best of preventive veterinary care, regular exercise, and nutrition will get sick on occasion. The bodies of our dogs, like our own, are complicated machines—although I like to think of them as miracles—that are constantly fighting for survival. Some of the challenges to health come from organisms that cannot be seen by the naked eye, but these viruses and bacteria are so powerful that they've been able to bring countries to their knees (think the flu pandemics of the early twentieth century) or change the course of history (think the Renaissance that followed the Black Death).

The advances of science and medicine have done a great deal to give us and our companion animals a fighting chance against disease. Vaccinations to prevent disease, antibiotics to fight infections, and even such advancements as the humble sewer have made the world safer for us all. Similarly, the achievements of pioneering doctors and veterinarians in understanding how bodies work, what's going wrong when they don't work, and how to fix them has extended the lifespan of pets significantly.

No matter how good your veterinarian is, however, you are the reason your own pet has a fighting chance at a healthy life. That's because not only are you the one who first notices when your pet needs a veterinarian's help, but you're the one who'll be caring for your pet after that appointment. It's a partnership with your veterinarian—and the hospital staff, plus any specialists brought in to help—and yourself, and the goal is your pet's recovery, or at least the management of a disease so your pet can live a normal life.

My favorite clients are the ones who want to know more, who challenge me, who ask questions, and who get the help they need to help their pets. I want to help you be one of those clients, for your pet's sake. So read on!

MAGIC WANTS, FAIRY DUST, AND INFORMATION FROM THE INTERNET

Pet lovers were second only to sci-fi fans in embracing the possibilities of the Internet. I've read—and really, there's no way to substantiate this, so I just can't—that the Internet has more images and video of pets than of people. I don't find it that hard to believe, really, considering how many pictures of the Almost Heaven Ranch animal family you can find online. I would bet my cover dog Quixote—the fourteen-pound Alpha Wolf of our animal family—has had more face time than I have. I can also tell you he's often recognized before I am.

The Internet is a great place to share the love of pets and connect with other pet lovers. And it's also a great place to look for information on pets and their care.

But as a veterinarian, I can tell you this: It's also one of the worst places to find information, not only because there's information that's wrong and can waste your time and your money, but also because there's information that's even worse—it's deadly. My pet care team of veterinarians, behaviorists, trainers, and other pet care experts has been working online longer than some of you have been alive. We get asked questions so often that we have most of the answers saved for a little cut-and-paste action.

The number one thing we tell people? *Get off the 'Net and call your vet.*

That's not because I'm trying to drum up business for my fellow veterinarians. It's because there's no way to offer treatment options that work without knowing what's actually wrong with a pet. And very few pet owners are knowledgeable or skilled enough to present their pet's symptoms accurately. Not to mention, they don't have access to diagnostic testing we veterinarians often need to know what's really going on. I tell my clients they're welcome to look things up on the Internet, but they should understand that every single case is different.

So let me stress this as strongly as I can: no Internet search and no book is a substitute for an in-person visit with your dog's veterinarian. And no magic home remedy you read about is going to help, either.

Now that I have that out of the way, let's give the amazing Internet some credit for what it can help you with, and that's improving the relationship you have with your veterinarian by giving you the information you need to be a better educated advocate for your pet. With the Internet, you can read many of the same peer-reviewed journal articles your veterinarian is reading. You can research the best care options and cutting-edge solutions. You can even—although this point is controversial among veterinarians, many of whom feel unfairly treated—see what other pet owners thought about how their pets were treated by a particular veterinarian. It's all there for the finding, but you have to know how to understand the respective value of a source to get the benefit of the information. Here are some suggestions:

- ❧ **Check the sources.** Look for citations to veterinary literature and specific references to studies and clinical research. While citations older than ten years may still be perfectly valid, claims based entirely on older research require additional scrutiny. Testimonials are not evidence, proof, or documentation. They are advertising. Don't rely on testimonials in making health decisions.
- ❧ **Look at the wording.** The best sites have straightforward language, free of sensationalism. If a site is badly organized, full of misspelled words and grammatical errors, and hard to navigate, the information is less likely to be reliable. Look for a track record of providing good information in the past and on other subjects.
- ❧ **What are they selling?** Websites with financial or professional affiliations that might compromise their objectivity should sound alarms. In particular, be extremely skeptical of information being provided by someone trying to sell something. Information providers with strong ideological beliefs, such as passionate agendas about health

and nutrition, could have had their objectivity tainted by them. Watch out for all-or-nothing statements praising or condemning a specific drug, procedure, therapy, or approach to health.

What you find on the Internet is best seen as a jumping-off spot for an open, thoughtful discussion with your veterinarian. And remember: when you show your veterinarian something she hasn't seen before, it's no sign that she hasn't kept up. The information may be wrong, in the first place, and in the second, there's nothing wrong with a medical professional saying, "I don't know"—as long as she's prepared to go find the answers.

You should also know that your local veterinary hospital most likely has routine access to online resources that could be described as a cannon to your BB gun. There is a sophisticated online resource for veterinary health-care professionals called the Veterinary Information Network (VIN) that tens of thousands of veterinary hospitals belong to. Besides being an accurate source of cutting-edge information, it's a place we go to access experts who know the very most about the condition we think your pet might have, to get a second opinion from another practitioner, or to share the results of the physical exam and test and, like viral medical rounds, ask a thousand other top vets what they think your pet might have and how it could best be treated. No, you can't access VIN, but if your veterinarian's a member, that's a sign you have a good one!

Find Team Becker on the Internet

In the last couple of decades, I can't tell you how many people have come to me with surefire ideas for making lots and lots of money on the Internet. The ideas have been varied, as have the offers. Some wanted me to invest, some wanted me to advise, and some…well, I just don't remember anymore. There really have been that many.

Most of them eventually started up, and most of those eventually closed up. Some of the ones that didn't make it had some really great people involved, and offered solid information for pet lovers.

In the meantime, I just kept doing what I do, sharing the best information I could find wherever I could share it—*Good Morning America* and *The Dr. Oz Show*, of course, and *Parade* magazine, the AARP website, and appearances all over the world. My writing partner, Gina Spadafori, and I combined our respective syndicated columns into one, and then we revamped her website, PetConnection, to add a decade's worth of articles. It's a blended family of a website: her work, my work, and our work. And then we've added some of the best pet care experts around to write for us as well. It's all searchable, and it's all free.

Drop on by at PetConnection.com. The website has been featured with cover pieces in the *L.A. Times* and *USA Today*, and is on every list of the best websites for pet lovers.

WHAT YOU NEED TO KNOW ABOUT WHAT EVERY DOG WILL DEAL WITH

It's hard to imagine a dog who will get through his life without dealing with two everyday realities of modern health care: taking medication and having surgery. And yet, few things cause more concern and problems than these common issues. So I want to cover them here so you can know the latest, and do your part to help your pet.

Pet Pharmaceuticals: Pet Meds, People Meds, and Even a Little Blue Pill

You're worried your dog is sick, so you take him in to see the veterinarian. After a thorough checkup, the doctor tells you she wants to put your neutered male dog on a drug you've heard a lot about: Viagra.

No, it's not your vet's idea of a joke. It's actually perfectly legitimate to prescribe Viagra for a dog, even if he's neutered—but not for the reasons you might think.

> **V**iagra, or sildenafil citrate, is best known for fixing what's referred to as erectile dysfunction in human males, but because it works by improving blood flow, it can also be effective in treating pulmonary hypertension, a disorder that causes high blood pressure in the arteries of the lungs. If your dog has a pulmonary problem, Viagra may be the key to his health.

And it's not the only human medication veterinarians can—and do—prescribe. Another surprising remedy is Botox, used to treat some eye problems in dogs. Most pet owners don't realize this, but aside from flea- and tick-control products, almost all of the medications their pets receive are crossovers from human medicine.

Some 80 to 90 percent of the drugs used in veterinary medicine come from human medicine. When you get into more specialized treatments, such as those for cancer, that figure goes even higher. This so-called off-label use of human drugs allows veterinarians to treat medical conditions (and species) that might not be priorities for big drug companies when it comes to developing and selling medications.

Knowing how and why certain drugs are prescribed can help pet owners understand health-care options—including some that save money. A good vet will discuss medications, tell you what side effects to look for, and encourage you to call with questions or concerns. Treatment can often be more complicated in animals than in humans.

Veterinarians need to know more about pharmacology than their physician counterparts. In human medicine, all drugs are FDA-approved, meaning that they have undergone significant scrutiny for safety and efficacy—but only in one species. Vets must often use fairly limited evidence to treat other species with differences in drug metabolism and action.

When a veterinarian believes that a particular human medication can help an animal, she'll prescribe it. This has been the case for decades, of course, but the practice has only really been legal since 1994, when Congress passed the Animal Medicinal Drug Use Clarification Act regulating the conditions under which such use is acceptable.

Even before the legislation was in place, however, there was a working system for prescribing human drugs to pets. Veterinarians relied on peer-reviewed studies, clinical trials, and published formularies that included suggestions for safe uses and dosages of human medications given to companion animals.

Today, with the legal issues cleared up, veterinarians and their patients have more options and better access to medications. Vets have always been glad to provide in-house pharmaceutical services, and general pharmacists, too, have usually been willing to fill prescriptions written by vets. But recently, online retailers and specialty pharmacists have also recognized that pets are an expansion market. These developments open the door to even more progress, including discussions on generic meds and price-shopping.

Chances are you won't be walking out with a prescription for Viagra or Botox the next time you go to the veterinarian's office, but you should still talk with the doctor about your pet's treatment options. More variety means better care for your favorite animal, and that's good news for everyone.

Good Stuff That's Not Really a "Drug"—Nutraceuticals

The word *nutraceutical* is a combination of *nutrition* and *pharmaceutical*, and refers to products, supplements, and dietary ingredients known or believed to have some kind of specific medical benefit. While not as well-tested or strictly regulated as drugs, nutraceuticals such as omega-3 fatty acids, glucosamine, antioxidants, and many other supplements and herbs have found their way into the world of veterinary medicine.

Conditions that can be helped by these kinds of supplements include age-related cognitive problems, arthritis, side effects of prescribed medications, and many kinds of skin and digestive problems. The next time your pet's veterinarian diagnoses a health problem, be sure to ask if there are any nutraceuticals that could be a helpful part of his treatment plan.

Medications Don't Work If You Don't Give Them

Only about 20 percent of pet owners are successful in getting the medication in the pet as directed by the vet. The reason is simple: it's hard to give medication to a pet who absolutely doesn't want it, and most medications end up in the cupboard rather than in the pet. Pet owners are embarrassed about their failures, assuming incorrectly that most other pet owners are successful in doing the deed, or feeling too embarrassed to call the veterinary hospital and admit failure.

However hard it is, your dog needs that medication in the dosage, for the length of time, and at the intervals his veterinarian has prescribed. Worse, by letting our pets sense that we're reluctant to give them medication, and then rewarding them for resisting, we are teaching them that medication is bad, scary, or otherwise unpleasant—and that they can get away with refusing to take it.

Fortunately, help is available. Ask your veterinarian for formulations of parasite control products, pain meds, even antibiotics that are in meat-flavored tablets that seem like munchies, not meds. Some newer antibiotics like Simplicef (once-a-day cephalosporin) or Convenia (an injectable cephalosporin that lasts up to two weeks) make fighting Fido two to four times a day a thing of the past. Compounding pharmacies can make big pills tiny, bitter pills sweet, and turn your dog's worst nightmare into his favorite tasty treat. How? By mixing the medication into savory liquids or pastes that pets will lap up eagerly, and even into transdermal medication that can be applied inside the ear. There are other alternatives like Greenies Pill Pockets (stuff the pill into a yummy treat that looks like an edible shot glass) and pill guns (that pop the pill safely past the teeth, over the tongue, and straight into your pet's throat).

- Three-treat trick—this is like the street game of three shells that hold one ball. The first bit of cheese or treat has no medication and is called "the promise." The second contains the medication and is called "the dead." The last treat contains nothing and is called "the chaser."
- With Greenies Pill Pockets, hold the pill pocket in one hand like you're holding a small glass by the base; drop the medication into the pill pocket with the fingers of the other hand, then use the fingers of the hand that were holding the base of the pill pocket but never touched

the medicine to pinch the pocket closed. Remember, dogs have forty times the smell receptors humans have, and some can easily smell the meds on the outside of the pill pocket, so you have to outsmart them.

If your pet's veterinarian prescribes medication and you find you can't follow his instructions, ask for help; there's plenty of it out there.

The Big Sleep: What You Need to Know about Anesthesia

If there's one part of veterinary medicine that seems to concern the average pet lover most, it's anesthesia. Some pet lovers consider anesthesia so high-risk that they hesitate to okay or even refuse entirely elective procedures that have long-term benefits to an animal's health and comfort. Other pet lovers think anesthesia is too expensive, blaming changes in protocols for increased cost.

The good news about veterinary anesthesia is that although it can never be risk free, it's safer and more comfortable than ever. The bad news is that those things that improve safety for pets do indeed increase the cost.

Anesthesia is absolutely safer now, and one of the reasons is because the monitoring of anesthesia has come over into the veterinary field from human medicine. Monitors checking pulse, respiration, and even blood oxygen levels warn of problems early, and it's more likely these days for there to be someone whose sole job is to watch those machines and watch that patient—not the person who's doing the surgery. Again, that's why you need to make sure you're comparing apples to apples if you're price-shopping for a procedure ranging from a spay to a dental. Even without monitoring machines, it's important to have someone checking heart rate and breathing. I tell you one thing, anytime any of the Becker pets is going to undergo surgery, it will always be at the place that offers the most sophisticated diagnostics, anesthesia, monitoring, and pain control.

The simplest definition of anesthesia is putting an animal into an unconscious state so the pet will be immobile and pain free while a procedure is performed.

While many pet lovers probably think of veterinary anesthesia as a gas given through a mask over the animal's face, in fact the modern practice of preparing an animal for surgery is a no-size-fits-all combination of injectable medications (often combining anesthesia and pain-control agents), anesthesia-inducing gas, and pure oxygen, the latter two delivered through a breathing tube to maintain an animal's unconscious state.

In addition to constant anesthetic monitoring by machines and trained technicians, the use of intravenous fluids during anesthesia is another safety measure, meant to allow a veterinarian to react rapidly if something unexpected happens during surgery. If there's an emergency, you want instant access to a vein. Another important safety protocol is keeping pets warm during surgery and recovery. A cold animal has delayed healing, and the shivering increases oxygen consumption.

Preanesthetic screening is also important when it comes to reducing risk. A good physical exam is the place to start. Your veterinarian needs to determine underlying problems and recommend preanesthetic blood work based on what's found on the exam. In a young pet, that could be just checking for anemia. In an older pet, that means a complete blood count, determining kidney and liver function, making sure all organs are okay.

Even in older pets, health problems don't necessarily rule out the benefits of procedures that require a pet be put under. You have to balance risks with the benefits and discuss them with your veterinarian. Is your pet in great pain? Has he stopped eating because of a rotting tooth? If these conditions are evident, they need to be addressed.

It's important to have a frank discussion with your veterinarian before your pet has surgery, to understand how your pet will be treated and why—and what you need to do before surgery to help keep your animal safe, such as withholding food and water as recommended. You'll also need to know what to look for after your pet goes home so you can call for help if anything abnormal pops up.

IS IT TIME TO CALL IN A SPECIALIST?

Although not as many specialists exist in veterinary medicine as in human medicine, the kinds and the number of certified veterinary experts grow every year. And that's good news for our pets.

Current companion-animal specialties include cardiology, dentistry, dermatology, nutrition, oncology, and radiology. Behavior specialists are becoming more common as well. These veterinarians help people and their pets work through such problems as house-soiling or separation anxiety with the aid of medication and behavior-modification techniques.

Many urban centers support independent specialists or specialty practices, but in less populated areas you're more likely to find a full complement of specialists at the closest university with a school or college of veterinary medicine. Only veterinarians who are board-certified are allowed to call themselves specialists.

Specialists are usually called on a case-by-case basis to work on specific problems in which they have more experience than most veterinarians. While it used to be that "primary care" veterinarians were reluctant to refer, these days the advances in veterinary medicine and the growth of independent specialist groups have made getting the help of a specialist much more common—and your veterinarian may even recommend sending your dog to one.

If your veterinarian doesn't suggest a referral and you believe it could help your dog, open the discussion. The final decision on what treatment and who offers the care is yours. If you have a good relationship with your veterinarian, bringing in a specialist should never be a problem. If you don't have a specialist group in your area, check with your closest school or college of veterinary medicine.

Don't count out an older dog! If you keep your older dog lean
and active and work with your veterinarian to provide supplements that help keep your pet's mind and body functioning well,
your dog will enjoy his senior years—and so will you.

Chapter 20

SPECIAL CARE FOR AGING DOGS

He has gone gray around the muzzle. She sleeps a little longer and doesn't seem to hear things that used to wake her up. He wants to chase the tennis ball just once or twice, instead of all afternoon the way he used to. When she looks up at you lovingly, her eyes are clouded.

Yes, there's no denying it: your dog is officially old.

No dog lover likes thinking about the fact that dogs have much shorter life spans than we do. But I want to make you feel better by making sure you know a couple things about the last few years of your dog's life.

First, the final third or so of your dog's life is often the best years you have together, the time when you understand each other well and work to make each other happy. You've reached the point where you're comfortable with each other, when your dog's behavior issues and training challenges are mostly behind him. You know where your dog likes to sleep and which treats are his favorites. He knows he can be a comfort when you've had a hard day—and that a daily walk does you both a world of good. There's an easy companionship with a dog you've loved for his whole lifetime that's one of the great pleasures you can share together.

The other thing you need to know: aging is inevitable, but suffering is not.

Since your dog may spend several years in this phase of life, try thinking of him not as a tired old guy, but as a pal just entering retirement. There are a million ways people tackle their own retirement years, and the happiest of them stay busy and fit.

Your dog can do the same. She will thrive on moderate, regular exercise, especially low-impact activities such as long walks and swimming. And she will bloom with toys that challenge her, learning new skills and spending lots of time with the family. With your veterinarian's help in providing guidance for new strategies to slow, stop, and even reverse the aging process, the senior years of your dog's life really will be the golden years instead.

HOW OLD IS OLD? FORGET THAT "SEVEN YEAR" THING

Better care at home and at the veterinarian's, and changes in the way dogs are protected from harm—very few dogs roam free to be hit by cars—have made the lives of many dogs not only longer but also better. But any middle-aged person who has dealt with the "weekend warrior" syndrome—the aches and pains of occasional overactivity—can well imagine that we need to change the way we care for our older dogs just as we change the way we care for our older selves.

But where's the line between active adult and older adult? In dogs, that depends on a lot of factors, from size to weight to breed or breeds that went into an animal's genetic code. The most long-lived, healthiest dogs are the ones in the middle—dogs of moderate size (less than thirty to forty pounds older weight), moderate build (no extremes such as short faces, long backs, and so on), and even naturally erect ears and shorter coats. The farther afield you get from nature's model of the pariah dog—what you get when feral dogs breed freely—the more problems you get with health and longevity. There are of course exceptions, but in general giant breeds such as Irish Wolfhounds have the shortest life spans, and can be considered middle-aged barely beyond their adolescence. In other breeds, closed gene pools guarantee shorter average life spans: it's not uncommon for Golden Retrievers to die before ten of cancer, and for Cavalier King Charles Spaniels to have their lives shortened by congenital heart defects.

Many veterinarians feel that canine cocktails—true mixed breeds, not overhyped designer dogs that often come from substandard high-volume breeders—are the healthiest and longest lived. But really, there's no definitive answer to these questions, just some good observations and decent hunches.

Aside from the congenital problems that throw all guidelines out the window, you can figure a giant breed dog—Mastiff, Irish Wolfhound, Great Dane—is "senior" at five or so. Large breeds such as Goldens, German Shepherds, and Rottweilers are senior at seven. Medium- and small-sized dogs (but not the teeny-tiny) of moderate build (not extreme, such as a Bulldog) act like young adults until ten or beyond.

The reason large dogs don't live as long as small ones is not well understood, even among experts in canine aging. The prevailing theory is that large breed dogs grow so much, so quickly, that their bodies and systems are stressed by the demand. You can appreciate the strain when you consider that large-breed puppies often grow fifty to one hundred times their birth size in their first two years. Small- and toy-breed dogs grow rapidly, too, but not at the kind of exponential rate their bigger cousins endure. It may be the physical stress of explosive growth that results in rapid aging.

Still, you know your dog best. You'll be able to see the signs of aging and start making adjustments for the best life possible when the prime of adulthood is past.

CHANGES IN VETERINARY CARE FOR SENIOR DOGS

Every dog's senior years should be kicked off with an expanded veterinary exam. This is the time for your dog to get the works—exam, blood screen, urinalysis, fecal exam, X-rays, and possibly ultrasound, depending on what kinds of health problems your dog might be prone to. The purpose of all the testing is twofold: First, your dog will have up-to-date baseline values on all his lab tests. If and when health problems arise, these results will make it easier for your dog's veterinarian to spot the cause. Second, as time passes, dogs are simply more likely to have ailments that go undetected. For example, a dog can have up to 75 percent loss of kidney function and still appear just fine during an exam. Lab tests are the key to discovering this kind of health problem early, so it can be treated or managed.

One common issue that comes up in senior exams is lumps and bumps—seems a lot of dogs start sporting them around the time they start their retirement. Growths are tricky business—they're worrisome to pet parents, and at the veterinary office, they can be anything from a "ho-hum" to an "oh my." Little skin tags and growths are very common in older dogs, and they're often harmless. You might think of them as a small sign that your dog's immune system is weakening over time—but not a warning that it's giving up. Larger lumps can be anything from a harmless accumulation of blood under the skin to a malignant tumor. There's no way to diagnose the average lump at home—let your dog's veterinarian take a look and a needle aspiration sample and fill you in on the details.

Consider your dog's senior exam a chance to ask the veterinarian what kinds of health concerns might be especially relevant for your dog. Does her breed have a predisposition to kidney problems? To diabetes or severe arthritis? Are there signs you should look for? Knowing what ailments are common to dogs like yours will help you be vigilant in watching for early signs of trouble.

Take time at your dog's senior exam to talk with the veterinarian about diet and exercise. If your dog is just reaching old age and still feeling fine, you may not need to change a thing about his lifestyle. If he's got some sneaky weight creeping on or issues with mobility or energy level, though, this is a good time to talk about what changes to your dog's diet and routine might be a good idea. And don't forget to ask about medications and supplements that will make his life more comfortable.

Once your dog has had that super-senior physical, make his appointments at six-month intervals for routine checkups and stick with them.

As your dog gets older, you may notice his hearing, vision, and sense of smell aren't as sharp as they used to be. He may get confused and do things like stand at the wrong side of the door or shy away from interactions he used to enjoy. Gradual slowing of the senses is a natural part of the aging process, but some dogs who have these symptoms bounce back with minimal treatment.

Instead of writing off slowing senses or confusion as just the price of time, ask the veterinarian if your dog may be experiencing cognitive disorder syndrome. This condition, with symptoms similar to Alzheimer's disease in people, affects up to 62 percent of dogs ten and over. In many cases, adding antioxidants to your dog's diet can help. There are specially formulated foods, supplements, and prescription medications that may help restore your dog's mental functioning.

One client brought me her aging Border Collie and told me about the dog's sensory loss, lethargic behavior, and confusion. She was expecting to hear her dog was beginning the last chapter of its life. Instead, we tried supplements to address cognitive dysfunction. After a week, this client called my office in delight—her dog was back in the toy box, prancing around the house, and begging for a walk—all with a treatment that required no shots, no incisions, no recovery time. It's days like that one that make me love my job as a veterinarian!

A REVOLUTION IN THE TREATMENT OF PAIN

One of the most important considerations of improving the quality of life of an older dog is making sure he is as pain free as possible. And while pain medications have become the gold standard in every phase of veterinary medicine, their use is extremely important in dealing with the chronic pain that comes from aging.

Just as with human medicine, advancements in the way we think of and treat pain for animals is improving the quality of life for pets, with veterinarians now being able to choose from a wide array of products and strategies to ease the hurt.

Animals can feel all the same aches and pains that we can because they share the same physiologic structures. Treating pain doesn't just make the hurting stop: it also promotes healthy healing.

Untreated pain slows healing time, interferes with sleep, and depresses the immune system. The treatment of pain improves respiration, shortens postsurgical hospitalization times, improves mobility, and can even decrease the spread of cancer after surgery.

Most veterinarians prescribe pain medication when needed, but some still believe a pet will move around less during recovery from surgery or injury if in pain—a belief no longer supported by studies. If an animal needs to be restrained, it's better to use a leash or a crate.

Still, many owners don't give pets pain medications—even if they are prescribed—because of concerns about side effects. All drugs can cause unwanted effects, but those risks need to be balanced against the problems caused by untreated pain. Side effects can also be minimized by using drugs appropriately.

The family of drugs known as NSAIDs (nonsteroidal anti-inflammatory drugs) can cause ulcers and damage the kidneys in pets, just as they can in humans. But in the same way that people continue to use these drugs for everything from headaches to back injuries, NSAIDs have a valuable role to play in the management of animal pain.

When NSAIDs are needed, it's essential to follow label recommendations for veterinary testing and monitoring of liver and kidney functions. Pet owners should review all potential side effects with the veterinarian and stop giving the drug immediately if vomiting or lethargy is observed, or if the pet stops showing interest in eating.

Pain-management experts also suggest asking the veterinarian about the human drugs misoprostol and sulcrafate, which can help protect the stomach lining and prevent ulcers. For dogs, the prescription of Tramadol has been on the increase, and many dogs unable to tolerate NSAIDs have benefited. Tramadol can also be used with NSAIDs and can be taken with steroids, which NSAIDs cannot.

Complementary and alternative medicine also has much to offer dogs and cats suffering from chronic pain. Acupuncture, physical therapy, and supplements such as glucosamine and chondroitin can relieve arthritis pain. The veterinary drug Adequan Canine, an injectable relative of glucosamine, can target inflamed joints and help rebuild cartilage.

Some dogs, such as those with certain kinds of cancer, need the powerful pain relief that only opiates can provide. Owners often dislike these drugs because they make pets groggy. Fortunately, if long-term use is necessary, the sedation effect usually lessens after a few days.

Opiates can also cause nausea and lack of appetite. A bit of peppermint or ginger—even in the form of a gingersnap—can make a dog feel better. There are also prescription medications that can help control nausea.

Pain control is never a one-size-fits-all prescription, and there are dozens of drugs that can be used alone and with other medications to relieve all but the most extreme pain in animals.

When a veterinarian isn't sure how to get to the bottom of a pet's pain, it's always worth asking for a consultation with a specialist to design a safe, individualized pain-management program. Veterinary specialists in oncology, surgery, and anesthesia are usually most familiar with the wide variety of drugs available today and their safe use.

Along with changes to diet, exercise, and environment, pain medications can make old dogs feel young again. Don't ignore their important benefits.

Stem Cells to the Rescue

Just as in human medicine, the use of stem cells—cells that are able to develop into specific kinds of cells to treat disease—has shown great promise in treating or slowing the course of many diseases. Recently, the use of stem cells in dogs has been proven helpful in addressing the pain of arthritis that often comes with age. It's also helpful in conjunction with surgery in dogs who have joint or ligament injuries or disease.

The Vet-Stem company is the world's leader in stem cell therapy, and I've had the pleasure of sitting down with veterinarians and other scientists to go over the procedures and look at the results. Stem cell therapy shows some of the ways veterinary care will be continuing to advance the frontiers of medicine for our pets. It's exciting stuff!

Even better, though still in its infancy, stem cell therapy is already making a difference for our pets today. Talk to your veterinarian!

MOVING MORE, AND MAKING MOVING EASIER

As your dog gets older, he may continue to do the leash dance when it's time for a walk, but what happens on the walk may change. Some senior dogs still have miles a day in them, but others run out of steam by the end of the block.

The key thing to remember about exercise is that your dog still needs it! Regular, gentle exercise is truly one of the keys to canine health and happiness. As your dog ages, try to build exercise habits that emphasize a steady buildup to moderate exertion more often than the intense, leaping games of fetch or pavement-pounding miles of running that may have gotten the two of you through his younger years. And break it up: instead of taking one long walk a day, take two shorter ones.

Do the same with your dog's other favorite activities. If it's fetch, make the throws shorter, and always keep them low. And don't forget to look for the opportunity to add low-key brain games using food puzzles or nose work that function as hide-and-seek for your pet.

Of course, above all, be sure the lowered activity level doesn't turn into weight gain. Extra weight puts more pressure on your dog's joints, and clogs up the efficient engine of his internal systems. If anything, keep your dog on the lean side of normal. And keep moving—it's great for you both.

Don't forget environmental adjustments: ask not what your old dog can do for you, but what you can do for your old dog. Keep in mind that for most dogs, your presence and affection are the most pleasing things of all. As they get older and when they're not feeling well, some dogs get a little extra clingy. You can accommodate that need for closeness by giving your dog easy access to you. Steps to help him get onto the couch or bed, or, if that's not your thing, more comfy beds around the house to give him a soft spot to ease those old bones. (And don't forget heating pads in the cooler seasons!) More options to consider include:

Stop slipping and sliding. A common problem among senior dogs is increasing unsteadiness on their feet. There are lots of possible contributing factors, including arthritis, hip dysplasia, nonspecific aches and pains, and the association of one unfortunate slip with more to come. This is one area in which you can offer your dog a quick, effective, and inexpensive fix. If one small area is giving your dog grief, firmly attach a throw rug with double-sided tape. If a whole room or a troublesome hallway causes the problem, head to the toy store for interlocking foam play mats. These mats, designed for toddlers, can be configured in any shape or direction you need, and they'll provide a soft, nonslippery surface for your elderly dog's paws. You can rearrange them or take them up at any time.

It's all about the bed. Many senior dogs sleep sixteen hours a day or more. With all that time spent snoozing, it's not surprising that the most important place to many dogs is the bed. Here's an area where you can reward your dog for a lifetime of love and companionship. Choose beds that are well-padded and warm. If your dog has arthritis, consider doubling beds up or adding egg-crate-type padding for extra cushion. Offering a couple different beds in separate rooms will give your dog ways to both catch his naps and stay close to you. If you do have multiple beds, try mixing up the fabrics—you may find your dog's favorites change depending on the weather and his mood.

Flavorful food. If your dog seems to be losing his appetite, try a little extra flavoring for his food. A few little jars of strained-meat baby food (look for no- or low-salt varieties, and skip labels with onion and garlic on them as well) in the pantry will give you lots of healthy options to kick it up for your pup. A small spoonful of baby food will add new flavor and texture to your dog's old food. To really amp it up, try putting the dog food in the microwave for a few seconds (no more than ten). Warming dog food releases its aromas and makes it more pungent. For a dog with sensory loss, the smell of his food warming in the microwave can be just the ticket to increase his appetite and his enjoyment of the meal. You can also make chicken or beef broth without salt, garlic, or onions, and add warm to meals.

Ramp it up or give him a lift. Many companies make stairs and ramps to help dogs get to their usual favorite places, including in the car. These are often lightweight, well-designed, and collapsible, or attractive

An Amazing Array of New Helpers

Every year, when I make the rounds of veterinary conferences and pet-product trade shows, I'm delighted to see all the new, clever, and innovative inventions to makes dogs more comfortable, and sometimes just more spoiled. Here are a couple that are perfect for dogs with old-age problems or chronic injuries:

🐾 **Pet therapy jacket.** This life jacket–looking invention comes with packs that can be heated or cooled and placed anywhere your dog needs them to relieve the aches and pains of sore muscles and arthritis.

🐾 **Bottoms-up leash.** If your senior dog suffers from hip dysplasia or arthritis, this leash can help her continue to have regular walks. The leash goes around your dog's rear legs instead of his neck. This design allows you to carry some of your dog's weight while he walks. Less weight equals less pain on sore muscles and joints.

🐾 **Canine wheelchairs.** A handful of companies make these, and you should not hesitate to look into them if your dog needs full support front or rear. Dogs don't feel embarrassed, and an otherwise healthy animal will adjust quickly and happily to the increased mobility. And this is a case where we can learn from our dogs!

enough (in the case of stair-steps) to leave as a permanent part of the decor. And while it's certainly possible to use old towels as slings to help old dogs up and down stairs, you'll find a wide variety of slings with easy-grip handles that make the lifting easier for you. Because after a dog's lifetime, you may be no spring chicken, either.

Be Realistic, Flexible, and Solution-Oriented

Your dog may breeze through years of senior citizenship without any significant health issues, but sooner or later, age catches up with even the most resilient of canine companions. You may one day discover your dog can't see or hear anymore, or that he's developed an irritable streak where he didn't have one before. In many cases, the first really distressing issue to come up is incontinence—an old dog may dribble urine in his bed or in the house—and suddenly you have a problem. Anytime a new health issue develops, the best course of action is to have it checked out by your dog's veterinarian.

The good news: many problems are treatable at any age.

If it turns out your dog really is just running out of time, it's time to double-down on the love and patience. Remember this is an animal who adores you, who lives for your approval and affection. As he begins to lose his health, he needs your assurance more than ever.

Some special situations you may deal with:

Blind dogs. Maintain your blind dog's environment with minimal change. Dogs actually adapt amazingly well when they lose their eyesight—as long as you don't start rearranging the furniture. If your dog knows his way around your house and yard and has a walking route that suits him, try to keep these things constant to prevent injuries and put him at ease.

Deaf dogs. For a dog who lives in a soundless world, sudden contact can be unnerving. It can also be dangerous for the person who delivers the shock, since your dog may nip out of fear. Learn how to let your dog know you're coming, and teach any children who have contact how to do so, too. Many dogs are hearing impaired but not completely deaf, and for those a couple simple hand claps are enough to get his attention. If your dog is completely deaf, step loudly as you approach him—your footfalls will cause vibrations that can be felt even if they're not heard.

Leaky dogs. If your dog has overnight incontinence, know that the situation probably upsets him even more than it upsets you. Take him out last thing before bedtime, and then provide a water-absorbent barrier in his bedding. You can use a puppy pad, cut up pieces of a water-resistant mattress pad, or an upside-down, rubber-backed bathmat. Whatever you use will need to be washed or replaced daily, but the extra loads of laundry are a small price to pay to ensure your senior dog is comfortable.

Will a Young Dog Make an Older Dog Young Again?

A lot of dog lovers wonder about the right time to get another dog. Usually loyalty to a senior dog drives the debate—after all, the last thing anyone wants is to add stress or anxiety to the life of a beloved pet. I recommend getting your next dog while your first is still in decent health and able to enjoy some companionship. After all, dogs are pack animals, and you can't have a pack with just one.

Pets who have a buddy are sick less often than those who live in one-pet households. When they do get sick, pets with partners are sick for less time. On average, pets from multi-pet households live longer than those alone. As long as he's not in very grave shape, your older dog may well grouch or growl a little bit if you bring home another pup, but he'll enjoy the addition. My experience with new dogs in old-dog homes has been overwhelmingly good—it's often like changing the batteries in your old friend—in his new companion, he may rediscover some of the energy and enthusiasm he's lost over time.

LIVING WELL WHILE DYING

At the end of your dog's life, you will have to make tough choices about what she can endure and what she should be spared. These are very personal decisions, and as you work with your dog's veterinarian to make them, know that there are no right or wrong choices—simply those that are best for your family and your dog.

Treatment, hospice care, and euthanasia are all options on the table, and it happens in the lives of many dogs that all three come to pass. When you choose treatment for your dog, consider what her quality of life is without it, what the treatment will involve, and what quality of life she can expect afterward. There are millions of pets whose lives are improved by veterinary care in their senior years, but there are also pets whose lives are prolonged by painful, costly procedures and treatments that do very little to improve their days. Ask your veterinarian what the reasonable expectations are for your dog's condition after any intervention.

Hospice care, no matter who gives or receives it, is all about comfort and pain relief at the end of life. It starts at the point where a patient is no longer being given treatment with the goal of cure or recovery, but instead simply receiving whatever contributes to comfort and ease. Many families successfully give their dogs excellent hospice care at home, buying weeks or months of high-quality time, especially with the advances in pain medications available today. Talk to your veterinarian about hospice options—you may be surprised at what can be done to care for a dying dog at home.

WHEN IS THE RIGHT TIME TO SAY GOOD-BYE?

Euthanasia is the last, hardest, and most loving decision any dog owner faces. No one can make this choice for you, and there is no wrong decision.

You know your dog best, so let him help you decide. Is his discomfort unmanageable, even with palliative care? Is food no longer of interest, even if made more palatable? These are often the questions that lead to the decision to end a pet's life, but sometimes it's deeper than that. You just...know.

As hard as it is, talk to your veterinarian about euthanasia options. Before the appointment, discuss your options for the remains (individual or group cremation, burial on your property if allowed by law, or simple disposal with no return). Your veterinarian and the entire staff are there to help you, to provide both you and your dog with what you need at this difficult time. They will help you through it, answering questions and scheduling your appointment so you won't have to wait.

It may be easier not to be alone, or at least, to have someone drive you home after. Friends and family members may wish to attend, to help you, and say their own good-byes. Child-development experts say that children may even be present, and saying good-bye to a beloved dog helps children learn to deal with the losses we all endure in our lives. You know your children—give them the opportunity to participate if they wish, and to find closure with memorials, such as drawings and storybooks, and even memorial ceremonies. (And do remember to tell your child's teacher, so she can be aware and help your child through this loss.)

Of course, the idea that children be present is astonishing to those who do not wish to be present themselves. As hard as it may be to get through, seeing that your pet did not suffer and knowing that you were there at the end is usually quite comforting once the initial waves of grief have passed.

The death of your dog is a tremendous loss, and you'll be surprised to find that there are people you know who completely understand how big a heartbreak this is, and others who just have no clue. Give yourself the time and energy to grieve. If you need someone to talk to, ask the veterinary office if there's a pet-loss support group in your area. Even if there's not a local group, there are pet-loss hotlines at many veterinary colleges and many online grief groups where dog owners can share their stories and struggles.

Memorials, from simple engraved slabs for the garden to necklaces with a bit of fur (or, astonishingly, DNA!) are available. Many people also like to do something for others in honor of their pet, from planting trees to making a donation to a canine health fund, veterinary school or college, or shelter.

In time, thinking of your dog will bring back happy memories along with your feelings of loss. Take comfort in everything you did to give your dog a good, healthy, happy life.

CONCLUSION: THE GREATEST DOG IN THE WORLD

As a veteran veterinarian (over thirty years), a lifetime pet lover (well over fifty years), and a communicator in person and in all forms of media, traditional and new, I find themes that get repeated. After reading these pages you know how sacred I hold the human-animal bond, the appreciation I have for the healing power of pets, and how much I stress to millions on TV in their living rooms or one-on-one in the exam room the importance for pets of daily oral care, high levels of preventive care, good nutrition, and keeping pets and people fit.

For more than three decades I've enjoyed asking individuals ranging from clients and neighbors, to celebrities and titans of industry, and groups ranging from ten to ten thousand the following question: who was the first pet you ever owned in your life? In the exercise I ask them to get specific: the species, breed, size, coloration, overriding memory of the pet, and of course, and my favorite...the genesis of the pet's name. In 99.99 percent of the cases, after asking the question I just sit back and watch the warm memories wash over the audience like a benediction. Most of these folks haven't thought about Skeeter, Ralph, or Luke (my childhood dogs in order) for a long time, but the vivid, warm memories come flooding back in an instant. They're warmed. Joyful. Thankful. First pets certainly rank ahead of first teacher, first kiss, or first car.

I trust that in this book I've given you the tactics and tools to help you better select the first pet for a child or your next pet as an adult. Pets picked with logic rather than pure emotion, and pets that are trained correctly (catching problems when they occur for the first time) will have manners that last a lifetime.

I used to end a radio show by saying "There's only one greatest pet in the world...and every family has that pet." I love talking with dog owners, whether it's in the exam room at one of the veterinary hospitals I work at, in my church, or on the street around different parts of the country (some people recognize me from a book or the media). They get so exuberant when talking about their pet(s), and they say in words and body language the same basic thing: "If you could just come over to where I live and be around _____ for a few minutes, you'd see why I'm so crazy about her!"

By harnessing the hundreds of secrets, surprises, and solutions in this book you'll raise a happier, healthier dog. You'll have the greatest pet in the world seen by the greatest veterinarian in the world.

Next time you see me, tell me about it.

ACKNOWLEDGMENTS

No book is ever written alone, nor even with the help of a coauthor such as I have been fortunate enough to have found in Gina Spadafori, with whom I have now written more than a dozen books.

But we could not have finished this one without the capable research, writing, and editing of some of our most talented friends. First and foremost, our lead writer, Jana Murphy, and our editor, Karen Murgolo and her most capable assistant Philippa "Pippa" White. Members of Team Becker who also contributed a great deal to the writing and editing of the book include Kim Campbell Thornton and Christie Keith. I'm grateful, too, to my longtime friend Dr. Nicholas Dodman for contributing the foreword.

Thanks, too, to the Team Becker folks who filled in on the writing and editing work we left to do this important project, or who contributed their considerable expertise, including veterinarians Drs. Tony Johnson, Robin Downing, Steve Garner, Rolan Tripp, and Narda Robinson, as well as dog trainers and authors Liz Palika and my daughter, Mikkel Becker. Thanks as well to Ericka Basile, Phyllis DeGioia, David S. Greene, and Susan Tripp. Thanks, too, to my agent, Bill Stankey, and to my attorney, Marc Chamlin.

Many, many other pet care experts have helped me a great deal over the years, and the list of folks would be longer than this book. To all of you, though, you know who you are and how much you mean to me. A special shout-out to fellow Washington State University College of

Veterinary Medicine alum Dr. Bruce King, who let us use his stunning new practice, Lakewood Animal Hospital in Coeur d'Alene, Idaho, for the pictures throughout and on the cover of this book, most of which were taken by Joel Riner and Dustin Weed of Quicksilver Commercial Photography, also in Coeur d'Alene. I'm grateful to our cover dogs: Henry the Golden Retriever, owned by Jill and Curtis Gibbs, and Ranger the Border Collie, owned by Carolynn Bernard-Harwell and John Harwell. Thanks to Dr. King as well for letting me be his colleague at Lakewood, and to Drs. Dawn Mehra and Robert Pierce for letting me do the same at the North Idaho Animal Hospital in Sandpoint. Finding time to work as a hands-on veterinarian is difficult with my schedule, but I love it so much I can't do without.

Thanks to my family, especially my incredible wife, Teresa. I just couldn't do what I do without her, and that's a fact. Thanks, too, to our son, Lex, our aforementioned daughter, Mikkel, and my mom, Virginia Becker. Love as well to the animal residents of our Almost Heaven Ranch in Bonners Ferry, Idaho, especially my "cover dog," Quixote.

Above all, the first mention in any of my books to my first grandchild, Reagan Avelle Shannon, to whom this book is dedicated with more love and hope for the future than I can possibly express.

Dr. Marty Becker
Almost Heaven Ranch
Idaho

RESOURCES

Dog Gear and Problem Solvers

AirCatditioner. A window litter box that vents odors outside while keeping litter out of the reach of dogs. www.aircatditioner.com

Anti-Icky-Poo. A cat and dog urine odor eliminator. www. antiickypoo.com, (866) 247–5221

Bamboo. A provider of pet home grooming products. www.bamboopet .com, (877) 224–PETS (7387)

Bissell. Manufacturer of vacuums and hard floor cleaners. www.bissell.com, (800) 237–7691

Bitter Apple. A bitter-tasting liquid that discourages dogs from biting themselves and creating hot spots. www.bitterapple.com

Brake-fast Bowl. A bowl designed to prevent dogs from eating too fast. www .brake-fast.net, (757) 339–5703

Bristle Bone. A dental chew toy, from Busy Buddy, with nylon bristles and rubber nubs; holds treats. www.premier.com, (800) 933–5595

Buster Cube. Toys for mental stimulation. One acts as a food bowl. www .bustercube.com

Busy Buddy. A line of treat-dispensing chew toys designed to keep dogs mentally stimulated while eating. www.busybuddytoys.com, (800) 933–5595

Chuckit. A ball-launcher that allows you to throw even slobbery balls good distances without touching them. www.chuckit.com, (800) 660–9033

DAP., or dog-appeasing pheromone. A synthetic copy of a natural appeasing pheromone that can help dogs remain calm in stressful situations. www .dap-pheromone.com

DentAcetic. A non-staining acetic acid tooth and gum gel or wipe that helps clean and deodorize a dog's teeth and remove plaque. Made by DermaPet. www.dermapet.com, (800) 755-4378

Dentastix. Made by Pedigree, these are dental treats that can reduce tartar buildup. www.pedigree.com

DenTees. Treats with limited antigen (for allergic dogs) and ingredients that neutralize stomach odors and freshen breath. Made by DermaPet. www .dermapet.com, (800) 755–4738

Dirt Devil. Vacuums and floor cleaners. www.dirtdevil.com, (800) 321–1134

Doggles. Shatterproof and 100 percent UV-protected eyewear for dogs, and other types of dog products. www.doggles.com, (866) DOG–GLES

Dremel. A cordless dog-nail grinder that uses rotary action. www.dremel .com, (800) 437–3635

Dyson. Vacuum cleaners, including the Animal line. www.dyson.com, (866) 693–9766

Eureka. Vacuum cleaners and accessories. www.eureka.com, (800) 282–2886

Flexi. Retractable leashes with a cord length that ranges from 10 feet to 26 feet. www.flexiusa.com, (800) 543–4921

FURminator. A de-shedding tool for long and short coats. www.furminator .com, (888) 283–1620

Genius. Connectable treat/release toys by Kong that can slow down gulpers and provide mental stimulation. www.caninegenius.com, (800) 523–7979

GoPet Exerciser. Electric treadmills and kennel or free-standing exercise wheel (like a hamster wheel). www.gopetusa.com, (717) 354–3399

Greenies. Dental treats and pliable treats in which to hide a pill. www .greenies.com, (866)–GREENIES

Kong. Toys, including some that dispense food, such as the Wobbler. Also, some toys for hard chewing and mental stimulation. www.kongcompany.com

Kool Dogz Ice Treat Maker. Makes iced treats that you can plant in the ground so your dog won't bring them inside. www.kooldogz.com

L.L. Bean. Dog beds, dog collars, place mats, and gifts for human dog lovers and more. www.llbean.com, (800) 441–5713

LeBistro Portion Control Automatic Pet Feeder. These are programmable automatic portion control food dispensers. www.petmate.com

Mars Coat King. Coat-stripping tool from a manufacturer of pet grooming products. www.marsgroomingproducts.com.au (Distributed worldwide)

Nail Grinder Kit. An electric nail grinder. www.osterpro.com, (800) 830–3678

Nature's Miracle. A liquid stain and odor remover. www.naturemakesitwork .com

Nina Ottosson. Offers a line of durable interactive games, including Dog Pyramid and Kibble Nibble, that dispense food or treats for mental stimulation while reinforcing relationships with people. www.nina–ottosson.com. (Based in Sweden and distributed worldwide)

Orvis. This is a large catalog company that mostly offers products for people, but also sells dog supplies such as beds, collars, feeders, and more. www.orvis .com, (866) 531–6188

Oster. This subsidiary of Jarden Corp. is a manufacturer of home-use and professional dog grooming equipment. www.osterpro.com, (800) 830–3678

Petmate. A pet-care company that manufactures many products key to the proper care of pets. Best known for revolutionizing the use of crates for house-training and behavior modification. www.petmate.com

Pledge Fabric Sweeper. A cleaning tool that slides. It's better than sticky paper for picking up fur from furniture and car interiors. www.pledge.com, (800) 494–4855

Puppy Bumpers. Stuffed pillow-like collars that help prevent puppies from escaping through fences or falling off fenced decks or balconies. www .puppybumpers.net, (804) 512–2553

Scat Mat. A Scat Mat emits a mild, harmless static pulse when touched and helps keep dogs off furniture and countertops. www.scatmat.com, (800) 732–2677

Squirrel Dude. For hard chewers, a durable toy from Busy Buddy that holds treats and bounces unevenly. www.premier.com, (800) 933–5595

Tagnabbit. This tag ring is designed to make it easy to add or remove collar tags and to switch tags from one collar to another. www.petmate.com

Through a Pet's Ear CDs. Music that calms dogs. www.throughadogsear .com, (800) 788–0949

Tick Key. A tool to safely remove ticks, including the heads. www.tickkey .com, (860) 618–3072

Ticked Off. A tool to safely remove ticks, including the heads. www.tickedoff .com, (800) 642–2485

Twist'N Treats. A two-piece adjustable rubber treat-dispensing toy from Busy Buddy. www.premier.com, (800) 933–5595

Dog Sports Organizations

American Kennel Club. A dog registry that also organizes many kinds of dog sports, including those for mixed breed dogs. An example: tracking, a sport where dogs track by scent. www.akc.org, (919) 233–9767

The Canine Freestyle Federation. An organization that promotes the sport of freestyle (dancing). www.canine-freestyle.org

Dock Dogs. An organization that promotes the sport of dock diving. www .dockdogs.com, (330) 241–4975

Iditarod Trail Sled Dog Race. An annual 1,150-mile race in Alaska. www .iditarod.com, (907) 376–5155

North American Dog Agility Council (NADAC). An organization that promotes the sport of agility. www.nadac.com

The North American Flyball Association. An organization that promotes the sport of flyball. www.flyball.org, (800) 318–6312

Splash Dogs. An organization that promotes the sport of dock diving. www .splashdogs.com

United States Dog Agility Association. www.usdaa.com, (972) 487–2200

Health-Care Management Products

Canine Heritage Breed Test. A DNA-based cheek swab test that can help owners answer "What kind of dog is that?" www.canineheritage.com, (800) DNA–DOGG or (800) 362–3644

CareCredit. A patient health-care financing program similar to a personal line of credit for treatments and procedures. www.carecredit.com, (866) 893–7864

VIN News. An independent news service that covers the veterinary and animal health industries and has a central reporting area for product recalls. www .news.vin.com

Veterinary Pet Insurance (VPI). Founded in 1982, the most popular supplier of pet health insurance, with more than a million policies sold. www .petinsurance.com, (800) 540–2016

Vet–Stem. A pioneering developer of stem-cell medicine for veterinary use. www.vet–stem.com, (888) 387–8361

Vetstreet. Private secure web pages that allow 24-hour web access to veterinarians, which can be used to request appointments, order pet products online, view pet's vaccine history, receive e-mail reminders, and research health information for pets. www.vetstreet.com, (888) 799–8387

Organizations of Interest

AARP. A nonprofit, nonpartisan membership organization that helps people over the age of fifty. www.aarp.org, (888) OUR–AARP, (888) 687–2277. Dr. Becker's pet-care column runs monthly on AARP.org, and he answers questions in the AARP Pet Pals section.

American Veterinary Medical Association (AVMA). A professional trade association for veterinarians. There is also information for pet-lovers on the website. www.avma.org, (800) 248–2862

ASPCA Poison Control Hotline. Animal-specific poison control center that provides informational articles and, for a fee, specific case information. www.napcc.aspca.org, (888) 426–4435

Orthopedic Foundation for America (OFA). An organization that offers testing for numerous diseases and conditions. OFA is best known for certifying the hips of dogs intended for breeding. www.offa.org, (573) 442–0418

U.S. Department of Agriculture. A US federal agency with oversight for protecting health through food safety, among other areas. www.usda.gov, (202) 720–2791

U.S. Food and Drug Administration. Responsible for recalls of animal medication and food. www.fda.gov

Over-the-Counter Treatments

NOTE: Check with your veterinarian before giving your pet any medications, even over-the-counter.

Benadryl. A human allergy medication that can also be used for allergic reactions in dogs. www.benadryl.com

Hextra. This is a brand of dental chew that reduces calculus by combining rawhide and the antiseptic chlorhexidine. One of several types of dental chews offered by C.E.T. www.virbacvet.com/cet, (800) 338–3659

Mars Wisdom Panel. Cheek swab test to help identify breeds in a mixed-breed dog. www.wisdompanel.com

Pedialyte. A childrens' over-the-counter liquid oral medication replaces lost fluids and electrolytes. Check with your veterinarian regarding dosages. http://pedialyte.com, (800) 227–5767

Pepto–Bismol. An over-the-counter liquid or tablet medication for humans that can be used to treat a dog's upset stomach and diarrhea. www.pepto–bismol.com

OraVet. Dental plaque and tartar prevention gel. www.oravet.com, (678) 638–3000

Zymox Otic Enzymatic Solution. A liquid once-a-day treatment for ear infections. www.petkingbrands.com, (630) 241–3905 or toll free, (888) PKB–5487

Pets in the Media: Broadcast, Print, and Web

Dr. Oz Show. A syndicated television show about health, starring Mehmet Oz, MD. Dr. Becker is the regular veterinarian. www.doctoroz.com

Fitness Unleashed: A Dog and Owner's Guide to Losing Weight and Gaining Health Today, by Robert Kushner, MD, and Marty Becker, DVM. Read about people and dogs exercising and losing weight together.

Good Morning America. Dr. Becker is the resident veterinarian on this ABC national morning news show. www.abcnews.go.com/GMA. You can find "The Pet Doctor" podcasts, with Dr. Becker and Mikkel Becker on the site.

Home-Prepared Dog & Cat Diets: The Healthful Alternative, by veterinarian Donald Strombeck. Has easy-to-follow recipes that can easily be prepared at home.

Parade magazine. Dr. Becker and Gina Spadafori regularly contribute to the Sunday newspaper supplement. www.parade.com

PetConnection.com. The website and blog for Dr. Becker and Gina Spadafori's nationally syndicated column.

Petfinder.com. A website to help you find adoptable dogs across the United States. Available dogs can be sorted by geographic area, breed, size, age, and sex. www.petfinder.com

Prescription Foods, Medications, and Therapies

NOTE: These items should be given by prescription only, in consultation with your veterinarian.

Adequan Canine. Injectable prescription medication for dogs with arthritis. Created by Novartis. www.adequancanine.us, (800) 637–0281

Advantage. A topical medication that kills fleas. www.advantage.petparents.com, (800) 255–6826

Atopica. A nonsteroidal oral medication for itching. www.us.atopica.com, (800) 332–2761

Botox. A medication used to treat increased muscle stiffness. www.botoxmedical.com, (800) 433-8871

Cerenia. A prescription medication used for motion sickness and nausea. www.cerenia.com, (800) 366–5288

Companion Therapy Laser, Litecure LLC. Cold laser therapy for faster post-surgery recovery times and pain relief. www.companiontherapylaser.com, (877) 627–3858

Comfortis. Chewable tablet medication made by Elanco that kills and prevents fleas. www.comfortis4dogs.com

Convenia. A prescription injectable cephalosporin antibiotic that lasts up to two weeks. www. convenia.com, (800) 366–5288

Frontline. A topical monthly flea and tick killer. www.frontline.com, (800) 660–1842

Heartguard (Ivermectin). A monthly heartworm preventive. http://us.merial.com/pet_owners/products.asp

Hill's t/d. A brand of prescription food formulated to keep teeth clean and help control the oral bacteria found in plaque. www.hillspets.com, (800) 445–5777 (Hill's is the manufacturer of other veterinarian-only therapeutic foods and the brand Science Diet, available through pet-care retailers.)

Neuticles. Testicular implants for neutered dogs. www.neuticles.com, (888) 638–8425

Porphyromonas Denticanis–Gulae–Salivosa Bacterin. A dental vaccine to prevent periodontitis. www.pfizerah.com

Reconcile. A chewable medication to treat separation anxiety in dogs. www.reconcile.com, (888) 545–5973

Simplicef. A once-daily oral cephalosporin antibiotic to treat dogs' skin infections. www.simplicef.com, (800) 366–5288

Tramadol. A prescription pain reliever for people and dogs that is not a non-steroidal anti-inflammatory medication (NSAID). www.ortho–mcneil.com, (800) 526–7736

Viagra. A prescription medication used to improve blood flow in dogs with pulmonary hypertension. www.viagra.com, (866) 706–2400

Xanax. A prescription medication to treat panic disorder in people and dogs. www.xanax.com

INDEX

ABOUT THE AUTHORS

Dr. Marty Becker

Dr. Marty Becker, "America's Veterinarian," is the popular veterinary contributor to ABC-TV's *Good Morning America*, the resident veterinarian on *The Dr. Oz Show*, and the pet expert for the American Association of Retired Persons (AARP). Along with his writing partner, Gina Spadafori, he is a regular contributor to *Parade* magazine. Dr. Becker is co-author of *Chicken Soup for the Pet Lover's Soul, The Healing Power of Pets*, and, with Spadafori, *Why Do Dogs Drink Out of the Toilet?* among other books.

Dr. Becker is an adjunct professor at his alma mater, the Washington State University College of Veterinary Medicine, and also at the colleges of veterinary medicine at both Colorado State University and the University of Missouri. He has been named Companion Animal Veterinarian of the Year by the Delta Society and the American Veterinary Medical Association.

Dr. Becker lives with his wife, Teresa, in northern Idaho, only a drive away from his daughter, Mikkel, his son, Lex, and his granddaughter, Reagan Avelle.

Gina Spadafori

A longtime journalist and editor, Gina Spadafori has been writing primarily about pets and their care for almost thirty years as a syndicated columnist and book author. She has written more than a dozen books with Dr. Becker. Gina has also headed the Pet Care Forum, America Online's founding source of pet-care information. She is the founder of PetConnection.com, consistently named one of the best pet-care websites.

Gina lives in northern California on a suburban micro farm with dogs, cats, chickens, and ducks. She rides horses as often as she can and is working on finding just the right horse to join her animal family.

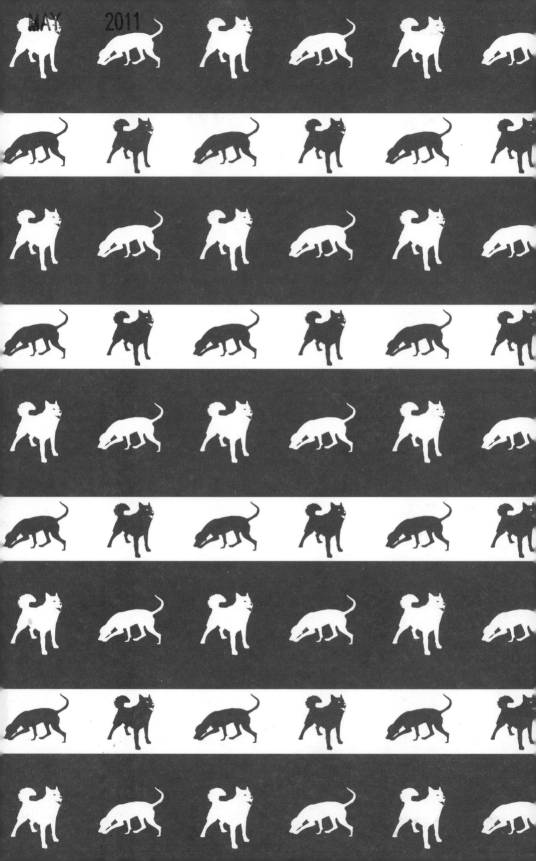